MONTH-BY-MONTH GARDENING

CALIFORNIA

First published in 2014 by Cool Springs Press, an imprint of Quarto Publishing Group USA Inc., 400 First Avenue North, Suite 400, Minneapolis, MN 55401

Cool Springs Press titles are also available at discounts in bulk quantity for industrial or sales-promotional use. For details write to Special Sales Manager at Quarto Publishing Group USA Inc., 400 First Avenue North, Suite 400, Minneapolis, MN 55401 USA. To find out more about our books, visit us online at www.coolspringspress.com.

Library of Congress Cataloging-in-Publication Data

Splan, Claire.
  California month-by-month gardening : what to do each month to have a beautiful garden all year / Claire Splan.
     pages cm
  Includes bibliographical references and index.
  ISBN 978-1-59186-609-1 (sc)
  1. Gardening--California. I. Title.

  SB453.2.C2S65 2014
  635.09794--dc23

                    2014030597

ISBN: 978-1-59186-609-1

Acquisitions Editor: Billie Brownell
Art Director: Cindy Samargia Laun
Layout: Danielle Smith-Boldt
Zone Map: Bill Kersey

Printed in China
10 9 8 7 6 5 4 3 2 1

MONTH-BY-MONTH GARDENING

CALIFORNIA

**What to Do Each Month to Have
a Beautiful Garden All Year**

CLAIRE SPLAN

COOL
SPRINGS
PRESS
Home and Garden Experts™

MINNEAPOLIS, MINNESOTA

Acknowledgments

I knew from the beginning that writing this book was going to be a substantial undertaking, and it was. Big time. I never would have gotten through it without the help and support of numerous people.

At Cool Springs Press, editor Billie Brownell was always helpful and encouraging and more patient and understanding than I had reason to expect. Project editor Tracy Stanley shepherded the book through production, making sure all the details came together. Art director Cindy Laun is responsible for the look of the book and making the text and art work together so well. I'm grateful for all of their efforts.

I'm also grateful to my family and friends, who I can always count on to be supportive of my writing.

Just before I began this book, I was lucky enough to find an amazing writing group called Shut Up & Write, which has bolstered my writing productivity and made writing this book a more pleasurable experience. Special thanks go to my writing buddy, Brian Higgins, who I met through Shut Up & Write and who was a constant source of encouragement from the beginning to the end.

Contents

Introduction

WELCOME TO GARDENING IN CALIFORNIA

California is not a place that lives or dies by the calendar. In a state that has a reputation for year-round living, months are more like suggested markers of time than fixed schedules or deadlines. And where seasons may be subtler and seem to come and go at will, with little regard for solstices and equinoxes, one could be forgiven for thinking that it matters not a whit when you do what you do in your garden.

But there is a certain wisdom in taking a month-by-month approach to a California garden. First, try though we might to feel unbound by the calendar, plants do have their own natural rhythms. They *want* to grow, but they know better than to grow at the wrong time, so feeding or pruning at the wrong time of year can work against them. Ditto for planting and transplanting. Second, it's easy to get overwhelmed by the particular needs of all the plants in your garden. A month-by-month approach breaks all the tasks down into bite-size chunks. It helps you to plan ahead without losing focus on what needs doing here and now. And it spotlights problems that might pop up at that time of year, so you know what to be on the lookout for and can be prepared to handle it.

Month-by-month gardening makes gardening more enjoyable by making it manageable and understandable, keeping you from ending up (forgive the pun) in the weeds. If you love your garden but find that you are always hopelessly behind in maintaining it, month-by-month gardening will help you find your rhythm with your garden again, making the time you spend in it a pleasure instead of a series of endless chores.

With our amazing Mediterranean climate, we Californians have always enjoyed our gardens. But now we, like the rest of the country, are returning to the garden with a renewed sense of purpose. Pressured by economic hardships, fearful of contaminated commercially grown produce, or lured by the thought of turning our home into a beautiful and tranquil oasis, we've gone back to the land, whether that land is measured in acreage or by flowerpots on a patio. But what is the number one factor that impacts our gardening activities? According to a 2013 survey of gardening trends conducted by the Garden Writers Association Foundation, it's not money, weather, or space. It's available time. Month-by-month gardening is the best way to make the most of the time we have available to garden, so let's get started.

MICROCLIMATES

It's hard to talk about gardening in California without dealing with the climatic elephant in the room—microclimates. The term "microclimate" refers to the climate in a small, specific area that is different from the climate of the surrounding area. Sounds simple. The thing is that California has a lot of microclimates, more than most other parts of the world, and even though microclimates are relatively small things, they can have a big impact, even for home gardeners. Even in your own garden you probably have more than one microclimate.

To identify specifically the different microclimates in your garden, you need to set one thermometer in a permanent location and then move a second thermometer to different locations in the garden each day, recording the different temperature readings at the same time of day. You will probably find a difference of several degrees in various locations and you can take advantage of that difference in deciding where to plant certain things. As a general rule, however, you can consider the following:

- **South- and west-facing walls:** These areas are likely to be among the warmest spots in your garden. Walls and fences (particularly when made of stone or masonry) absorb heat through the day, keeping the area warmer into the night. Plant heat-loving plants here, such as tomatoes, pomegranates, and other edibles that need heat to ripen fruit.

- **North-facing walls:** These areas are cool and best for shade-loving or woodland plants. In hot-summer parts of the state, plant shrubs like hydrangeas, viburnum, or other plants that might burn with too much direct sun.

- **East-facing walls:** These areas get morning sun so plants that like light but not too much heat, such as azalea, rhododendron, and fuchsia, prosper here.

- **Under the eaves of houses:** This area will provide a bit of shelter and a few more degrees of warmth during a frost. Use this area for frost-tender plants or move container plants here during a period of frost for extra protection.

- **At the bottom of a slope:** Cold air will flow down a slope and hang in the low ground below, which makes that area unsuitable for frost-tender plants but better for plants that need more chill hours to set flowers or fruit, such as peonies or apples.

The old joke is that everybody talks about the weather, but nobody does anything about it. When it comes to microclimates, however, you *can* do something about it. You can use them to garden more successfully.

START WITH THE SOIL

Perhaps you live in an area with dark, nutrient-rich loam. When you squeeze a handful of soil, it forms a clod that then crumbles in your hand. When you breathe it in, it doesn't smell like salt or chemicals; it smells fresh, moist, and alive. Lucky you! From a gardener's perspective, sitting on good soil is like sitting on a pile of gold. Odds are, however, that your soil is less than perfect. You may have sandy soil that has the benefit of good drainage but is deficient in nutrients. Or you may have clay soil that turns to hard rock in the summer and waterlogged muck in the rainy season. Maybe your soil is highly acidic or highly alkaline. Whatever your soil conditions are, there are pretty simple ways to improve them. It will take some time and diligence to work your way toward having that lovely loam that makes plants thrive, but it can be done.

Good soil is loose soil. Good soil crumbles in your hand but doesn't slip through your fingers like sand through an hourglass. Good soil yields to a shovel rather than meeting it the way cement meets a toothpick. This may not describe your soil as it is now, but your soil can become loose, or friable, as gardeners like to call it.

Many people think the way to get loose soil is to get out a rototiller and till it. Double-digging is another technique people have used. These techniques work, but they can also break down the structure of the soil and are usually not necessary (unless you have very rocky soil). Working compost into the soil and adding a layer of organic mulch on top will, over time, accomplish the same thing as rototilling, and it will improve the soil structure rather than destroy it.

■ *Common organic materials for improving garden soil include (A) manure, (B) peat moss, (C) chopped leaves (D) straw, (E) grass clippings, and (F) compost. Coarser materials work best for improving dense, clay soils, while finer materials are best in sandy soils.*

If you have heavy clay soil, there is another step you can take to make your soil looser and more workable. Buy a few bags of gypsum (calcium sulfate dehydrate) and spread it liberally over your soil like a light dusting of snow. Then spread a few inches of an organic mulch over that and water. Keep watering regularly and in a few months, you will find that your hard clay has become friable. This is not a one-time fix; in time it may become hard again and you will have to repeat this procedure. For sandy soil that is too loose, compost (or any organic matter) and mulch are all you need. This too is not a one-time fix; you'll need to constantly add organic matter to keep your soil loamy.

THE IMPORTANCE OF DRAINAGE

We tend to think of soil as a solid, but in fact it is highly oxygenated—or at least it should be. In dense clay soils, water drains slowly, pushing out the oxygen and leaving delicate roots unable to reach it—in other words, drowning. In sandy soils, on the other hand, there is so much space between soil particles that water passes through it quickly, giving roots a quick drink but no consistent moisture, so they dry out faster. In a healthy loam, drainage is fast enough to allow roots to still get oxygen but slow enough that they get all the moisture they need.

For the most severe drainage problems, you may need to install French drains or pipes, but often humus is what makes the difference in soil drainage. Humus is organic matter that has broken down completely and when combined with clay or sandy soil, it not only adds nutrients, it also improves the drainage. You add humus to your soil by working in compost, aged manure, rotted leaves, grass clippings, and other organic matter. It doesn't improve the soil overnight, and you may need to look to raised beds, container planting, and other techniques to get you through to the day when your soil drains properly. But over time you should see your soil drain more efficiently as the overall soil quality improves.

It makes no difference whether you're planting radishes or pecan trees, roots need to grow *down*. In California, where some housing developments were built on a few scant inches of imported topsoil, that can sometimes be a problem. So how deep is your topsoil? The only way to find out is to take a shovel and dig. You may find that the only way you can provide your plants with enough loose soil to grow healthy root systems is to garden *up*, by building raised beds or using lasagna-style planting methods. Over time, you can change not only the quality of your topsoil but also its depth.

Before you plant anything, however, you should also run a soil test to find out how your soil rates in terms of nutrients and pH. (See March for information on how to test your soil and April and September for information on selecting fertilizers and soil amendments to improve your soil's health.)

GROWING FROM SEED

There are a lot of advantages to growing from seed, the most obvious one being cost. Seeds are by far the most inexpensive way to grow. In addition, with seeds you'll have a much wider range of plant varieties to choose from, including interesting heirloom varieties that you will never find in the stores. And I've often found that plants I've grown from seed in my garden become better established than transplanted seedlings from the nursery.

You'll find information on the seed packets about whether the seeds should be started indoors or planted directly in the ground. There are a few factors that determine whether a plant is a good candidate for direct sowing or not, including the germination time and the type of root system the plant has. Plants that are slow to germinate may benefit from the head start of growing indoors. On the other hand, some plants have taproots or delicate root systems that don't tolerate transplanting well and are better off taking their chances outdoors right from the beginning. Some plants can go either way, but starting indoors will give them the advantage of a few additional weeks growing indoors before temperatures permit moving them outdoors.

■ *To plant tiny seeds like moss rose, mix the seeds with sand before planting to help spread the seeds evenly over the soil.*

DIRECT-SOWING SEEDS OUTDOORS

For plants that can be direct sown, a good deal of their survival depends on how well you prepare the ground for them. The planting bed should be free of weeds, rocks, and other debris and the soil loose enough to accommodate tender roots. For root crops like carrots and parsnips, be sure that the ground is loosened and all rocks are removed to the depth that the roots will grow. Planting these crops in soil that is rocky will lead to roots that are forked and deformed as they try to grow around the stones. It's always helpful to work compost into the soil before sowing seeds as well. It helps the soil to retain moisture and has nutrients to provide the seedlings as soon as the roots develop.

Once the soil is loose enough, smooth it out with a rake and trace out a seeding plan in the ground. If you're planting in rows, use a rake handle or the narrow side of a board to impress the row into the soil. Drop in the seeds at the recommended spacing and cover with soil. A rule of thumb is to cover seeds to the same depth as the width of the seed, so tiny seeds are scantly covered and bigger seeds are planted more deeply.

Some seeds, like wildflowers or lettuces, for example, can be broadcast, or sprinkled generally over a prepared area. With really fine seeds, it can be hard to tell if you're distributing them evenly enough. A good trick is to mix the seeds with horticultural sand or vermiculite and sprinkle the mixture over the soil. The sand or vermiculite is easier to see and you'll be able to get a more even broadcast.

Tamp down on the seeded area well to make sure that the seeds and soil are in good contact and there are no big air pockets left. Then water well with a fine mist. Be sure to label what you've planted.

Did you get the feeling someone was watching you while you were planting? There was—birds. And they are waiting for you to go inside so they can swoop down and steal the seeds you just planted. To spoil their plans, you can invert plastic strawberry baskets over the larger seeds or use floating row covers over the entire seeded area. Row covers allow sunlight and moisture to get through, but keep pests away and can protect tender seedlings in case of a late light frost.

SOWING SEEDS INDOORS

For plants that can be transplanted, you can get a jump on the growing season by sowing seeds indoors. The optimal conditions for starting seeds involves grow lights and heating mats, but most seeds can be started easily under less than optimal conditions. There are some things you can't compromise on, however: sterile soil and growing containers, adequate moisture, and warmth.

It's not necessary to use "seed-starting" mixes. It is necessary, though, to use soil that is sterile. There are methods for sterilizing soil yourself, but honestly, it's not worth it. Just buy bags of good quality potting mix. I prefer to mix it in equal proportions with perlite, a naturally occurring, lightweight volcanic material that helps to improve the drainage. While seedlings definitely need adequate water, tender roots will drown if not in a mix that drains well.

To plant seeds individually, you can use recycled plastic six-packs and small (2-inch or 4-inch) pots from the nursery or even yogurt containers (with holes cut in the bottom for drainage). Some people use egg cartons, but I don't think they are deep enough to give the roots much room. Other people use peat pots that can be planted directly in the ground, but I've found that in sandy, fast-draining soil like I have, the peat decomposes far too slowly, keeping the roots inhibited. And you should definitely not use peat plugs to start seeds in. (Peat has all the wrong drainage properties for seeds.) Whatever container you use, make sure it is completely clean; use a 10 percent bleach solution to make sure it is free of bacteria as well.

Some people prefer to plant in flats, but that can make transplanting a little more stressful for the plants that have to have their roots detangled. One way I've found to get around that problem is to make soil blocks in flats. Some of my most successful seed starting has been done in soil blocks in those clear plastic clamshell boxes you get take-out food in. (Having the closed lid keeps in more moisture.) You can buy handy-dandy gadgets that form soil blocks quickly in multiples and if you're starting a lot of seeds, that may be a good investment for you. Since I usually start seeds a few small batches at a time, I just use a square 2-inch plastic pot as the form. All you do is prepare your soil mix and moisten it enough so that it will hold together in a clump in your hand. Fill your soil block form with the mix, packing it in tightly, and then releasing it upside down into the flat. Keep repeating until the flat is filled with blocks that are touching on all sides but not firmly packed together. Use a pencil or chopstick to make an indentation in each block and drop in the seed at the proper depth. Cover the seed with soil and water lightly.

Before the seedlings emerge, what seeds need more than light is warmth. Professional propagators use heat mats for that purpose, but you can improvise. Find a warm spot in your house and set up the seed trays there. I've started seeds on top of my refrigerator and on a cookie sheet placed over a radiator. (That worked great, actually.) As soon as the seedlings emerge, however, move them to a place where they can get the best light possible. Insufficient light will cause seedlings to get leggy, a weakness that some plants never really recover from. If you notice your seedlings getting leggy, add additional light and direct a fan blowing gently over the seedlings for an hour or two each day. The movement caused by the breeze helps to strengthen the stems. If weather permits, start hardening off the seedlings (see the next section) as soon as possible.

In addition to soil, containers, heat, and light, the last thing that seeds absolutely must have is consistent watering. While many mature plants can handle the stress of drying out and come back from it when they finally do get water, seedlings just can't. Check the soil daily; it should be moist but not waterlogged (too much water is as damaging as too little). Add water as needed.

MOVING SEEDLINGS OUTDOORS

Once your seedlings are big enough for transplanting and the last average frost date has passed, it's time to get them ready for life outside. This process, called *hardening off*, is a little like sending your kids off to school—you want to send

them out for just a short time each day and let them get used to the new environment slowly.

Find a spot outside that is protected from wind and animals that can knock the seedlings around, and leave them there, first for an hour or two, and then for longer and longer periods of time. Indirect light is best at first, and then gradually work them toward full-sun exposure. Since the plants are still very tender, check them when you bring them in each day to make sure they aren't getting attacked by bugs.

If at first you're not noticing any discernable difference in your plants as you begin hardening them off, then you know you're doing it right. But as the amount of time the plants spend outdoors increases, you should notice the plants looking a bit more vigorous, with thickening stems and fuller foliage. That's when it's time to transplant.

Plant them in their new location, disturbing the root systems as little as possible, and water them well. If after a few days you see signs of transplant shock (wilting or dieback), try trimming the plant back by as much as a third. Keep watering and give it a chance to redirect some of its energy back toward the roots. With a little bit of luck, the plants will settle into their new home and get growing.

SAVING SEEDS

Farmers have been saving seeds since the earliest days of agriculture, but we've learned a thing or two along the way to make the process more efficient. There are good reasons for saving seeds, first of which is the money it saves. Instead of having to purchase new seeds year after year for your favorite crops, often at $1.50 or more a packet, you can save the seeds of the plants you know you were able to grow successfully. Even the best seed companies have occasional crop failures and saving your own seeds will ensure that you'll have the seeds you want each year.

Another reason to save seeds is to be able to participate in seed exchanges. These seed swaps are becoming more and more common lately and you can find them through gardening groups, on the Internet, or maybe even your local library. My city

■ *Harden off plants by setting them on your porch or patio during the day and bringing them in at night until they are acclimated to outside conditions.*

library recently started a seed library where you can take out seeds contributed by other gardeners and deposit seeds that you have saved. As with seeds saved from your own garden, you can be fairly confident that seeds from a local seed exchange will grow well in your garden.

To collect seeds, you have to be willing to sacrifice the fruit or flower on one or two plants. Select your healthiest and most vigorous plants to save seed from; after all, you want to carry on the genetic characteristics of the best of the crop. After the fruit has fully matured, open up the fruit and collect the seed. Wash the seed well to make sure all of the flesh from the fruit has been removed, then spread the seed out in a single layer on paper towels on a cookie sheet or plate. Put the seeds somewhere out of direct light but with good air circulation and let the seed dry *completely*. When you think the seed is completely dry, spread them out on a fresh paper towel and

dry them another day just to make sure. When they really are completely dry, package them for storage. Ultimately, seeds should be stored in an airtight container, but you can package the different varieties in envelopes, plastic containers, or zip-top plastic bags, and then store those labeled packages together in an airtight container. (If you want to get fancy, you can do a Google search for "seed pack templates" and find all kinds of designs for seed envelopes to download and print from your computer.) Once the seeds are all packed, store the container in your refrigerator. Heat and sunlight can damage seeds, so the refrigerator provides the best, most consistent climate for seed storage.

If you're wondering how long you can store seeds, there's no one answer to that. Some seeds simply have a longer shelf life than others. But if you store them properly, most seeds will last more than a year.

A word of warning about saving seed: Many plants, such as apples, for example, do not grow "true" from seed. You can plant the seed and grow an apple tree from it, but the fruit you'll get from it will not be a genetic match to the fruit the seed came from and will most likely be inferior to that original (parent) fruit. If you want seed that is going to produce a plant with certain exact characteristics, you should buy seed from a reputable seed company. If you want a fruit tree that will produce a particular variety of fruit, you need to buy a grafted variety from a nursery or learn to graft one yourself.

THE BASICS OF WATERING

Before you get to the question of how you should water, it helps to understand some basic tips about watering:

- The best time to water is early morning, just before dawn. Water will have time to penetrate the soil before it can evaporate and plants will have the moisture they need during the heat of day. Also, roots are less likely to rot when they haven't been sitting in water throughout the night.

- The best method of watering is drip irrigation or soaker hoses, which get the water directly to the root systems with little or no evaporation and no splashing water to carry fungal diseases.

- Consistency matters. Inconsistent watering can stress a plant and cause fruit to split. Blossom end rot in tomatoes can also be caused by inconsistent watering.

- If you recycle water from your household (grey water), do not use it on your edible plants. Use the grey water on ornamental plants and lawns and save the fresh water for your fruits and vegetables.

- Infrequent and deep watering beats frequent light watering. Why? Because deep watering encourages deeper, healthier root systems. For trees in particular, a deep root system will lead to better overall health and fruit production.

With this information in hand, as well as an understanding of your soil type and particular plants' water needs, you can create an optimal schedule for watering.

IRRIGATION TECHNIQUES AND RAIN HARVESTING

There are three general methods of irrigating your garden. The first is drip irrigation, which uses narrow aboveground tubing and drip emitters to deliver water in small amounts to the precise locations you want in the garden. This is the most efficient irrigation system because it gets the water directly at the roots and loses the least amount of water to evaporation. This kind of system needs to be monitored regularly to make sure emitters are working correctly and also to ensure that the water is not dripping directly against the plant stems or tree trunks, which can cause crown rot.

Another type of irrigation is a sprinkler system. These systems use underground pipes and sprinkler heads (stationary or pop-up) to spray water in a certain direction. Sprinklers use considerably more water than drip systems—gallons per minute as opposed to gallons per hour. It also loses more water to evaporation and because it sprays at or over plants, it can leave foliage wet, which can be conducive to the spread of fungal diseases. It can also cause a lot of runoff because it can deliver water faster than the ground can absorb it. You can control runoff by setting the system to go on and off for short intervals, allowing the water to penetrate in between.

If you don't have an irrigation system in place, that leaves hand watering. While hand watering does use more water than a drip system and leaves water on the foliage, it has the advantage of getting the water directly to the intended areas in easy-to-control amounts. It can be time-consuming, of course, especially for a larger garden. One way to minimize the hands-on time of hand watering as well as maximizing the water efficiency is to use soaker hoses. These are either flat hoses with holes on top or round hoses that ooze water all around. By winding the hoses throughout the garden bed, you can deliver the water close to the root systems in much the same way that drip emitters do.

One of the simplest and most common water conservation techniques is very low-tech: rain barrels. Large waterproof barrels strategically placed around your house to collect water from rain gutters can save many gallons of water that you can use for your garden. If you live in a region with a fair amount of rain throughout the year, rain barrels are great but in dry-summer regions (and that's most of California), they're of limited use. They fill up fast in the rain and the water gets used up fast. And then there may be weeks or even months where it doesn't rain again and the barrels just sit there empty, taking up

■ *Select a location for a rain barrel under a downspout. Locate your barrel as close to the area you want to irrigate as possible, and make sure the barrel has a stable, level base.*

space. And there's another problem—rain that runs off roofs may pick up bacteria from birds and insects as well as chemicals used in some roofing materials. That water should not be used on edible plants. As with grey water, rain barrel water should be used on ornamental plants only so that you can save the fresh water for the fruits and vegetables.

FERTILIZING

The first step in fertilizing your garden plants should always begin with a soil test. Your local nursery or garden center has soil test kits that will tell you how much of the major nutrients or micronutrients your soil has. Or you can take the standard soil test offered by the University of Massachusetts Amherst (www.umass.edu/soiltest/list_of_services.htm). For a reasonable fee they'll measure the pH, major nutrients, heavy metals, and more. Once you've determined what nutrients your soil needs, you can find the fertilizer that will supply it.

N-P-K

The three main nutrients (also called *macronutrients*) that plants need are nitrogen (N) for green growth, phosphorous (P) for blooming and fruiting, and potassium (K) for overall vigor. When you look at fertilizer packages, you will often see three numbers, such as 10-0-10 or 5-20-10. Those are the N-P-K indicators that tell you what the proportions are of each nutrient in that fertilizer. A *complete fertilizer* will contain all three macronutrients. For lawns you should look for a high-nitrogen fertilizer with a higher first number. If you want to encourage flowering or fruiting, look for a higher middle number. Often you want a little bit of everything; in those cases look for a *balanced fertilizer*, indicated by the same number for each nutrient, for example, 10-10-10.

FERTILIZER TYPES AND HOW TO USE THEM

Fertilizers can be organic (made of plant or animal products) or inorganic (made of synthetic chemicals). From a plant's point of view, there isn't much difference. Organic nitrogen and synthetic nitrogen work just the same. But there are other differences to consider. While organic fertilizers, such as compost, manure, and fish emulsion, improve the biodiversity of the soil, they can also contain pathogens and their nutrient values can be more variable. On the other hand, inorganic fertilizers may not replace trace nutrients in the soil and are produced in ways that are not sustainable.

Whatever fertilizer you use, you should be sure to water plants well *before and after* applying the fertilizer. Fertilizing a plant that isn't hydrated will cause it to burn. Apply the fertilizer in the amount recommended on the package—don't overdo it! Plants should only be fertilized when they're actively growing and not stressed.

For trees, keep in mind that roots don't just grow down, they also grow out, so you need to apply the fertilizer in a way that will reach all the roots. The bulk of the root system for a tree will be contained with the drip line, the area around the trunk that is covered by the entire canopy of the tree. To adequately fertilize a tree, you should apply the appropriate amount of fertilizer evenly within that drip line.

BASIC TOOLS

There are a few tools every gardener should have on hand. Here are the essential and near-essential garden tools and other items I'd recommend you invest in.

- Shovel
- Trowel
- Pruner and lopper
- Rake
- Garden fork
- Hoses and watering nozzles
- Garden cart
- Composter
- Hat
- Gloves

■ *Tools come in a variety of sizes and shapes. Before buying any tool, try it out at the store to make sure that it's comfortable to hold and use.*

There's no point in investing in good tools if you aren't going to take care of them. Tools need to be regularly cleaned, sharpened, and oiled if you want them to last. For pruners and loppers, keep a sharpening stone on hand. A few quick swipes of the stone across the blades give you a sharp blade. Sharp blades make clean cuts and clean cuts are less susceptible to disease. Pruners should also be oiled periodically to keep them moving smoothly and resistant to rust. And here's the best tip of all: Keep a container of disinfectant wipes with you whenever you're pruning. After you finish pruning each plant or tree, wipe your pruners and loppers down with the disinfectant so that you don't spread bacteria or fungi onto other plants.

INTEGRATED PEST MANAGEMENT (IPM)

California doesn't have quite as serious a problem with destructive bugs as some of the more tropical areas of the world, but bugs are still treated as a serious threat here. The reason? The state's $45 billion agriculture industry. California farmers can't afford to let an infestation get out of hand so the state is vigilant about containing any real threat posed by an invading insect and has in the past instituted spraying programs and quarantines to eradicate or control problems with the Mediterranean fruit fly, the light brown apple moth, and the Asian citrus psyllid, just to name a few.

But most bug problems are not that serious. And it is important that our responses to any insect problem be proportional to the actual threat. You don't have to go nuclear on every bug that deigns to feed on your tender little plants. Your garden is a complex biological community and almost any attack you launch against insects will certainly affect more than the targeted bug and the plant it's living on.

The law of unintended consequences says that any intervention in a complex situation will result in unanticipated and sometimes undesirable outcomes. The same controls that kill pest insects also kill beneficial insects. That's an unintended consequence. The same controls that kill pest insects can also lead to the building up of a genetic immunity to that control so that we create super-bugs that we need even more lethal controls to kill. That's one heck of an unintended consequence.

Gardeners who practice sustainable gardening methods believe that we should have more of a "let's all get along" approach to pest control. This is called *Integrated Pest Management (IPM)*, and its goal is to reduce or eliminate the use of pesticides by practicing prevention, observation, and when necessary, intervention to control significant pest damage. For the home gardener, this is by far the safest and in many ways the easiest strategy. It means accepting minor bug damage but foregoing the most toxic weapons of mass destruction to combat every little pest. By using biological controls, mechanical controls, and good sanitation practices, we can in most cases keep our gardens healthy while we keep the thugs of the insect world in check.

GOOD BUGS/BAD BUGS

It took me a while to come to terms with the idea that not all bugs are bad. Except for the obvious ladybugs and butterflies, I wasn't inclined to give any of them a pass. But I've since learned to welcome certain bugs in my garden and encourage them to keep coming back.

First, let's welcome the pollinators. God bless every one of them! All kinds of bees, butterflies, moths, beetles, and even ants pollinate the flowers necessary for fruit to set. (Yes, even beetles and ants, regulars on the pest hit list, do us the favor of spreading a little pollen as they weave their path of destruction!) Without them, we might as well hang up our trowels and call it quits.

Then there are the predator insects that keep the pests in check. Ladybugs eat huge numbers of aphids and other small insects that suck on plants. Trichogramma wasps, or stingless wasps, ingeniously inject their eggs into the eggs of codling moths, European corn borers, and other pests. Their larvae then consume the contents of the other eggs, limiting the pest population. Praying mantises are voracious predators and will consume all kinds of insects from aphids on up. They are effective controls for serious infestations, but if there are not enough pests to satisfy them, they'll consume other beneficial insects as well.

These are just a few examples of the insects that we should be encouraging in our gardens and that would be killed by some of the heavier-handed chemical controls we might use. With that in mind, let's look at more environmentally friendly tactics to employ.

MECHANICAL CONTROLS

Let's start with the simplest and easiest-on-the-environment methods of pest control:

- Handpicking caterpillars and beetles off of your plants is both effective and immediate. Wear a glove if the "ick" factor bothers you at all and drop the bugs into a jar of water and dish detergent before disposing of them in the trash.

- For tinier bugs like aphids and scale, a blast of water from the hose will wash them away in an instant.

- Many bugs such as aphids, scale, and mealy-bugs become a problem because there is an existing ant problem. Ants basically "farm" these insects for their honeydew secretions. If you control the ants, you will have an easier time controlling the other bugs. One way to keep ants off of fruit trees is to use a product to "trap" them, such as a nondrying, sticky paste that you paint around the base of a tree to keep ants from climbing up. Check online for products.

- Diatomaceous earth (DE) is a good barrier for crawling insects. This natural product is made from the fossilized remains of tiny fresh-water organisms. Its granular texture has the effect of scraping the undersides of the bugs crawling over it so that they end up dying of dehydration. It is completely safe for pets in the garden, but be sure to use "food-grade" DE only. This is most effective in gardens that do not use sprinklers since wet DE does not work as intended.

- Push a cardboard toilet paper roll over a seedling and into the ground and you've created a barrier for cutworms. When the plant is more mature you can just tear the barrier away.

■ *Protect young seedlings from cutworms with a short section of a cardboard tube.*

- Slugs and snails love a good beer. Put a shallow pan of it in the garden at the end of the day and in the morning you'll find out exactly how many came for the party and never left.

- Earwigs, on the other hand, like a good roll—the cardboard or newspaper kind. Place a paper towel roll or rolled-up newspaper in the bed and the next day you'll find that earwigs used it as a tent all night. You can just pick up the loaded tube and dump it in the trash.

BACTERIAL CONTROLS

One popular pesticide that is a microbial control is *Bacillus thuringiensis* or Bt. Bt, which is considered an acceptable control for organic farming and gardening, is very effective against caterpillars and worms. When they eat the leaves of a plant sprayed with Bt, they become infected with the bacterium and die. The problem is it kills *any* caterpillar, including those of butterflies and moths that are not pests. For that reason it should be applied very specifically and not sprayed in any general way around your garden.

PESTICIDES DERIVED FROM PLANTS

Next up on the weapons list are pesticides created from plants. While these plant-derived controls may sound "natural," that doesn't mean that they are harmless and care should be used in their application.

The safest of the plant-derived pesticides is Neem, an oil derived from the seeds of the Neem tree. Neem is an effective control for many kinds of pests, including aphids, mites, and nematodes. It is safe for animals and humans and many beneficial insects aren't harmed by it. Neem doesn't directly kill the insects; instead, it disrupts their behavior, affects their growth, or even paralyzes them so they can't reproduce.

Pyrethrins are insecticides derived from the flowers and seeds of the chrysanthemum that target the nervous systems of insects, causing them to die. Pyrethrins are toxic for humans, pets, and fish and care should be used when applying it. Rotenone is another naturally derived control that comes from the roots and stems of certain tropical plants like the jicama vine. It effectively kills all kinds of beetles and was thought to be safe for humans, but recently there has been some question that its use may be linked to the development of Parkinson's disease. Personally, I would not use either of these last two products.

Before using any of these pesticides, please read the instructions carefully, especially the fine print about the precautions you need to take when applying them.

CHEMICAL CONTROLS

With the poisonous legacy of DDT and other chemical pesticides lurking in the background, it is easy to assume that every chemical control is a nightmare of unintended consequences. But it's not that simple. It seems odd, but some synthetic controls are actually less toxic than some of the naturally derived pesticides. And then there are other chemical controls that are widely used that I won't go anywhere near.

Horticultural oils are synthetic but most of them are generally considered acceptable for organic gardening. The oils, which may be petroleum- or vegetable-based, are sprayed onto plants and coat the insects, effectively smothering them. Different types of oils are used at different times—dormant oils are sprayed on during a plant's dormant period and summer oils are used in summertime.

Insecticidal soaps are made from potassium fatty acids and are effective against soft-bodied insects like aphids, mites, whiteflies, and mealybugs. The soap works by disrupting cell membranes in the insects, causing them to die, but it leaves most beneficial insects unharmed. It can be toxic for some plants, however, and you may want to test a few leaves to see how the plant reacts before applying more broadly. A 2 percent solution is what is usually recommended, but the solution can be made stronger or weaker as desired. Insecticidal soap is also an effective control for powdery mildew but generally needs repeated applications.

Beyond these controls, however, things get more serious. Neonicotinoids, synthetic versions of nicotine, have been used extensively in agriculture and considered safe, but there is now concern that they may have played a role in the Colony Collapse Disorder that has decimated so many bee colonies in recent years. Pyrethroids are synthetic versions of pyrethrins and are toxic to fish and other aquatic life so there is great concern about contaminated runoff getting into water systems. Carbaryl, also sold under the name Sevin, is effective and widely used on food crops in the United States, but it kills insects indiscriminately—beneficials as well as pests. It's also classified as a likely human carcinogen, which I translate to mean, "It's not worth it."

As with the plant-derived pesticides, do not apply any of these controls without reading all of the instructions for application and taking the appropriate precautions.

PRUNING

The purpose of pruning is to selectively remove parts of a plant to train it into a particular shape; control the plant's size; encourage flowering, fruiting, and new growth; improve air circulation and light penetration to the center of the plant; maintain health and vigor; and rejuvenate mature plants. Pruning at regular intervals should be a routine part of garden maintenance in order to maintain the health and appearance of your plants.

THE MAIN TYPES OF PRUNING

There are two main types of cuts made in pruning: heading cuts and thinning cuts. *Heading cuts* cut a shoot back to a bud, a stub, or a lower lateral branch. *Thinning cuts* completely remove a branch all the way back to its point of origin. Thinning cuts open up space in the tree canopy while heading cuts lead to a denser canopy because the cuts typically encourage new shoots to emerge.

Timing of pruning is important. Dead, diseased, or damaged parts of a plant can be removed at any time of year, but removing living wood is best done at certain times. In general, you should avoid pruning in spring when the cambium layer of the wood is forming and in fall when fungal diseases are most easily spread. On deciduous trees, winter pruning is done to manage the structure of the tree and encourage new growth. Summer pruning is done to control the size and improve the appearance.

Some trees, such as birch, maple, dogwood, elm, walnut, and cherry, will "bleed" sap from the cuts when pruned at certain times of year, usually late winter and early spring. This bleeding is not harmful to the tree, but it can leave unsightly marks on the bark. Trees that have this tendency to bleed should usually be pruned in late fall or early winter to avoid this.

When you make a pruning cut, you should remove only the branch wood and not cut into the stem or trunk to which the branch is attached. Cutting into the stem wood will create a larger wound that will be harder for the tree to seal off. At the same time, when you remove a branch, you should not leave a stub behind. Cut it off cleanly enough that there's nothing left to hang your hat on. Similarly, when you are removing the end of a branch, cut back to about ¼ inch above a bud that is pointing in the direction you want the branch to grow. Leaving more than ¼ inch above the bud will result in a dead stub.

THE THREE-PART CUT FOR TREES

When removing large branches, it's often necessary to make a three-part cut called a *jump cut*. This kind of cut prevents a branch from falling midway through a cut and tearing bark

■ *Start by undercutting from beneath the limb with your bow saw or chain saw.*

■ *Finish the cut from above. This keeps the bark from tearing when the limb breaks loose.*

■ *Trim the stub from the limb so it's flush with the branch collar.*

and underlying tissue from the trunk as it falls. The first cut is made from the bottom of the branch upward about 15 inches from the trunk. Cut upward until the weight of the branch presses against the saw and prevents you from cutting further. The second cut is made from the top of the branch downward about 18 inches from the trunk. This cut should go all the way through the branch so that you are left with a stub of about 18 inches. The third and final cut should begin at the top of the branch just outside the ridge where the branch connects to the trunk. Cut downward in a straight line to the outside of the trunk collar, a swollen area on the underside where the branch connects to the trunk. Hold the stub with your other hand to prevent any tearing and avoid cutting into the trunk itself.

As a rule, it's best to remove no more than one-third of a tree canopy at any one time. If a tree has not been pruned for a long time, plan on taking a few years to get it back into shape by taking one-third of the old wood away at a time.

There is no need to "seal" pruning cuts with paint or any other kind of sealant. In time a healthy tree can seal off a cut to prevent moisture and pathogens from penetrating.

Pruning is a skill that is learned with practice, but I've found that seeing an experienced gardener or arborist prune a tree is the best way to begin. Many nurseries offer demos and clinics on proper pruning techniques; these present a great opportunity to ask questions and see the proper way to make cuts.

SUSTAINABLE GARDENING

Sustainable gardening is hot term these days but sometimes the definition seems opaque. What is sustainable gardening, really? It's an assortment of gardening practices designed to create balance in the garden by using nature's own systems to encourage growth, manage resources, control waste, and establish an ecosystem that is in harmony with wildlife.

The primary elements of sustainable gardening include:

- **Organic gardening:** Using biological and mechanical controls rather than chemical pesticides and herbicides and natural soil amendments rather than synthetic fertilizers

allows gardens to achieve a natural balance of predators and prey and avoids the use of petrochemicals that are produced from irreplaceable resources and polluting processes.

- **Native plants:** Plants that have for many generations become adapted to an environment will have a greater ability to survive with fewer resources and without attracting new pest and disease problems.

- **Soil management:** Healthy soil is the basis of a healthy and successful garden. By feeding soil with compost and natural amendments, you build up a growing medium that can support plant life and harbor fewer pest and disease problems.

- **Composting:** Home composting reduces waste that must be removed from your property and creates a healthy amendment to add to your garden soil.

- **Drip irrigation:** This most efficient watering method delivers water directly to plants' roots, minimizing the amount of water that is lost to evaporation and reducing the risk of spreading diseases through water splash.

- **Mulching:** Applying a 3- to 4-inch layer of materials such as bark or wood chips, straw, pine needles, or other organic matter helps to keep soil temperature even, reduce water lost to evaporation, minimize soil erosion, and feed the soil as the organic matter decomposes.

- **Integrated pest management (IPM):** Rather than aiming for total eradication of pests, IPM methods aim to control pest problems by allowing a tolerable amount of insect pests, encouraging beneficial insect predators to keep pest populations in check, practicing good sanitation in the garden, and when organic methods are not sufficient, using the least toxic methods of pest control.

- **Recycling:** Re-using and recycling containers and hardscape elements in the garden keeps those items from ending up in the landfill.

One of the most productive things you can do to create a sustainable garden is to allow and encourage beneficial insects and other animals, including the following:

- **Ladybugs:** Everybody loves ladybugs, but not everyone appreciates the major job they do by eating aphids that suck the juices out of plants.

- **Spiders:** They may creep us out but the average spider eats about 100 insects a year.

- **Toads:** Just one toad can eat up to 20,000 slugs, flies, grubs, cutworms, or grasshoppers in a single year. That's a lot of pest management right there.

- **Bats:** Bats consume large quantities of insects and then do double-duty by acting as important plant pollinators.

- **Bees:** In California alone, 42 different nut, fruit, vegetable, forage, and seed crops depend specifically on bees for pollination.

- **Green lacewings:** Green lacewings eat aphids, mites, mealybugs, and other small insects.

- **Ground beetles:** Ground beetles go after cutworms, grubs, root maggots, slugs, and snails. If you have a log or piece of wood lying around your garden, you'll often find ground beetles underneath.

- **Hover flies:** These flies feed on flower nectar, which makes them excellent pollinators. They also eat aphids and mealybugs.

- **Hummingbirds:** These small birds are not only busy pollinators, they also consume a good many insects as part of their daily diet.

You can purchase and release some of these beneficials, such as ladybugs or green lacewings, into your garden. But if you avoid using pesticides, you will usually find that when your garden develops a problem with a pest, such as aphids, the beneficial insects will find their way to your garden—and their potential food source—soon enough.

GARDENING TO ATTRACT WILDLIFE

For many of us, one of the biggest benefits of gardening is that it creates a point of contact between us and the creatures of the wild. But when people think of encouraging wildlife to come into their gardens, they're often thinking only of birds, bees, and butterflies. To really establish your garden as a place that is welcoming to wildlife, you need to broaden the scope and make it habitable to all kinds of creatures, including reptiles, amphibians, mammals, and yes, even insects.

A garden that is wildlife-friendly provides for all the needs of the animals within—that means food, water, shelter, and places to raise their young. Follow these general principles and practices to welcome as many kinds of wildlife as possible:

- No chemical pesticides! This is the single biggest step you can make to creating a healthy garden for wildlife. While you may use pesticides with the intention of killing only the "bad bugs," beneficial insects will inevitably die as well, and larger animals may be affected as well. In addition, by killing the bad bugs, you've removed an important food source for other animals.

- Remove or reduce the lawn. Large lawns don't provide areas of shelter or as many food

Anna's hummingbirds are busy pollinators as well as insect predators that should be welcome in any California garden.

■ *Animals such as this rough-skinned newt will appreciate your efforts at natural gardening.*

sources for many animals. Using that space to grow a more diverse palette of plants is like opening up a smorgasbord for wildlife.

- Use native plants to attract native wildlife. Native plants tend to attract a greater number of insects that in turn attract larger animals.

- When planting to provide food sources for wildlife, consider all types of food: pollen, nectar, berries, seeds, stems, leaves, and the bugs that are attracted to these foods.

- When planning a water source for wildlife, keep in mind that moving water attracts more wildlife than still water. If a still water feature is all you can arrange, make sure it is kept clean and consistently refilled and that precautions are taken to prevent mosquitoes from breeding there.

- Although it's important to practice good sanitation in your garden, a certain amount of dead and decaying plant material provides both shelter and food for all kinds of wildlife. Leave some leaf debris on the ground and use mulch.

- Diverse plantings offer the optimal setting for wildlife, but don't just plant different types of plants. It's also helpful to select plants that will grow to different heights and have different flowering times, shapes, and sizes.

- While you should grow a wide variety of plants, it's also helpful to plant some things *en masse* rather just one or two of everything.

DIG IN

Grab a pencil, paper, and tape measure. Take the measurements of the space that you plan to plant and sketch out a simple grid marked off by feet. Indicate where North is on the diagram. Take the list of what you want to grow and use it to map out a plan with the proper spacing for all the plants. Consider the mature height of each plant so you can avoid having taller plants shading out shorter ones. The plan doesn't have to be complex or perfect. Odds are, you won't follow it exactly anyway. But creating this visual aid in advance forces you to think through how the garden will look, not just at the beginning but as the plants grow and mature as well. If you are technologically inclined to the point where you no longer own pencils and paper, there are software tools you can find to map out a garden plan.

Take notes as you go along. Whether you start a garden journal or a blog or just scribble a few notes on a calendar, it helps to have something to look back on that reminds you of when you planted or transplanted, the last time you applied fertilizer, or what varieties you tried and how they turned out. That information will help you make decisions in the future about what to grow and what you might want to do differently. It doesn't have to be anything fancy or well written, but having one fixed place where you log the important details of your garden will pay off more than you might imagine.

Here's one last piece of advice: Don't just take my advice. Talk to other gardeners. Talk to the staff at your local nurseries. Call your County Extension office if you have specific questions; they train master gardeners who have a good deal of gardening knowledge and are happy to share it. And use the Internet's vast gardening resources when you need to quickly search for information, identify a plant, or buy seeds or plants you can't find locally.

Those are the basics. Now let's start the gardening year!

HOW TO USE THIS BOOK

California Month-by-Month Gardening is designed to be an easy-to-use, all-purpose guide to garden care and maintenance in the Golden State. In spite of the wide range of climates throughout our state, certain tasks are best-suited to particular times of the year. By identifying those tasks that are best handled each month, your garden becomes more manageable, and you'll do a better job of meeting your plants' needs.

Each month, there are six basic categories for activities: Plan, Plant, Care, Water, Fertilize, and Problem-Solve. Everything you need to do that month will fall into these categories. Care covers tasks such as pruning, harvesting, dividing, and deadheading. Problem-Solve includes advice for handling disease and pest problems that may occur.

Plants are categorized in general plant groups: Annuals (ornamental plants with a life cycle of one year); Bulbs (including corms, tubers, and rhizomes); Edibles (fruits, vegetables, and herbs); Houseplants (any indoor-grown plants); Lawns; Perennials (plants, including succulents and ornamental grasses, with a life cycle of more than one year); Roses (all forms of roses); Shrubs; Trees (ornamental as well as fruit and nut trees); Vines & Groundcovers; and Water Gardens.

To use this book effectively, begin by compiling a general inventory of your garden by plant group. Knowing what plants you already have will not only help you plan their care, but will also help you identify what type of plants you might still want to add.

Read through the activities for each month and determine which tasks need to be done in your garden. Then prioritize the tasks based on your available time and the window of opportunity to get the task done. For example, bare-root plants are only available for planting for a limited time and once purchased, they must go in the ground before they break dormancy. Gardening is most successful when you don't try to fight nature's timeline.

Variations in soil types, microclimates, and other factors can influence the timing of life in your garden. Use this book as your guide, but get to know the rhythms of your own garden. With a month-by-month approach, you'll find that you're working more in sync with nature, so you can better appreciate the joys of gardening instead of seeing it as one long to-do list.

Dig in and get your hands dirty. California gardens are meant to be enjoyed all year long.

USDA COLD HARDINESS ZONES

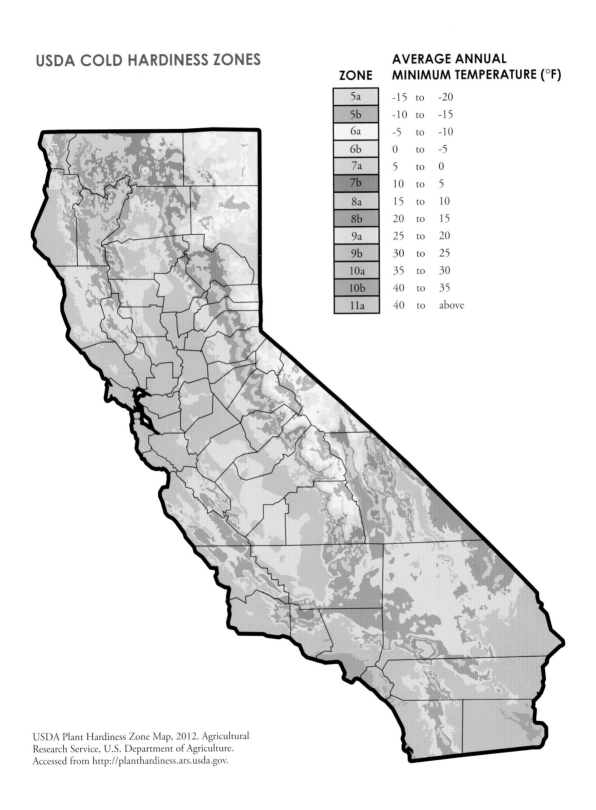

ZONE	AVERAGE ANNUAL MINIMUM TEMPERATURE (°F)		
5a	-15	to	-20
5b	-10	to	-15
6a	-5	to	-10
6b	0	to	-5
7a	5	to	0
7b	10	to	5
8a	15	to	10
8b	20	to	15
9a	25	to	20
9b	30	to	25
10a	35	to	30
10b	40	to	35
11a	40	to	above

USDA Plant Hardiness Zone Map, 2012. Agricultural Research Service, U.S. Department of Agriculture. Accessed from http://planthardiness.ars.usda.gov.

APPROXIMATE FROST DATES IN CALIFORNIA

These dates will help you to know when you might safely plant frost-tender vegetables in your garden or the length of your growing season. The following table provides approximate dates where there is a 10 percent chance and a 50 percent chance for frost (temperatures that are 32°F or lower) and the number of days at 32°F and 28°F and above for various California communities.

COMMUNITY	PROBABILITY OF FROST (SPRING) (MONTH/DAY)		PROBABILITY OF FROST (FALL) (MONTH/DAY)		# OF FROST-FREE DAYS* AT 32°F OR ABOVE	# OF DAYS* AT 28°F OR ABOVE
	50%	10%	10%	50%		
Alameda	—	1/17	12/26	—	365	365
Auburn	2/18	4/02	11/09	12/01	232	312
Bakersfield	1/25	2/24	11/15	12/11	277	321
Berkeley	—	1/18	12/25	—	365	365
Bishop	5/04	5/25	9/29	10/15	137	157
Chico	3/21	4/24	10/29	11/14	196	258
Davis	2/26	4/08	10/31	11/28	226	282
Eureka	1/27	3/12	11/13	12/16	274	365
Fairfield	2/07	3/16	11/14	12/06	255	306
Fresno	2/04	3/20	11/06	12/03	246	300
Half Moon Bay	—	3/07	12/09	—	306	365
Lakeport	4/16	5/07	10/11	11/03	163	197
Lompoc	2/08	3/23	11/11	12/14	259	329
Long Beach	—	1/08	12/23	—	365	365
Los Angeles	—	—	—	—	365	365
Marysville	1/25	2/26	11/17	12/09	280	320
Modesto	2/01	3/03	11/16	12/08	268	313
Mendocino	2/19	4/12	11/05	12/07	229	332
Monterey	—	1/27	12/18	—	365	365
Napa	2/22	4/06	11/05	12/05	277	310
Palm Springs	1/04	3/07	11/29	2/01	309	359
Pasadena	—	2/08	12/12	—	365	365
Paso Robles	4/05	5/14	10/11	10/29	160	217
Placerville	4/10	5/10	10/20	11/09	171	214

COMMUNITY	PROBABILITY OF FROST (SPRING) (MONTH/DAY)		PROBABILITY OF FROST (FALL) (MONTH/DAY)		# OF FROST-FREE DAYS* AT 32°F OR ABOVE	# OF DAYS* AT 28°F OR ABOVE
	50%	10%	10%	50%		
Riverside	1/26	3/07	11/18	12/23	272	365
Sacramento	2/10	3/20	12/04	1/01	250	306
Salinas	7/22	3/01	11/17	12/10	217	365
San Bernardino	1/21	3/09	11/23	12/24	265	365
San Diego	—	—	—	—	365	365
San Jose	1/11	2/10	11/24	12/26	301	365
San Luis Obispo	1/24	3/29	11/10	12/30	247	352
San Rafael/ Marin	1/24	4/15	11/19	1/02	242	365
Santa Rosa	2/21	4/05	11/05	12/07	228	291
Sonora	4/19	5/17	10/11	11/04	164	200
Stockton	2/13	3/14	11/14	11/30	254	293
Ukiah	3/18	4/17	10/29	11/16	203	266
Victorville	4/02	4/24	10/22	11/03	189	226
Visalia	1/28	3/02	11/12	12/06	267	315
Woodland	1/31	2/28	11/13	12/04	267	307
**Yuba city	—	4/08	11/08	—	—	—

* Indicates a 90% probability for number of days at 32°F and 28°F or higher.
Data compiled from: National Weather Service Data, Climatography of California Freeze/Frost Occurrence Data, 1971–2000.

** Data from county Agricultural Commissioner's Office.
Publication and web links: cdo.ncdc.noaa.gov/climatenormals/clim20supp1/states/CA.pdf
— Copyright © 2009, The Regents of the University of California. Used by permission.
ucanr.org/sites/gardenweb/files/29030.pdf

January

A fresh start—isn't that what we're all hoping for in January? And where can you get a fresher start than in the garden? Although this month may be very different in the southern part of the state than it is in the northern, and it may seem like a different world in the mountains compared to the coast, gardeners throughout the state should use this month to evaluate their gardens, determine what is working and what needs reworking, and ask themselves this all-important question:

What do I want to accomplish in my garden this year? Perhaps there is a big landscaping project that's been on the back burner that you're finally ready to tackle. Or maybe your garden's gotten a little out of control and you just want to establish a little more order. Never is your garden more full of possibilities than in January.

But as important as this longer-term planning is, there are actions that should be taken this month. Whether your garden is bathed in winter sunshine, soggy with rain, or buried under a foot of snow, keep in mind that "garden" is a verb as well as a noun, and there's always something that needs doing in a California garden. The nurseries are brimming with winter annuals, bare-root trees, and more goodies than See's Candies, and the temptations are many. You'll have plenty of opportunities to get some dirt under your fingernails with winter planting, but there are also some chores to get out of the way. Get ready to plant, prune, spray, fertilize, and maybe do some storm cleanup. In most parts of California, winter does not allow gardeners a hiatus.

But it won't be all work. The garden is a special refuge in the winter, a place of stark beauty. The hours you spend in the garden this month may be cold or wet but they can be rewarding.

PLAN

ALL

It's the start of a new year. What do you want your garden to grow into over the next twelve months? This month is the perfect time to start imagining the garden of your dreams and making plans to put it in place. Is this the year you'll start a vegetable garden? Or will you finally install the water feature you've been thinking about? Maybe you've been meaning to carve out a space in the garden to put a bench or a couple of chairs for reading. Perhaps you've been dreaming of turning your landscape into a tropical oasis or a native garden or a succulent garden. Oh, the possibilities!

But don't devote the entire month to dreaming of what's desired. Spend some time taking stock of where you're at right now. Now, in midwinter,

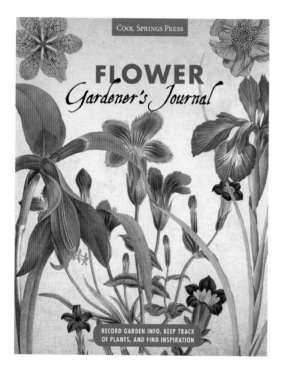

■ *A garden journal gives you a place to document what's going on with your plants and prompts you to be a more keen observer of the happenings in your garden.*

your garden is showing you its bones. With most of the deciduous trees and shrubs laid bare and the tender perennials died back to the roots, you can see the existing structure of your garden and decide what you like and what you want to change. Look for trouble spots—areas that are too bare or too overgrown or lacking seasonal color or interest. Take photos and date them. Make notes in a garden journal so that in the lush days of spring you'll remember why you thought a particular corner or flower bed needed special attention. This is where dreams can begin to morph into the actual plans that you'll put into action over the coming months.

And get ready for seed-starting! Winter days are a great time to spend poring over seed catalogs and placing orders for those heirloom flowers and vegetables that aren't easy to come by in six-packs or 4-inch pots in the spring. For some of the best selections, check out the Resources section for contact information. And all those seed packets you have left over from previous years? Time to sort through them and toss the ones that are too old to be viable. Flower seeds vary a great deal in the length of time they will remain viable, but most vegetable seeds, if properly stored, will usually be good for up to five years:

1 year	Onion
2–3 years	Bean, carrot, corn, pea, pepper, spinach
4–5 years	Beet, broccoli, cucumber, eggplant, kale, lettuce, melon, radish, squash, tomato

Test the viability of older seeds following the directions in the "Here's How" box. To keep seeds at peak freshness, store seed packets in an air-tight container in the refrigerator (never in the freezer!).

LAWNS

Take the time this month to clean and prep your mower and other tools so they'll be in good shape throughout the year. Set the blades higher during the winter months (2 inches for warm-season grasses and 3 to 4 inches for cool-season grasses) and sharpen and oil them for a cleaner cut and rust-free operation. Alternatively, this is a good time to look into hiring a lawn service.

HERE'S HOW

TO TEST THE VIABILITY OF SEEDS

Spare yourself a disappointing spring by testing the viability of the older seeds in your collection before planting time. A simple procedure requiring nothing more than a paper towel, some water, and a plastic bag will give you the information you need to easily calculate the germination rate.

- Spread ten seeds (all of the same variety, all from the same seed packet) across half of a clean paper towel, fold the other half of the towel over to cover the seeds, and dampen the paper towel until it's completely moist.

- Place the paper towel with the seeds in a zip-top plastic bag on which you've written the date. Attach the seed packet to the plastic bag with a paper clip or tape and set the bag someplace dark and at room temperature where it won't be disturbed.

- Check every three to four days to make sure the paper towel is still moist. If it is drying out, dampen it again.

- After about ten days unfold the paper towel and count how many seeds have germinated. (Some types of seeds are slower to germinate even when they're fresh, so consult the seed packet to see if you should allow more than ten days.) If at least seven seeds have sprouted (a 70 percent germination rate), the seeds still should be viable enough to plant. If only four or five seeds have sprouted (a 40 to 50 percent rate), you can still use them but you should probably plant them twice as thickly as the packet recommends. With less than a 40 percent germination rate, it's probably not worth your time to plant those seeds. Toss them and treat yourself to packed-fresh-for-this-year seeds.

ROSES

Nurseries are filled with bare-root roses at this time of year, but don't be seduced too easily. Give careful consideration to how much space you have where roses will receive a minimum of six hours of sun a day. Then decide what type of rose (hybrid tea, shrub, climber) would best fill the space. Last but definitely not least, give serious consideration to the disease resistance that any cultivar offers, especially for the most common rose diseases: blackspot, rust, and powdery mildew.

TREES

You can shop for a wide range of bare-root fruit trees in local and online nurseries, but keep in mind that hardiness zones are only one criterion to consider when making your selection. Pay close attention to the chill hours needed (see October to find the number of chill hours recorded for your region) as well as whether or not the tree needs another variety planted nearby as a cross-pollenizer.

VINES & GROUNDCOVERS

Watch for areas with soil erosion problems; in the spring you can plant a groundcover in those areas to improve the problem for the following year.

WATER GARDENS

Plan ahead for renovations or improvements to be done in the spring. It can take time to source parts or identify professionals to install lighting, pumps, or entirely new water features. You can also shop for plants now, although online nurseries will usually hold your order until the proper time to plant based on your U.S. Department of Agriculture (USDA) plant hardiness zone. But doing the research and ordering now will guarantee that you'll get the plants you want before they sell out.

PLANT

ANNUALS

Pot up some containers of colorful cool-season annual flowers to brighten a bleak winter landscape. Pansies, Iceland poppies, stock, dianthus, cineraria, and snapdragons (actually a perennial, but they're sold as an annual) make a colorful splash to fill in bare spots around dormant shrubs and trees.

BULBS

Still haven't gotten your spring-blooming bulbs planted? It's not too late, as long as your

PLAN YOUR GARDEN PROJECTS ON PINTEREST

Are you a Pinner? If you're an active member of the Pinterest community, you may already know what a great site Pinterest is for discovering ideas, finding instructions, and making plans for garden projects. If you're not on Pinterest yet, this may be the reason to finally join.

Pinterest is a social media website where you can collect images, articles, videos, and other online content and organize them on subject boards that you create for your own interests. Whatever your hobby or passion is, it's likely that you'll find content of interest to you as well as fellow Pinners for you to follow on Pinterest.

You can join Pinterest using your Facebook or Twitter account or just your email address. Once you've joined you'll be asked to indicate what topics you're interested in. Gardening happens to be one of the very active topics on the site and you'll find more garden-related items that other users have already pinned than you'll know what to do with. You can repin items that other users have already pinned, or you can add a Pin It button to your browser's toolbar and use it to pin items you find anywhere on the Internet (unless a website's owner has blocked his site or images from being pinned). Create a few boards for yourself that will help you organize your garden pins. Some of my boards include "Garden Scenes I Love," "Fairy Gardens," "DIY Gardening Techniques," "Garden Wildlife," and "Garden Organization." I use these boards to pin ideas and instructions for projects I might like to try in the future. For me, Pinterest has replaced the manila folders stuffed with pages I used to tear from magazines. It was always a challenge trying to keep my idea folders organized and usable, but Pinterest makes it a breeze. Not only can I get inspired by other gardeners' pins, I can also create boards for any projects I'm planning and pin ideas, tips, instructions, or cautions for those projects, whether it's for building a new garden shed, decorating a deck, designing a water feature, or planting a butterfly garden.

If you're ready to join the Pinterest community, you can start by following me and my boards. You'll find me at pinterest.com/alamedagardener/. Come join the fun and get inspired to plan your best garden yet.

ground isn't frozen. And in warmer parts of Southern California, it's not too early to plant summer-blooming bulbs or tubers, such as begonias, cannas, or tigridias, as long as danger of frost has passed. (See October for information on planting bulbs.)

EDIBLES

The number of crops you can grow right through the winter in California is rather stunning. In areas that don't experience hard frosts, the edibles you can plant this month include artichokes, asparagus, broccoli, cabbage, carrots, cauliflower, kohlrabi, lettuce, onions, peas, peppers, potatoes, radishes, and spinach, as well as grape and kiwi vines and a wide range of fruit and nut trees that are available in bare-root form. Some of these vegetables, like spinach, don't germinate well in cool soil so they

need to be grown from nursery starts or planted from seed indoors, but others, like lettuces and radishes can be direct-seeded outdoors in mild-winter regions.

Successive plantings of cool-season crops can keep your edible garden producing until the warmer weather comes, but be prepared to provide some protection from frosts (except for kales and cabbages, whose flavor gets sweeter with frost).

In the colder parts of California, you may have to take extra steps to extend the growing season for edibles. Cold frames, typically constructed as a four-sided, open-bottomed box with a clear glass or plastic lid that can open, are one way. They offer enough protection from cold, frost, and snow to give you weeks or even months

◼ *A cold frame can extend the growing season in your garden to almost—or truly— year-round. Use an oversized cold frame like the one here and there may be no need to put up vegetables in the fall, because you'll have all the fresh produce you can handle.*

more of growing time. A more flexible option is to create a mini-hoop house by anchoring semi-circles of PVC pipe into the ground and covering it with a floating row cover made of a spunbond fabric like Reemay cloth, which lets in light and air but keeps frost off plants. When the weather warms up, simply remove the cloth and hoops and let the plants keep growing where they are.

ROSES

In the mild-winter parts of the state (zones 9–11), you can start planting bare-root or container-grown roses. (See February for instructions on planting bare-root roses.)

TREES

In the winter, you'll often find nurseries stocking bare-root trees. These are young (usually less than two years old) saplings in their dormant state that are shipped from the growers without a container. The bare rootball is wrapped up during shipping to keep it from drying out and then stashed in a bed of sawdust, wood chips, or leaves when they arrive at the nursery. Because growers are spared the labor costs of potting up the trees and the shipping costs are much lower, bare-root trees generally sell for 30 to 50 percent less than container trees. Not only do you get a better price buying a bare-root tree, but you get the chance to really see what you're buying.

◼ *Bare-root trees are the most wallet-friendly, but you must plant them during the dormant season before growing begins.*

HERE'S HOW

TO READ A SEED PACKET

When it comes to the information provided on a packet of seeds, there is a great deal of variation from one seed company to another. Some provide a great deal of information, not just regarding growing, but also harvesting and use. Others, unfortunately, can be rather stingy with the specifics. Here are some of the details you should look for on a seed packet:

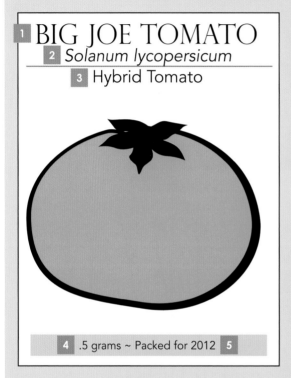

1 BIG JOE TOMATO
2 *Solanum lycopersicum*
3 Hybrid Tomato

4 .5 grams ~ Packed for 2012 **5**

1 Common name

2 Scientific name

3 Type of plant
Either "hybrid" (a plant bred from two different varieties of the plant) or "heirloom" (a plant that was more commonly grown in the first half of the 20th century and has not been hybridized)

4 Weight or seed count
Many seed companies package seeds by weight but some sell seeds by number.

5 "Packed for" date
All seeds must be sold to customers before the end of the "packed for" year.

6 When to plant outside
The packet may have a zone map or just list the months that are appropriate for planting.

7 Light requirements
Most vegetables require full sun, but the tag will note the requirements.

You can make sure the roots are healthy and not damaged or girdling the trunk. You can easily see if the trunk is straight. Everything about the tree is right there, exposed to view.

When you get the tree home from the nursery, brush any sawdust or wood chips off of the roots and let it soak in a bucket of tepid water for several hours to make sure the roots are completely hydrated. When you're ready to plant, dig a hole twice as wide but the same depth as the rootball. Loosen the soil at the bottom of the hole and mound it a bit so that the roots can extend comfortably out from the center of the hole. Begin filling the hole back up with soil, making sure that the tree is straight and that you aren't burying it too deep. The soil should cover the rootball entirely but not pile any deeper around the base of the trunk.

It's not usually necessary to stake a young tree unless it's in a particularly windy spot. If you do stake it, use flexible ties to secure the trunk to two stakes, one on each side. The idea is to allow the tree to move a bit, which helps to strengthen the trunk, but not let it fall over. Don't leave the stakes and ties in place for more than the first year or the ties will end up cutting into the tree as it grows.

Bare-root fruit trees should be cut back by at least one-third, or as short as 18 inches

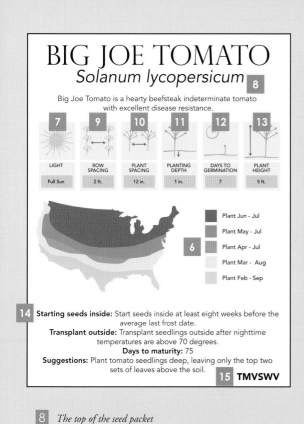

BIG JOE TOMATO
Solanum lycopersicum 8

Big Joe Tomato is a hearty beefsteak indeterminate tomato with excellent disease resistance.

7	9	10	11	12	13
LIGHT	ROW SPACING	PLANT SPACING	PLANTING DEPTH	DAYS TO GERMINATION	PLANT HEIGHT
Full Sun	2 ft.	12 in.	1 in.	7	5 ft.

Plant Jun - Jul
Plant May - Jul
6 Plant Apr - Jul
Plant Mar - Aug
Plant Feb - Sep

14 **Starting seeds inside:** Start seeds inside at least eight weeks before the average last frost date.
Transplant outside: Transplant seedlings outside after nighttime temperatures are above 70 degrees.
Days to maturity: 75
Suggestions: Plant tomato seedlings deep, leaving only the top two sets of leaves above the soil. 15 **TMVSWV**

8 *The top of the seed packet*
Usually has information about the type of plant you're growing. Indeterminate tomatoes keep growing and growing—like a vine—while determinate tomatoes stop.

9 *Row spacing*
Space needed between rows (if you're planting in rows).

10 *Plant spacing*
The amount of space required between individual plants.

11 *Planting depth*
The depth at which you'll plant the seed if you're sowing the seeds outside, as opposed to planting transplants.

12 *Days to germination*
The number of days between when you plant the seed and when it sprouts. Most vegetables require certain soil temperatures for germination. Radishes germinate in 50-degree soil, while tomatoes require warmer soil. You can buy soil thermometers to take the temperature of the soil.

13 *Plant height*
The height of the mature plant.

14 *Starting seeds inside*
Warm-weather vegetables are started inside to give them a head start on the growing season. All vegetables have a "days to maturity," which is the number of days between sprouting the seed and harvesting.

15 *TMVSWV*
For vegetable seeds, more and more companies are starting to provide information on disease-resistance. The code above indicates this plant will be resistant to Tobacco Mosaic Virus and Spotted Wilt Virus.

above the ground immediately after planting, depending on how low you want the branching to start. I know it sounds severe, but cutting back at planting encourages better root and branch development.

The first tree you might want to plant this year may be the one sitting in your living room. That living tree left over from Christmas? It's time to decide what to do with it. Unless you live in a rural area with plenty of room in the back forty, it's almost certainly a bad idea to plant a Christmas tree in the ground. These trees grow big—really big! Scotch pines will grow to 30 to 100 feet tall, Douglas firs will reach 80 to 160 feet, and Noble firs top out at a whopping 90 to 200 feet; all of them will eventually take up 20 to 30 feet in width. Unless you have enough space to accommodate that growth, away from where people or property can be damaged by the falling branches these varieties are known for, plant your living Christmas tree in a large container, such as a wine barrel planter, where its growth will be restricted. Plant it in full sun in a well-draining potting mix; water regularly, then stand back. Eventually (and with some varieties, sooner than you would expect), it will outgrow its container. At that point, it's best to either donate it to a park or someplace else that has the room to grow it in the ground, or decide that it's outlived the promise of its Christmas tree farm beginnings and send it to the chipper.

CARE

ALL

Sharpen your pruners! The most significant care that your garden will require this month will be in the form of pruning. It offers an excellent opportunity to correct structural problems, rein in out-of-control growth, and generally rejuvenate plants for the coming season's growth. It also is the perfect time to check for signs of disease or pest problems that may require further care and attention.

Except for most of the San Francisco Bay Area and select areas in Southern California, frosts continue to be a possibility. (See November for information on how to best protect your plants from frost damage.)

ANNUALS

If you planted sweet peas in the fall, you may already be seeing blooms. If you keep picking the flowers, the bloom period will continue until heat causes the plant to shut down in late spring or early summer.

EDIBLES

Winter pruning is essential for fruit-bearing trees and vines. It clears away dead wood and stimulates new growth to keep the tree productive. (See Trees this month for information on pruning fruit trees.)

DON'T FALL FOR THIS OLD WIVES' TALE

It was once a common practice to seal pruning cuts on any woody plants with latex paint, wax, or even white glue. The conventional wisdom was that sealing the cuts prevented moisture from getting into the tissue of the plant where it could cause rot or carry disease. Now, however, horticulturists know that sealants are more likely to trap in moisture and pathogens, not keep them out. So just make clean pruning cuts with sharp, disinfected pruners and forget about sealing. Plants have ingenious ways of sealing off the cuts all on their own.

Pruning is also necessary to establish and maintain the right structure for grapevines and keep them productive. The trick is achieving the right balance of shoot growth and fruit production.

There are three methods of grape pruning: cane pruning, head training, and spur pruning, which is the method most commonly used by home gardeners. (See Here's How to Spur Prune Grape Vines for details on the spur-pruning method.) Grape pruning for some reason just seems harder to grasp without seeing it done first by someone who knows what he or she is doing, so I'd recommend getting a demo from a knowledgeable expert or at least watching a few YouTube videos on the subject first. But, as with most kinds of pruning, you are unlikely to do any real damage if you don't do it exactly right and you'll learn and gain confidence as you do it year after year.

Onions that were planted from sets in November should be mature enough to harvest now (fifty to sixty days after planting). Allow harvested onions to dry and cure before storing.

ROSES

For most of California, January is the usual time to prune roses, but if you live where hard frosts are still a possibility, it's probably best to wait until February. In areas that don't experience hard frosts, roses don't really go into full dormancy, and pruning in January is like hitting a reset button, clearing away the previous season's growth and giving them the fresh start that they would usually get following a dormant period.

Don't be intimidated—pruning is the single best thing you can do for roses and even if you do a less-than-stellar job, they will likely reward you with loads of blooms in the spring. Pruning correctly is not difficult, however, so sharpen your pruners and let's do it.

Begin by thinking about the shape you'll be defining with your pruning cuts. Roses are usually pruned to an open vase shape, which allows air to circulate and sunshine to penetrate into the center of the plant. Exceptions include climbing roses (see Here's How to Prune Climbing Roses), standard roses, and espaliered roses; these should be pruned

HERE'S HOW

TO SPUR PRUNE GRAPE VINES

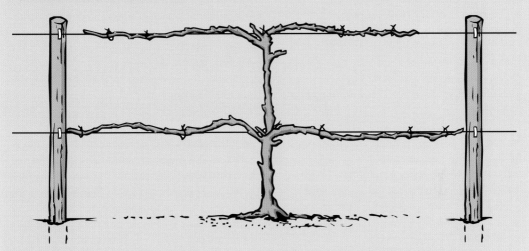

Spur pruning is done on grape vines that have been or are being trained against a fence or trellis. The vine is trained to have just one or two branches (called cordons) growing laterally and secured to the support structure. The cordons produce spurs that grow new budwood each year. With each year's pruning you'll reduce the budwood and remove excess growth and dead wood.

- Along each cordon examine the spurs that have one-year-old shoots. (These shoots will be smooth wood approximately the width of a thick pencil.) Select one healthy-looking shoot on each spur to keep, preferably the shoot that is closest to the cordon. Cut that shoot back to leave just two or three buds and completely remove any other shoots

from that spur. Continue down the cordon, cutting back shoots on each spur in this way.

- Make another pass along each cordon to remove any spurs that had no budwood and have stopped producing. Removing this dead wood will keep the cordon from getting too gnarly and crowded.

- Make a last pass over the vine to remove any remaining budwood that might make the vine too congested and limit the air circulation and light penetration. This is the part that really takes some experience because you're sacrificing some fruit production in order to have a healthier vine. It takes a season or two to get the hang of this and find the right balance for your particular vines.

to allow air and light to reach all branches but not in the open vase shape.

Your first cuts should be to remove dead, diseased, or damaged canes. Look for branches that are blackened or shriveled and cut them back to healthy wood, which should be green on the outside and cream-colored inside. Next, remove any suckers, which are shoots growing up from the rootstock. These can grow up through the

soil directly from the roots or from the trunk of the rose below the graft union. Select four to six healthy canes that will give you the shape you want and trim them back to approximately 18 to 24 inches in length. These cuts should be made just above a bud eye, the spot from which a new branch will grow. It can be tricky to spot bud eyes at first, but look for a crescent-shaped leaf scar on the cane (a spot from which a set of leaves had grown); the bud eye will be right above that scar.

Try to find outward-facing bud eyes so that the new branches will grow out instead of toward the center of the plant. Make a diagonal rather than straight cut so that water will not pool on the cut. As a last step, clean up any dead leaves or debris on the ground and wipe your pruner blades with a disinfectant before moving on to the next bush to be pruned—those two actions will help prevent the spread of pest and disease problems from one rose to another.

That's all there is to it. Keep in mind that roses tend to be hardy and rather forgiving plants so they will probably survive anything you do to them. If the results are not quite what you intended, you can always do some cleanup pruning later in the year when you can see how the rose is growing.

TREES

Winter-pruning deciduous fruit and nut trees is simpler than many people think and the payoff is significant. Pruning during the dormant stage allows you to really see the structure of the tree and shape it to its best advantage. Trees that are pruned regularly tend to be healthier, more productive, and more attractive. Regular pruning also keeps the tree's size under control, which makes for easier harvesting.

Ideally, prune when the tree is dry and no rain is forecast. Dry conditions allow the tree to begin compartmentalizing the pruning cuts so that it can better resist the attack of water-borne pathogens. Begin by studying the tree and making a plan of action. It's best to remove no more than one-third of the tree canopy at one time, so think about how

HERE'S HOW

TO PRUNE CLIMBING ROSES

For the first two or three years a climbing rose is in the ground, it's best to prune it lightly, just enough to keep it attached securely to the support structure. After that, however, climbers benefit from a serious pruning in the winter, revitalizing it for spring growth. The exception is the once-blooming rose, which is best pruned right after it is finished flowering. Repeat bloomers flower once on older wood, then later in the year on new wood, so they really depend on their winter trimming.

- Begin by removing the 3 Ds: dead, diseased, or damaged branches.

- Remove as much of the remaining foliage as possible. Disease-carrying fungal spores can linger on last year's leaves, so stripping these off the vine and clearing them off the ground cannot only keep the plant healthier but also give you a better view of what needs to be pruned.

- Take a moment to look the whole plant over carefully and identify the best-looking canes that you'll want to keep. Look for healthy canes with multiple buds swelling up on them. These buds will become the lateral branches on which the flowers will grow. If it helps, you can tie brightly colored ribbons to the branches you want to keep so you don't get carried away and accidentally remove them. Then clip off all the other canes.

- Starting at the bottom, trim each remaining branch to fit the support structure and secure it to the structure with a clip or tie, keeping the branches as horizontal as possible. Then clip the lateral branches, leaving two to five buds on each. Make the cuts at an angle that is parallel to and about ¼ inch above the last bud. Work your way up the plant, pruning each cane in the same way.

- Finally, check the base of the plant for suckers, that is, any shoots growing from below the bud union, the bulging, knobby mass just above the soil surface. Trim the suckers off by cutting as close to the stem as possible. Suckers are an endless battle and they will continue to grow back over and over again, so you'll need to watch for and remove them throughout the year.

■ *Fruit trees such as peaches are pruned to an open center (top), while apple trees are pruned to a central leader (bottom).*

using thinning cuts. Make heading cuts on the remaining main branches, leaving them 24 to 30 inches in length. Make heading cuts on smaller, lateral branches, but be careful not to remove or trim fruiting spurs, short 3- to 5-inch woody sprouts that bear blossoms and fruit on some types of trees. Some spurs are only productive for three to five years but others produce for ten or more years, so you will greatly diminish your harvest if you remove too many good spurs. Old, unproductive spurs can be removed later in the year when you can see that they are not fruiting.

Wipe your pruner blades with a disinfectant or dilute bleach solution before moving from one tree to the next in order to prevent the spread of disease. There is no need to seal the cuts you made with latex paint or any tree-sealing product. That is an older practice that has been proven to be ineffective and sometimes even damaging.

Just as deciduous fruit and nut trees are pruned at this time of year, deciduous ornamental trees also need pruning. The same pruning techniques used on fruit trees apply to ornamentals; however, different species of shade trees may be better suited for a central leader shape rather than the open vase shape recommended for most fruiting trees. With this form, one branch is selected to grow vertically with lower branches trained horizontally; the result is a shape somewhat resembling a Christmas tree form. Another common form for ornamental trees is a modified central leader shape, which has a more rounded top created by cutting back the leader and allowing other branches to grow upward as secondary leaders. Whichever form is used, it's important that branching be evenly spaced around the trunk, vertically as well as radially so that the branches are strongly attached to the trunk and air is able to circulate throughout the canopy.

VINES & GROUNDCOVERS

This is the time to prune most vines. Two important exceptions are wisteria, which should be pruned immediately following its bloom period, and clematis, which should be pruned at other times of the year depending on when it blooms. For vines such as Dutchman's pipe, honeysuckle, passion vine, and, in areas that are past danger of frost, bougainvillea, pruning time is nigh.

much you want to cut and what shape you want the tree to have. An open-vase shape is the most commonly recommended form because it allows light to penetrate into the center of the canopy and air to circulate through the branches, all of which help to lessen the likelihood of fungal diseases taking hold.

There are two types of pruning cuts: heading and thinning. Heading cuts remove only a part of a branch, cutting back to a shoot that you want to develop into a branch. Thinning cuts remove the entire branch all the way back to the trunk or larger branch it sprouted from.

If pruning a young tree, select three or four main branches evenly spaced around the tree to form the vase shape and remove any other large branches

As with most plants, it's usually best to remove no more than one-third of the plant at one time. But if the vine is a vigorous grower, even a severe pruning is not likely to hurt it and may well be necessary to keep it under control. One approach is to trim away one-third of the vine, but every third year give it a more severe pruning to keep its size in check.

However often you prune, the guidelines are pretty much the same as with any other pruning job. Remove dead, diseased, and damaged branches first, then thin and shorten the remaining branches to increase air circulation, control the size, and clear out dead foliage. Closely check clinging vines growing on the side of a building to ensure they're not

HERE'S HOW

TO CARE FOR YOUR GARDEN TOOLS

Banish dull, dirty, rusty tools from your gardening life.

If well cared for, most good-quality gardening tools can last a lifetime, but to keep them in working order you need to make sure they stay sharp, clean, and rust-free. An annual once-over for all your tools each January will keep them reliably functional and make you a happier gardener all year long.

For pruning shears and loppers, disassemble the tool and use steel wool and oil (such as linseed oil) to remove built-up layers of dirt, sap, and rust. Sharpen the blades with a sharpening tool (these can be purchased at hardware stores and nurseries for $10 to $20), drawing the tool across the blade at a 45-degree angle. Wipe the sharpened blade using a clean rag and some more oil.

■ *Use a file or sharpening stone to sharpen hoes and other garden tools.*

damaging surfaces they're attached to; the suckers they use to hold on can easily take off paint and damage plaster underneath. For vines that twine or send out tendrils, as you trim the branches, you can wind them lightly around the support structure—it won't take them long to "grip" on and secure themselves in place again.

Pruning saws should also be cleaned with steel wool and oil. Wiping the blade with a thin coat of paraffin will help it cut more smoothly.

Shovels, spades, trowels—any digging tools—can also be cleaned using steel wool or a wire brush and the edges sharpened in the same way the shears and lopper blades were.

Lightly sand all the wooden handles on your tools, then wipe them down with oil to keep them conditioned and easier on your hands. Better yet, you might want to prime and paint the wooden handles in bright colors that will make them easier to spot among all the greenery.

Here are two of the best tips I've come across to extend the life of your tools and keep them in good shape throughout the year:

- Take a bucket with a lid and fill it with clean horticultural sand. Pour in a couple of quarts of motor oil. Keep the bucket handy where you store your tools and each time before you put away your shovel, spade or trowel, thrust it deeply into the sand a few times. It will keep the blades a bit sharper and the light coat of oil will help prevent rust.

- Keep a container of disinfectant wet wipes with your tools and give them a quick swipe before you put them away. Not only will it keep dirt from accumulating on the blades, but it will also help to prevent the spread of some plant diseases.

You depend a lot on your tools. Don't they deserve this little bit of TLC?

■ *Keeping a rain gauge in your garden will help you know when or if your plants need water.*

WATER

ALL

January is typically a month when nature takes care of the watering chores for you, but we Californians are no strangers to drought, so keep an eye on the rainfall levels and be prepared to provide supplemental watering if needed. Install a simple rain gauge in your garden to help you track precisely how much water your garden is getting. When the gauge shows rainfall of ½ inch or more, you can safely skip your next scheduled watering. If nighttime temperatures are anywhere near freezing, when you do water be sure to do it at midday so there is time for the water to be absorbed into the ground.

Conversely, if you have poorly draining soil, watch out for yellowing and dropping leaves on evergreens and hardy perennials—signs that your plants are drowning. Heavy clay soil that hasn't been sufficiently amended can hold too much water around roots. Consider moving vulnerable plants to containers until the drainage problem can be improved.

HOUSEPLANTS

Shorter days mean less light coming in through the windows so houseplants will be growing less and requiring less water than usual. The finger test is always the best way to determine your watering schedule: Stick your finger into the soil to a depth of 1 inch. If it's dry to the touch at that level, water.

Interior heating greatly reduces the humidity in your home during the winter months and tropical plants especially can suffer in the drier air. Fill a shallow tray with pebbles and add water to almost cover them. Set your houseplants on top of the pebbles and let them absorb the humid air as needed.

FERTILIZE

ALL

The only plants that might benefit from fertilizing this month are those that are actively growing. As a rule, however, less is more at this time of year. More plants are killed by overfeeding than underfeeding, and applying chemical fertilizers during the rainy season just adds to the problem of chemical run-off getting into open waters and groundwater.

BULBS

Apply a sidedressing of compost to spring-blooming bulbs when their leaves start to emerge. The boost of energy will support not only this year's flower, but also help keep the foliage healthy enough to absorb nutrients for next year's flower to form. Avoid high-nitrogen fertilizers around bulbs; they lead to excessive foliage growth and are associated with bulb rot.

TREES

Citrus trees are heavy feeders and they require more nitrogen to support their evergreen growth

■ *Citrus trees are heavy feeders.*

than phosphorus and potassium. Look for a fertilizer with a 2-1-1 NPK ratio (such as 10-5-5 or 20-10-10), meaning that it has twice as much nitrogen as phosphorus and potassium. For the essential trace minerals they require—particularly iron, zinc, and manganese—spray the tree with a liquid solution of a kelp-based or other water-soluble fertilizer. Combine the foliar spray with a slow-release granular fertilizer to cover all the bases and provide a balanced diet. Follow the directions on the package for application amount and frequency; as a general rule, organic fertilizers will be less concentrated than synthetic fertilizers and therefore will need to be applied more often.

HERE'S HOW

TO FEED ORCHIDS

One exception to the fertilizing rule of thumb is orchids. Whether they're growing indoors or outdoors, orchid growers recommend a "weakly weekly" approach to feeding—that is, apply a weak solution of a fertilizer specifically formulated for orchids every week. Mix the fertilizer at one-half to one-quarter the strength recommended on the fertilizer package. To prevent "burning" the roots, water the orchid thoroughly first to get the growing medium completely wet, then apply the fertilizer solution, making sure that the plant drains completely afterward. If the orchid leaves are a dark green, it's an indication the plant is getting too much nitrogen and you should weaken the concentration of the fertilizer or adjust (lessen) the frequency of application.

■ *Be sure to use protective gear when spraying trees.*

PROBLEM-SOLVE

LAWNS

If there are persistent problem spots in your lawn, this is a good time to test the soil in those spots, as long as the ground isn't frozen. Take several samples on a dry day. (See March, Here's How to Test Your Soil's pH and Nutrient Level, for instructions on how to take soil samples and get them tested.)

TREES

If you had problems with pests or diseases on your deciduous fruit trees in the previous year, you can spray the trees while they're dormant to control the problems. This is best done after you have finished the winter pruning. (See February for instructions on dormant spraying.)

WATER GARDENS

If you live in a region in which ponds freeze over, you'll need to make sure that methane and other toxic gases are not trapped beneath a layer of ice where they can poison your fish. A heater or pump will keep some surface area open, but if you don't have either of those, you can create a hole in the ice by pouring boiling water near the edge of the pond. Never punch through a layer of ice on a pond—doing so can injure or shock the fish.

■ *Lady's slipper orchid,* Paphiopedilum

February

It's time to fall in love with your garden again. This month, which can feel so much like the winter of our discontent with its gray skies, cold ground, and bare branches, is actually the beginning of a love story. Think of it as a romantic comedy in which, true to the formula, you and your garden meet and . . . you don't like each other at all. Or maybe you like each other a lot, but you just can't seem to hook up. It's all bad timing and missed connections. You're full of fresh ideas and lusting after new plants, but your old plants are demanding your attention and whispering, "Prune me, baby, prune me!" Can true love ever be found here?

Spoiler alert: The answer is "yes!" First, though, there will be obstacles to overcome (late frosts, battering rains, damaging winds) and misleading crossed wires (those inevitable days of false spring). New characters will be introduced. Some will flash briefly across the screen, never to return (annual flowers and vegetables), and others will be around for a long, long time (bare-root roses and perennials). Some will brighten the scene and add promise; others will seem needy and difficult and complicate your life.

This month the garden can feel like it's nothing but complications and contradictions when it's really just the natural way of things. The lush, romantic garden we imagined and the fresh start we mapped out just last month is meeting cold reality and the result can be many things—soggy, wind-ravaged, frost-bitten—but not necessarily romantic.

No doubt, there will be cleanup to do this month, but there will also be new plants to install and old plants to reshape. In the hazy light of February we can begin to see the garden unfold in our mind's eye. Clarity comes, however, when we realize that winter is not a problem to be solved but a necessary shift in the garden's energy.

And just when it seems that nothing could flourish under such daunting conditions, buds will swell and break, bulbs will send up green shoots, and the landscape will be made anew.

In other words, love.

PLAN

ALL

Make a list of all the winter chores you have yet to complete and draft a plan for finishing the highest-priority ones this month. In particular, that means doing all the things that should be done while plants are still dormant: planting or transplanting, pruning, or spraying. Other tasks are less time-sensitive and can be done later if necessary, but once plants break dormancy (which they will in just a matter of weeks) they become much more sensitive to having their roots disturbed or being heavily pruned, and you'll completely miss the opportunity to use a dormant oil spray.

BULBS

Set aside a cold, damp day to page through colorful catalogs of summer-blooming bulbs and order now for the best selection. The list of possibilities is long, thank goodness, and unless you have deep pockets and a large garden, you'll have a hard time narrowing your selection to a reasonable amount. My favorites include dahlias, Oriental lilies, calla lilies (well, pretty much anything with the word "lily" in the name), crocosmia, freesia, watsonia, and tuberous begonia. But don't stop there. Try out some of these beauties as well: *Agapanthus, Alstroemeria, Amaryllis belladonna, Chasmanthe aethiopica* (note that in mild climates like the Bay Area, *Chasmanthe* can be mildly invasive), *Dierama pulcherrima, Eucomis comosa, Galtonia, Gladiolus, Incarvillea, Ixia, Liatris, Nerine bowdenii, Polyanthus tuberosa, Ranunculas, Schizostylis coccinea, Sparaxis, Tigridia pavonia*, and *Tritonia*.

EDIBLES

What are you growing that's good to eat right now? If you've let the edible part of your garden lapse during the winter, think about what you can plant now that will be ready for harvest in short order. In most parts of California, that includes lettuces and many kinds of greens. If nothing else, you might try growing some nutrition-packed microgreens, which are just lettuces, greens, and herbs that are harvested when they are about an inch high, generally around 10 to 14 days after planting.

HERE'S HOW

TO PLANT A SALAD BOWL

This is a fun project that gives you lettuce longer. The bowl is portable, so you can move it around on colder or warmer days to give the lettuce the conditions it needs to grow.

1   *Purchase wide, shallow pots to plant salad bowls, or if you have an old plastic salad bowl, you can drill holes in the bottom and plant it. Fill the bowl about halfway with potting soil.*

2   *Plant the lettuce bowl with lettuce transplants. For extra taste, plant some bunching onions in the center of the bowl and a dill plant or two on the edges. Fill in around the plants with potting soil and water the plants. On hot days, move the bowl into some shade. On cool days, move the bowl into the sun. If temperatures are forecast to drop below freezing, bring the bowl into the garage.*

SHRUBS

Watch for the spots in your garden that are lacking color at this time of year—they might be good places to fill in with winter-blooming natives like ceanothus and manzanita. Ceanothus can fill a dull area with broad swatches of blue, purple, pink, or white from midwinter well into spring. Manzanitas sport clusters of bell-shaped white or pink blossoms from winter to spring, but are eye-catching all year long for their red, polished-looking wood.

PLANT

ANNUALS

If you did not sow wildflower seeds in the fall, you can do so now. Look for mixes containing California poppies (*Eschscholzia californica*), farewell-to-spring (*Clarkia amoena*), California bluebells (*Phacelia campanularia*), and mountain phlox (*Linanthus grandiflorus*). The spring rains should help them germinate, but in periods of drought you'll need to provide supplemental water.

California poppies

EDIBLES

This is a busy month for getting the edible garden growing and a good time to get lots of annual veggies and even a few perennials in the ground. Let's start with some perennials: asparagus and strawberries.

Asparagus varieties fall into two categories: "Traditional" or "all-male." Traditional varieties are open-pollinated and will produce male and female plants. "All-male" may still produce an occasional female plant, which you can spot by its red berries. But because the male plants don't have to put energy into producing seeds, they produce more and larger spears. The "all-males" are also more resistant to diseases such as rust, fusarium crown rot, and root rot. For "all-male" plants, try 'Jersey Giant' (especially recommended for zones 7 and below), 'Jersey King', and 'Jersey Knight'. For open-pollinated plants, try 'Purple Passion' or 'Viking'.

To plant asparagus root crowns, prepare a trench 1 foot wide and 8 to 10 inches deep in a spot with full sun exposure and well-draining soil. If you are planting in rows, space the trenches 4 to 6 feet apart. Mound loose soil that's been mixed with compost or composted manure at the bottom of the trench and soak it well with water. Lay the crowns 1 foot apart with the tops 6 to 8 inches below ground level and spread the roots out across the soil mound. Cover with 2 inches of the soil and compost mixture and water again. As the plants grow, fill in more soil and compost, a few inches at a time, making sure not to cover the tips of the plants. Stick a finger into the soil to test the moisture level and water deeply whenever it feels dry around the roots.

When planting strawberries, make sure you select a variety that will deliver the kind of harvest you want. Strawberries are divided into three types: June-bearing, which produce a heavy crop in May and June; everbearing, which produce two or three crops between spring and fall; and day-neutral, which produce continually from spring into fall but will not fruit in temperatures over 90 degrees Fahrenheit. In reality, the line between everbearing and day-neutral is a bit fuzzy, but all that matters is that you know when to expect your plants to bear fruit.

Mulching around strawberry plants will keep the weeds down.

Plant bare-root crowns for spring-bearing and everbearing strawberries 6 inches apart in rows 12 inches apart. Day-neutral berries should be spaced 4 to 5 inches apart. Plant so the crown is right at ground level. If you plant them too deep, they may rot and if they're not deep enough, they will dry out. If your soil doesn't have good drainage, build up mounds of soil in which to plant the crowns. Water well and mulch. A thick layer of pine needles is an excellent mulch for strawberries since the pine makes the soil more acidic.

Continue to plant cool-season annual crops. (See the list of possibilities in January.) In areas that are past the danger of frost, this is a great time to sow mesclun seed mixes in containers or raised beds to keep as a cut-and-come-again crop that will keep producing until the hot weather comes.

HERE'S HOW

TO START SEEDS INDOORS

Growing plants from seed is easy as long as you provide the basics that all plants require and then pay attention to those plants that may have a few special needs. First, let's take care of the basics: soil, heat, light, and water.

- Begin by purchasing a commercial seed-starting medium or mixing your own blend. Whichever way you decide to go, you need the medium to be sterile and fast draining. I often use a good-quality potting soil (as opposed to a seed-starting mix) that I lighten by adding perlite to improve the drainage. I avoid using seed-starting media that is primarily made of peat, especially those tablet-like peat plugs. Peat has a weird relationship with water—it repels it and repels it, then it sucks it up like crazy and won't let go of it. Either way, that's no way to treat tender roots of new seedlings.

- Fill small, clean containers with the soil mix, slightly moistened. (If using recycled containers, wash them first in a solution of nine parts water to one part chlorine bleach, allowing them to soak for a minimum of 10 minutes.)

- Plant seeds at the depth advised on the seed packet (usually the same depth as the size of the seed). Sprinkle very small seeds over the top of the soil and then press them down on the soil surface to make sure the seeds have made good contact with the soil.

- Water the containers thoroughly, preferably by setting the containers in trays of water and allowing them to absorb the water from the bottom up. Once the soil is completely moist, you can empty the trays of excess water.

- Until seeds have germinated they need heat more than they need light. Heat pads made especially for seed starting can warm the soil to speed germination, but even placing the seed trays on a sun-warmed windowsill will help.

- Check the seed containers daily and keep them evenly moist but not overly wet. Once the seeds germinate and the first leaves emerge, move the seed trays to a place where they will get direct sunlight or light from a UV-light bulb.

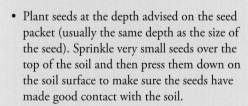

There's still time to get bare-root fruit trees or kiwi vines planted, but don't wait much longer. Depending on what part of the state you're in, they could be breaking dormancy soon. (See January for instructions on planting fruit trees and December for information on planting kiwis.)

Once seedlings develop their first set of true leaves, they'll be able to utilize more nutrients and you can begin feeding with small amounts of a timed-release fertilizer. Keep seedlings indoors or in a protected and covered place until outdoor daytime temperatures are above 50 degrees. At that time you can begin moving the seedlings outside for a few hours each day to begin hardening them off.

Refer to the sidebar below for more tips on raising healthy seedlings.

HERE'S HOW

TO PREVENT LOSING SEEDLINGS TO DAMPING-OFF DISEASE

Damping-off disease, which causes tender seedlings to wilt, discolor, and ultimately die, is not one disease but a general term applied to the affliction of any of a number of fungal diseases, including botrytis, Fusarium, and Phytophthora that affect seeds and seedlings. There's no cure for damping off, so prevention is the best course of action. If you want to give your seedlings the best possible odds of avoiding damping off and surviving those tender early days, here are seven tips to follow:

1. Start with as sterile an environment as possible. That means using a sterile potting mix; cleaning pots or seed trays with a diluted bleach solution; treating tools such as trowels, soil blockers, hand seeders, and labeling stakes with disinfectants; and using seeds that have been properly stored in a cool, dry, air-tight container.

2. Improve the drainage of the potting mix by adding perlite, vermiculite, or clean horticultural sand.

   Avoid overwatering and if possible, avoid watering from above. A better approach is to set the pots or trays in a tray of water long enough to moisten the soil completely. Then empty the bottom tray of excess water.

3. Do not add fertilizers to the potting mix when you sow the seeds. Until they have more developed root systems, seedlings can't use all that excess nitrogen and it can encourage the growth of fungal diseases. Seedlings will not really benefit from fertilization until after the first set of true leaves has emerged.

4. Good air circulation is necessary, so putting a fan on a low setting over the seed trays can be helpful. A light breeze on young seedlings can also strengthen the stems.

5. Proper light from above and heat from a heating mat below will also keep moisture under control and encourage healthier seedling growth.

6. Avoid touching seedlings unnecessarily, especially when wet, as that can spread fungal spores, if they are present.

7. Once you see signs of damping off, dispose of any affected plant material as well as the soil right away before it spreads further.

With these precautions your young seedlings should have an excellent chance of growing up strong and healthy.

ROSES

In warmer regions (zones 8 to 11) plant bare-root or container-grown roses. Before you plant, make sure you've chosen the right location. Choose a bed that will receive at least six hours of direct sun a day. Also, never plant a rose in the same spot where a rose was previously growing. The roots of roses secrete a substance that will stunt the growth of the next rose. Wait at least two years in between rose plantings in any one spot.

Planting bare-root roses is a straightforward process, but there are a few important points that you shouldn't overlook. Check Here's How to Plant Bare-Root Roses to guide you through it.

If, for some reason, you can't get your bare-root roses planted right away, unwrap them and store them in a bucket with moist compost, soil, sawdust, or peat moss covering the roots and bottom third of the canes. Put the bucket somewhere cool (between 35 and 40 degrees Fahrenheit) and check periodically to ensure it's all staying moist. When you're ready to plant, gently brush off the soil or whatever the roots were packed in, and plant according to the instructions.

SHRUBS

You'll find lots of azaleas and rhododendrons in the nurseries now in full bloom, which makes selecting ones to take home either really easy or really hard, depending on how you look at it. Azaleas and rhodies somehow manage to be dormant at the same time they're in bloom, which means it's the perfect time to plant them. These shrubs love acidic soil, so it doesn't hurt to add sphagnum peat when planting to lower the soil's pH level.

This is also a good time to shop for and plant camellias. Examine the blooms closely for any signs of brown on the petals, which could indicate the plant is suffering from camellia petal blight. Don't buy any camellia with this problem and be sure to clean up fallen blossoms surrounding any camellias you do plant so as not to introduce the disease.

■ Shop for rhododendrons while they're in bloom. Add sphagnum peat to the soil when planting to make the soil more acidic.

HERE'S HOW

TO PLANT BARE-ROOT ROSES

- Remove the rose from its packaging and brush away any wood shavings or other material that may have been packed around the roots.

- Trim the canes back to about 8 inches in length. Make the cuts on a diagonal just above an outward eye. You'll recognize the eye as a slightly swollen spot on the cane from which leaves will sprout. You can also trim the roots back by as much as an inch to stimulate new root growth.

- Soak the rose in a bucket of lukewarm water for at least a couple but no more than twenty-four hours. This will ensure the entire plant is hydrated before it goes in the ground.

- In a location that gets at least six hours of direct sun a day, dig a hole that is 18 inches wide and 12 inches deep. Amend the soil you removed from the hole with compost, mixing it well, then mound some of that soil in the bottom of the hole.

VINES & GROUNDCOVERS

Look for vines to fill in bare fences or walls or cover a pergola or arch. Evergreen varieties of climbers like jasmine, clematis, trumpet vine, Carolina jessamine, or honeysuckle add a layer of texture, colorful blooms, and in some cases heady fragrance to what might otherwise be dull hardscape. Choose vines that are lush rather than leggy, and once they're in the ground, pinch back the tips to encourage new growth.

CARE

ALL

Try to avoid handling wet foliage, which can spread diseases from plant to plant. Also, as much as possible, avoid digging in or walking on wet soil, which compacts it and worsens drainage.

ANNUALS

Prolong the bloom of cool-season annuals by deadheading faded blooms.

BULBS

If you potted up bulbs to force last autumn and have had them in cold storage, now is the time to bring the bulbs indoors and water them. (Check the table in October to make sure you've allowed them the full amount of chill time needed.) Find a cool spot for them to hang out until they sprout and are actively growing, then move them somewhere that is both warm and brightly lit, like a sunny windowsill. Keep the bulbs evenly moist throughout the bloom period and enjoy the show. Aren't you glad now that you took the time in October to do a little forcing?

If you forced an amaryllis into bloom, the flowers may now be fading, but you can keep the bulb alive for reblooming next year. Just remove the flower stalk but keep the foliage intact. It needs lots of bright light now in order to feed the bulb to form the next flower, so move it somewhere where it will get as much light as possible. If your area is out of danger of frost, you can place the potted bulb outdoors in partial to full sun.

- Place the rose in the hole, spreading the roots out over the mound. Adjust the depth of the rose so that the graft union (the gnarly-looking knuckle toward the top of the main stem) is at or just a couple inches above the soil level.

- Add the soil back into the hole. When the hole is about two-thirds filled, add water to help the soil settle and fill in air gaps. Fill in the remaining soil and water well again.

- If you live in an area that is still cold or windy, mound soil up around the base of the rose to cover the stem and the bottoms of the canes to keep the rose from drying out. Leave the soil mound in place only until the leaf buds break out, which should happen in just a few weeks. Then carefully brush the soil away from the plant, leaving the rose exposed from slightly below the graft union up. (In milder climates, it's not necessary to create this protective soil mound.)

■ *Move forced yellow narcissus bulbs to a sunny spot indoors and water them through their bloom period.*

EDIBLES

Kiwi vines need pruning at this time while they are dormant. For newly planted or one-year-old vines, train one strong shoot up the support structure and tie it in place. Prune out all the other shoots coming from the crown. When the shoot grows to the top of the structure, pinch out the tip to encourage lateral growth and tie it in place. Train two lateral branches and take off any other lateral branches coming off the main stem.

In the second year train two shoots at the top of the main stem out horizontally and tie in place. In the second winter, trim each one back to 12 to 18 buds. The next year, clean up the vine, removing water sprouts and dead or weak wood, but be sure not to remove the fruiting spurs on the lateral branches. In later years, thin the fruiting lateral branches to 6 inches apart and cut the remaining laterals to 18 inches.

Onions that were planted from transplants in November should be mature enough to harvest now (seventy to ninety days after planting). Allow harvested onions to dry and cure before storing.

PERENNIALS

Divide herbaceous perennials that have gotten too full as soon as they begin to sprout green growth again. Dig up the entire rootball and shake loose as much soil as possible. Some plants can be gently pried apart and separated with your fingers; others will need to have the rootball cut into divisions with a sharp, sterile knife. It may seem brutal, but they will benefit from the procedure and it's certainly better than leaving them crowded and competing with each other for food and water. Make sure each new division has at least one healthy green sprout and that the roots are white and plump rather than black, mushy, or dried out. Cut away any roots that do not look healthy. Replant

■ *Smaller rootballs can usually be cut into pieces using a sharp knife. Larger clumps can be sliced with a sharp spade or pried apart using two back-to-back garden forks.*

the divisions, allowing enough space between them for them to fill out. Repeat this process every three to four years or whenever they show diminished flowering or start to look dead in the center.

ROSES

In regions with snow, remove heavy piles of snow that can break the canes. Also, periodically brush away lighter loads of snow on the canes or piled around the trunk to check for signs of damage from mice or other rodents. If there is damage, you may want to set traps or provide some protection for the plant.

There's still time to finish winter pruning.

SHRUBS

Clean up fallen camellia and azalea blossoms; they can spread fungal spores into the soil, causing petal blight on blossoms in subsequent years.

Cut back woody shrubs like artemisia, fuchsia, salvia, butterfly bush, and Mexican brush sage to keep their size under control. Trimming the plants back to about 1 foot above the ground will keep them from getting leggy or hollowed out in the center from light not being able to penetrate.

TREES

If you've had a serious problem with pests or disease on any of your deciduous fruit trees, this is the proper time to apply an appropriate dormant spray. Dormant sprays can be fungicides, horticultural oils, or a combination of an oil and a pesticide. They should be applied now because the active ingredients in the sprays can damage foliage and blossoms and could be deadly to bees and other pollinators if applied when trees are in bloom.

What kind of spray you use depends on which problem you're dealing with. Oil sprays can control overwintering pests like scale, European red and brown mite eggs, blister mites, pear psylla, and aphid eggs. For diseases like leaf curl, shot hole, powdery mildew, and scab, sprays of copper, lime sulfur, Bordeaux mixtures, or a synthetic fungicide provide some control.

Spraying is best done after winter pruning so that the tree can be covered more completely

and during a stretch of dry weather. How well the spray works depends to a large extent on how well you spray. Refer to the steps in Here's How to Spray for Pests or Diseases During the Dormant Season, below.

You can repot or transplant Japanese maples that are in containers late this month. Pruning the roots before repotting will help stimulate new root growth.

HERE'S HOW

TO SPRAY FOR PESTS OR DISEASES DURING THE DORMANT SEASON

Follow these steps for the most effective dormant spraying:

1. Choose a day that is dry with temperatures above freezing and no rain forecast for at least the next 36 hours.

2. Prune out dead and damaged branches and remove any fruit or foliage that may still be on the tree.

3. Cover nearby evergreens or perennials with a tarp so the spray won't damage them.

4. Prepare the spray according to the directions on the package and put on protective eye gear and gloves. (Even though the spray may be organic, you don't want to get it on your skin or in your eyes.)

5. Fill your pump sprayer with the mixture.

6. Begin spraying at the top and middle of the tree and move toward the outer branches. Cover the branches thoroughly so that they are dripping with the spray solution. Once the branches are covered completely, spray the entire trunk down to the ground. Let the solution dry on the tree before removing the coverings on the nearby plants.

7. If you feel the need to treat a tree with both an oil spray and a fungicidal spray, allow at least thirty days to pass between each spray.

WATER GARDENS

Keep a sharp eye on the water level of your pond or fountain throughout the rainy season. An overflowing pond can be dangerous for the fish in it and the spillover can damage surrounding plants and wash away soil. Install an overflow pipe at the natural water level of the pond that will drain away excess water. Cover the opening of the pipe with a mesh screen to prevent fish and plant material from getting carried into it.

WATER

ALL

Continue to monitor the rainfall and provide supplemental water when necessary. Watch as well for wilting or foliage turning a lighter-than-normal shade of green, signs that plants are suffering from too much water, particularly in areas surrounding downspouts. Potted plants may need to be tipped over sideways to drain excess water. The appearance of toadstools or excessive mossy growth in a lawn or flowerbed is an indication that drainage is poor. Soil drainage can be improved by working organic matter into the soil and applying a layer of mulch on top. You may also need to find ways to divert water from downspouts to other areas of the garden.

FERTILIZE

BULBS

Stop fertilizing spring-blooming bulbs as soon as flowering starts. Excessive feeding at this time leads to bulb rot and can actually shorten the life of the flower.

ROSES

Apply a sidedressing of compost to rose bushes that have already been winter-pruned.

TREES

In all areas except for where there is still snow on the ground, fertilize deciduous fruit trees now. Mature trees require the equivalent of 1 pound of nitrogen; younger trees require less.

In coastal areas, fertilize avocado and citrus trees now; in interior regions, wait another month.

Both of these trees are a little fussy when it comes to their nutritional needs (particularly related to things like iron and zinc) so to make things simple, I prefer to use a fertilizer specially formulated for citrus and avocado. Follow the feeding instructions on the package based on the maturity and size (trunk girth) of the tree. Opt for a timed-release formula, unless you're willing to spread the feedings out four or five times over the growing season.

Water well after applying fertilizer.

PROBLEM-SOLVE

LAWNS

Even a respectably healthy lawn can develop thatch, which is a layer of partially decomposed leaf matter, stems, and roots that settles on top of the soil. The problem is that when thatch builds up too much, it prevents water and nutrients from passing through to get to the roots, resulting in ugly brown patches. Grass types that reproduce by runners, like Bermudagrass, are more likely to have a thatch problem than other types.

If you have warm-season grass, you should dethatch every two or three years in the late winter or early spring as soon as it's actively growing again. Do it when your lawn is neither dry nor soggy—just a bit moist. Begin by moving your lawn shorter than usual, making two passes in opposite directions in order to get a good, thorough cut. Now comes the actual dethatching. If you have a small lawn and a desire to build a little muscle, you can use a thatching rake, which has a row of knife-like blades to cut through the grass and thatch and into the soil. For anything larger than a very small lawn or for tougher grasses, it's easier to rent a vertical mower. Either way, make two passes with the thatching rake or vertical mower, each time in a different direction. Rake up all the debris and dump it (only compost it if it's pesticide-free and doesn't contain hard-to-compost stolons). Finish by watering the lawn well.

TREES

In recent years, a new disease has moved into California that is threatening homegrown citrus trees of all kinds, as well as the state's multi-billion

■ *Citrus greening disease is spread by the Asian citrus psyllid (below).*

dollar citrus industry. Huanglongbing (HLB) disease (also called citrus greening disease) is a bacterial infection spread by the tiny Asian citrus psyllid insect *Diaphorina citri*. The disease is, so far, incurable and ultimately fatal to any tree that becomes infected. While there's nothing that you can do to treat the disease, it's important that you inspect any citrus trees in your garden every month for signs of infection or the presence of the psyllid.

The first symptoms to look for are yellow splotches on the leaves. Unlike the yellowing that often occurs on citrus trees that's caused by mineral deficiencies, the yellow splotches on HLB-infected leaves are asymmetrical and can extend through the leaf veins and down the leaf shoots to the branches. The fruit will be small, deformed, and not fully colored. Both the flesh and the juice of the fruit become more bitter and inedible. As the disease progresses, entire branches will turn yellow and die, eventually leading to the death of the tree.

As you're examining the leaves, look for signs of the Asian citrus psyllid, which have already been found in parts of Southern and Central California. The psyllid and its eggs are more likely to be found on new green shoots, so check those carefully.

If you suspect that your citrus tree is showing symptoms of HLB, report it through the Save Our Citrus website (www.saveourcitrus.org) or using the Save Our Citrus iPhone app, which is available for download from the iTunes Store. You can also call the California Department of Food and Agriculture hotline at 800-491-1899. Inspectors will come out to your home to inspect the tree and if it is infected they will remove it.

HERE'S HOW

TO PREVENT THE SPREAD OF HUANGLONGBING (HLB) DISEASE

Since Huanglongbing, or citrus greening disease, has no known cure, the best you can do is take some simple steps to avoid the spread of the disease to your garden:

Check the quarantine status. A number of California counties are under quarantine for the Asian citrus psyllid. Yours may be one of them. Before you move citrus plants or fruit over county lines, call the California Department of Food and Agriculture hotline at 800-491-1899 to find out what counties are currently affected. Knowingly violating the quarantine could result in a whopping big fine anywhere from $1,100 to $60,000.

Examine your citrus trees monthly to look for signs of the disease or the presence of the Asian citrus psyllid or its eggs.

Purchase new citrus plants only from reputable, licensed California nurseries.

Whenever you prune your citrus trees, dry the clippings for a few days in the sun or double-bag them and dispose of them in the trash. Do not compost citrus clippings!

March

There is a wildness to March that even the most elegant and well-groomed garden cannot deny. It comes from the explosion of new growth played out against a background of unpredictable weather. Winter does not always fade gently into spring; sometimes the two seasons mix it up, battering us with cold, wet storms one week, then seducing us with blue skies and sunshine the next. Bright, tender sprouts burst forth from old wood or newly planted seeds, sometimes to be met with killing frosts or wicked winds that scatter blossoms, sacrificing the harvest to come.

But this is why we garden, is it not? To bring the wildness home, to inject a little "wild life" into our everyday lives. We plant and prune and weed to tame the wilds, but it is what we cannot or would not want to tame that is most likely to quicken a gardener's heart—the flare of blossoms on the fruit trees when they break out of their winter dormancy, the random effusion of daffodils naturalized from a few bulbs planted long ago, the tiny specks of green poking up through the soil, welcomed whether they were carefully sown by the gardener or dropped by nature's other helpers.

We may still be picking up the pieces from a wicked winter or taking cover from battering storms ushered in by spring—reminders of how fragile gardens can be when nature is doing its worst. We suffer most when we forget that we live and garden at nature's pleasure, but when gardening becomes a battle against the mighty forces of nature, we have already lost.

As we go about the chores that this month brings—planting new crops, battling weeds, taking on the early attacks of garden pests—let's not make it an "us vs. the wild" kind of effort. Trying to impose our will over nature is a fool's game. Let us instead welcome the wildness into our gardens and work with it, complementing its beauty, carving out our place in it, and creating a space that isn't wilderness tamed so much as wilderness cultivated, collected, and contained.

PLAN

ALL

Save yourself a lot of frustration and money by determining the condition of your soil now so that you can devise a plan for improving it to follow throughout the year. (See Here's How to Test Your Soil's pH and Nutrient Level, below.)

EDIBLES

Map out a plan for your warm-season edibles. A simple diagram of your planting space will help you determine how many plants to buy, as well as what other accessories will be needed (teepees for beans, cages for tomatoes, trellises for cucumbers, and so forth). In addition, plan to rotate your crops so that members of the same plant families (such

HERE'S HOW

TO TEST YOUR SOIL'S PH AND NUTRIENT LEVEL

The wise gardener feeds his soil rather than his plants. But to do this effectively, you have to know the current condition of your soil—whether it's acidic or alkaline, if it's deficient in any macro- or micro-nutrients, and whether it has unacceptably high levels of lead. To get that information, you need to test your soil.

There are soil tests that you can buy at the garden center that will give you some of that information. These kits are quick and easy to use and will give you general readings on

the pH level and nitrogen, phosphorus, and potassium levels of your soil. It's then up to you to determine what to add to your soil to adjust it appropriately.

For just a few dollars more, however, there's a mail-in test that you can run that will give you specific readings as well as recommendations for correcting your soil for specific crops. The University of Massachusetts at Amherst Soil and Plant Tissue Testing Laboratory (http://soiltest.umass.edu/) will run an inexpensive soil analysis that gives you good, detailed

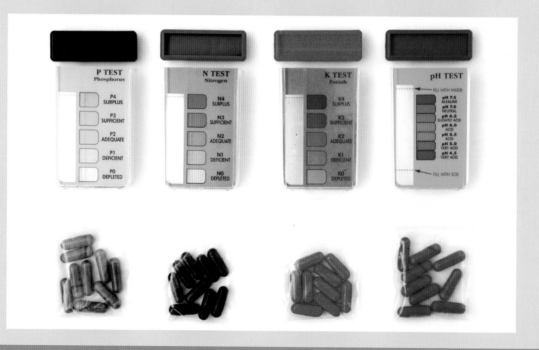

as *Solanaceae* family members tomatoes, potatoes, peppers, and eggplants, and *Brassica* family members broccoli, cabbage, cauliflower, and Brussels sprouts) are not growing in the same soil they grew in the previous year. Rotating crops from year to year helps to break pest and disease cycles. (See September for more information on rotating plant families.)

LAWNS

Although fall is a better time to plant a new lawn, you can sow a new lawn or install sod in the spring, as long as you don't anticipate any water rationing in the summer that would prevent you from keeping it sufficiently watered. If you're thinking about putting in a new lawn, you'll need to decide what kind to grow—warm-season grass or cool-season grass.

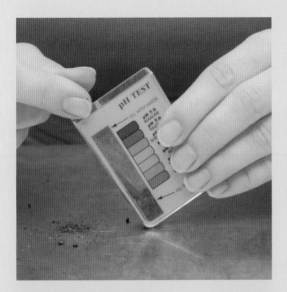

information that will make it easier for you to correctly amend your soil. See the lab's website for information on the routine soil analysis as well as additional tests available.

However you test your soil, it's important that you collect good soil samples. To do this, take a bucket and collect a trowel-full of soil from 6 to 8 inches below the soil surface (or 4 to 6 inches in lawns) in at least 12 places in the area you want to test. Mix all the samples together in the bucket, breaking up soil clods and removing stones, roots or any other kind of debris, then spread it out on clean paper to air-dry. When it's completely dry, collect 1 cup of soil to test, and send it to the testing service.

HERE'S HOW

TO ADJUST YOUR SOIL'S PH LEVEL

If your soil test comes back showing that your soil is either more alkaline or more acidic, you may want to amend it to raise or lower the pH level, depending on what you want to grow in that soil. Most edible plants, as well as ornamentals like roses, azaleas, rhododendrons, and many others, grow best in acidic soil. There are some plants that prefer alkaline soil, including ceanothus, daphnes, lilacs, hellebores, and clematis.

The pH scale is measured from 0 to 14 with 7 being neutral, below 7 being acidic, and above 7 being alkaline (also called *basic*). Soils in California tend to be between 5.0 (acidic) to 8.5 (slightly alkaline), with most areas having soil that is near neutral or slightly alkaline. The reason that pH level matters is that plants growing in soil that has either too high or too low a pH level will not be able to fully access the nutrients present in the soil. In that case, adding fertilizers won't help the plant at all. Most plant nutrients are available in a pH of 6.0 to 6.5, so that range is generally considered ideal for growing.

The pH level cannot be changed overnight but you can change it over time, and it's not difficult to do. To lower the pH level, making your soil more acidic, the most common remedy is to add organic matter such as sphagnum peat to the soil and work it in to a depth of 4 to 6 inches. Acidic mulches like pine needles can help to lower the pH level as well. It can take one to two years for organic matter to make a significant difference in the pH, however. For quicker action, you can add sulfur, but even that will take a while to work, especially in heavy clay soil. To raise the pH level, making the soil more alkaline, you can add pulverized limestone. (Be careful not to add dolomitic limestone, which also contains magnesium, unless you know your soil is deficient in magnesium, because too much magnesium could be detrimental.) Raising the pH is also a slow process and amendments will need to be added repeatedly to maintain the desired pH level once it is achieved.

Warm-season grasses include Bermudagrass, zoysia, buffalo, and blue grama grasses. On the plus side, these grasses are drought-tolerant and able to survive on about half as much water as cool-season grasses. On the minus side, the same qualities that make these grasses stubbornly survive without water also make them somewhat invasive. (Author's note: I say "somewhat invasive," but honestly, there are times I would like to do serious harm to whomever it was who first planted Bermudagrass in my garden years before I bought my house. If you plant Bermudagrass, you had better really love it, because good luck getting rid of it.) Warm-season grasses also turn brown in winter, although some new varieties of zoysia grass will stay green all year. These grasses have a coarser look than cool-season grasses and tend to grow better in southern climates.

Cool-season grasses include fescues, perennial rye, and Kentucky bluegrass. They will give you that lush-looking lawn that's more typical of eastern gardens and that stays green all year, but only if you provide enough water—and these grasses are very thirsty. Cool-season grasses tend to grow better in northern and coastal climates.

Most lawns are a mixture of warm- and cool-season grasses to provide the advantages of both types. Before you purchase lawn seed or sod, make sure you know what kind of grass is in it and whether it is suited for your growing conditions, primarily sun exposure and watering schedule.

Although it may seem like an odd recommendation for a gardening book, if you love the look of a lawn but don't like the watering and maintenance demands of most lawns, you might want to consider installing artificial grass. Particularly in gardens that only have a small area to devote to lawn or for households with dogs, today's artificial lawns are actually an eco-friendly alternative worth looking into. Check the Resources section for more information.

WATER GARDENS

Make a plan for managing disease-carrying mosquitoes and preventing them from breeding throughout the spring and summer. Stock up on mosquito dunks (also called mosquito doughnuts), which can be floated in bird baths, ponds, or any standing water to prevent mosquitoes from breeding on the water surface without harming birds, fish, or pets. Many counties in California will also provide mosquitofish (*Gambusia affinis*) to you free of charge to stock your pond. Contact your local mosquito abatement program or vector control office for information. Now that mosquitoes carrying West Nile and yellow fever viruses have been found in California, this kind of pest control is more important than ever.

PLANT

ANNUALS

Continue sowing seeds. In areas that are past the last-frost date, you can start moving seedlings outdoors. Harden off seedlings first by reducing the amount of water and fertilizer you give them. Keep them moist enough to just keep them from wilting. Then begin moving them outdoors for a brief period during the warmest part of the day. Set them in a spot where they will get filtered light and be protected from the wind. Bring them back inside after a few hours, but increase the amount of time they stay out each day. In a couple of weeks, they will be acclimated enough to the outdoor temperatures to withstand being transplanted.

Although you'll still find cool-season annuals available in many nurseries, they're not a great investment at this point, except to fill bare spots quickly for a short time. Warm-season annuals are a better choice to plant now, including ageratum, coleus, cosmos, impatiens, lobelia, marigolds, nierembergia, petunias, salvia, snapdragon (sold as an annual although it's effectively a perennial in much of California), stock, sweet alyssum, and verbena. Many of these grow easily from seed; some, such as cosmos and marigolds, can even be direct-seeded into the garden, saving all the steps of sowing indoors, then hardening off and transplanting outdoors. Planting from seed is not only more cost-efficient, it also gives you more varietal options and, when direct-sown, avoids the risk of transplant shock.

BULBS

It's time to plant summer-blooming bulbs. You can get hardy bulbs like lilies in the ground now, but only plant tender bulbs (which are affected by cold weather) once you are safely past the last frost date for your region. Be sure that the soil you are planting in has good drainage and amend it if necessary with organic matter to improve the drainage. Plant bulbs at a depth of two to three times the diameter of the bulb; you can plant a little deeper in sandy soil than in clay soil. Be sure to label bulbs as you plant them so you won't disturb or damage them with other plantings.

■ *Cosmos is a warm-season annual that grows easily from seed and reseeds itself for crops year after year.*

EDIBLES

The edible garden really heats up (figuratively even if not exactly literally) this month. There are many things that can be planted this month, especially in the milder climates where another round of cool-season vegetables can be squeezed in while also putting in some warm-season plants.

The warm-season edibles that can be planted now include artichokes (see October for information on planting artichokes), carrots, cauliflower, kohlrabi, peas, potatoes (see Here's How to Plant Potatoes), and New Zealand spinach. Other edibles that can be planted this month include beets, broccoli, chard, lettuce, and radishes.

The warmest parts of the state can begin planting beans, cucumbers, squash, and tomatoes as long as nighttime temperatures are above 50 degrees. In zones 10 and 11, bananas can be planted now through April.

In the coldest parts of the state, you can still plant asparagus, Brussels sprouts, collards, garlic, kale, leeks, onions, and turnips. This is also the preferred time to plant blueberries in zones 7 and lower (zones 8 and higher should wait until fall). Bare-root grape vines can also go in the ground in colder regions up to three weeks before the last expected frost date.

HERE'S HOW

TO PLANT POTATOES

Potatoes can be grown throughout California as long as they have full sun and sandy, fast-draining, slightly acidic (pH 5.0–6.0) soil.

The first step to a successful potato crop is buying certified disease-resistant seed potatoes. (Even organic potatoes bought at the supermarket or farmers' market will not give you reliably disease-resistant plants, and the diseases that potatoes are prone to are not worth dealing with.) Cut them into 1½-inch cubes, each with at least two eyes. Small seed potatoes can be planted whole. Dry the potato pieces for a couple of days, then plant them 2 inches deep and 1½ feet apart in loose, prepared soil. Water well. As the plants sprout and grow, add loose soil or compost around the stems, always being sure that the top leaves

are still above the soil. The potatoes will grow from the roots that sprout all along the buried part of the stem.

An alternative method is to plant in 3- to 4-foot-high "towers" constructed of reed fencing wrapped around large wire tomato cages. The seed potatoes are planted in a layer of compost mixed with straw and then the tower is filled with more of the compost-straw mixture as the plants grow up. Because the plants grow so much taller this way, the yield can be two to three times larger than what you can get by growing potatoes in the ground. Potatoes also work well as a container crop and some garden supply companies sell "grow bags" that make it easy to grow potatoes on a patio or deck (see Resources for more information).

PERENNIALS & SHRUBS

Although fall is really the best time to plant any permanent additions to the garden, this is the next-best time. That goes for transplanting as well, so this is a good time to review all the permanent plantings already in your garden to see if any of them show signs of being in the wrong place (such as legginess from lack of sun or sunburn from too much sun). If so, scout out a better location and transplant them now. If you're unsure whether a plant will do well in another location, and if it's small enough to fit in a container, you can plant it in a container in the new spot and try it out there for a few months. If it does well there, you can take it out of the container and give it a permanent home there in the fall.

Choose your potato variety based on what you want to use the potatoes for. For baking and mashing, try 'Butte' and 'Russet Burbank'. 'Carola' is good for soup-making, and 'Reddale' is good for boiling, stewing, and salads. 'All Blue' is a beautiful bluish purple that looks great in salads. For areas with short growing seasons, try 'Yukon' or 'Yukon Gold'. 'Nooksack' can handle particularly wet growing conditions better than most. If you have soil that seems prone to diseases, try (late blight–resistant) 'Island Sunshine' or (verticillium wilt-resistant) 'Reddale'. For container growing, recommended varieties include 'All Blue', 'Yukon Gold', 'Red Pontiac', or any fingerling varieties.

ROSES

There's still time for planting bare-root roses in cooler regions (zones 6 and 7) and container-grown roses in zones 6 to 11. (See February for instructions on planting bare-root roses.)

TREES

While most fruiting trees are best planted during their winter dormant period, some trees are best planted now. Avocado and citrus, both evergreens, do well planted now when most danger of frost are past and temperatures are still mild enough to allow them to settle in before things really heat up. Avocados (zones 9 to 11) have shallow, tender roots so take care to be gentle with them when planting. Citrus (best in zones 8 to 11 but can grow anywhere they can be protected from frost) are not as tender-rooted, but take care to plant with the graft union above the soil line. Mulch the trees heavily after planting, but take care to keep the mulch away from the trunk. Both avocado and citrus are thin-barked trees and can develop crown rot easily if the trunk stays too moist.

Another evergreen tree to plant now is the loquat, which is becoming increasingly common in California (zones 7 to 10), appreciated both for its fruit and its striking appearance as a landscape tree.

Bare-root persimmon trees can also be planted now (container-grown trees can be planted through the summer). Asian persimmons will grow in zones 6–10. American persimmons are hardier and can grow in zones 4–10. If you live in a colder region and want to grow an Asian persimmon, look for an Asian variety grafted onto American persimmon rootstock. Plant in full sun (American persimmons will tolerate some shade). Persimmons are self-fruitful but do better with a second tree as a pollinizer.

VINES & GROUNDCOVERS

Plant a groundcover now so it can take advantage of late spring rains to get established. Plants that trail or spread can quickly fill in empty spaces in your garden, minimizing evaporation, preventing soil erosion, and adding another layer of color and

■ *Ice plant forms a dense, drought-tolerant groundcover that blooms in a carpet of brightly colored flowers.*

texture. Here are a few great-looking, drought-tolerant groundcovers to consider:

- **Ice plant:** These quick-growing succulents have gotten a bad rap as an invasive plant, but in fact there are many varieties of ice plant classified under several genuses, and some are not invasive at all. One good option is *Delosperma cooperii*, a low-growing, small-leaved ice plant that forms a dense mat of pink or purple flowers in spring and summer.

- **Hen and chicks:** Another succulent, *Echeveria* lays down a carpet of rosettes that multiply by offsets. The larger, older rosettes are the hens, and the smaller, newer offsets are the chicks. The leaves range from green to blue-green to gray-green to red-tipped, and they produce clusters of bell-shaped flowers in red, pink, or yellow.

- **Creeping thyme:** *Thymus praecox arcticus* spreads into a soft, fragrant blanket that will

fill in nicely around steppingstones or patio pavers. It can handle light foot traffic and produces purple, pink, white, or red flowers in the summer.

- **Lantana:** While not all lantana varieties are groundcovers, *Lantana montevidensis* maxes out at about 2 feet high and can spread to as much as 6 feet wide. The dark-green leaves can take on a red or purplish tinge in colder weather, and the flower clusters of purple, white, or purple-and-white are popular with birds and butterflies.

- **Sedum** Another succulent choice, sedums come in many varieties that grow as low as 2 inches high and provide evergreen coverage in well-draining soil. Foliage can be light green (*Sedum acre*), dark green (*S. anglicum*), blue-green (*S. spathulifolium*), or a number of other variations. Most varieties bloom in spring or summer in shades of yellow, white, or pink, but the real show is the foliage itself.

HERE'S HOW

TO EXPAND YOUR PLANTING SPACE BY GROWING VERTICALLY

If you're looking for new ways to garden, you may need to grow up. Vertical gardening is not just one of the latest trends, it's also a smart technique that maximizes space, lessens the impact of some garden pests, and provides great visual interest.

Vertical gardening refers to any method that emphasizes growing plants up (or down) rather than spreading out horizontally. The techniques for growing vertically certainly aren't new, but they are particularly relevant in today's smaller gardens where every square foot of ground is precious.

Vertical gardening can make a small garden seem bigger because it directs the eye upward, drawing the focus away from horizontal boundaries, and adds another layer of interest and complexity to your garden design. Plants grown vertically are also less susceptible to garden pests that attack from below because less of the plant is in direct contact with the soil.

Here are a few ideas for using vertical growing techniques on annuals, perennials, and edibles in your garden:

- **Hang it up:** Almost any plant that can grow in a container can be grown in a hanging pot. For dramatic pops of color, try pots of impatiens, pansies, or petunias. But don't forget about vegetables and fruits too. Tomatoes can be grown upside-down in topsy-turvy hangers and strawberries will happily grow out the sides of coir liners in wire hangers.

- **Trellises make a blank wall interesting:** Climbing roses, clematis, jasmine, and wisteria make quite an impact when grown on a trellis or arbor. Lush, colorful vines can even make a drab cyclone fence look great. But don't stop at flowers. You can also grow cucumbers, squash, and pumpkins against a trellis.

- **Teepees stand above the rest:** A basic teepee of bamboo poles tied with wire or jute rises up to grab the sunlight and show off its vines. Plant it with sweet peas for color, or go the edible route. Pole beans and peas do great on a teepee.

- **Stack up levels:** Stacking pots is perhaps the simplest method of all, but the results can be amazing. For a stacking herb garden, try planting the perimeter of a large oak barrel planter with mint or basil, then add a smaller pot in the center, and another pot in the center of that, each with another herb that will fill out and spill over the side. For a fun, quirky look, anchor a metal rod in the ground and stack terracotta pots by running the rod through the drainage holes, tipping each pot in a different direction. Plant strawberries, calibrachoa, or lobelia in the pots so they can spill out the sides.

- **Espalier a tree:** Lots of trees, including fruit trees, can be trained to grow flat against a fence or wall. Plant young trees and prune them to the formal or informal shape you want, or look for trees in the nursery that have already been pruned to an espalier form.

CARE

ALL

Plan to spend a fair amount of time this month pulling weeds. Weeding is a nonstop effort in most California gardens, but March is a time when you are more likely to get the upper hand in the battle. By pairing relentless weed-pulling before weeds get well established with the use of a pre-emergent herbicide like corn gluten meal (CGM), which prevents weed seeds from germinating, you can really make a difference now in the amount of weeding that will be necessary the rest of the year.

Look for good tools to make your weeding efforts effective and a little easier on the back. A few that are worth investing in are:

- **CobraHead weeder:** This hand tool has an arching arm that ends in a pointed oval shape and is great for breaking through all kinds of soil to get at weed roots and runners.

- **Hori Hori knife:** A sharp serrated blade that is not only good for getting at weeds in cracks and other tight spots but also is handy for dividing plants.

- **Fiskars UpRoot:** This long-handled weed-puller has a foot lever you step on to plunge into the soil and pull out dandelions or any long or taprooted weeds. It works quickly and since you use it standing up, it saves a bit of wear and tear on your knees.

Clean up and refresh the mulch around your plants. You don't necessarily have to remove the mulch you laid down in the fall. Many plants will send shoots through the mulch layer. Other plants may need to have the mulch pushed away a bit so that the shoots can break through. The only time you really need to remove the mulch entirely is if it is surrounding plants that are vulnerable to soggy conditions. In those cases, the plants will appreciate having the mulch cleared away completely so that they don't rot.

Early in the month keep watch for late frosts, particularly in the interior part of the state. In addition to the usual frost-tender plants to care

■ *The CobraHead weeder is a good tool for removing weeds that form invasive runners.*

for, you'll need to protect any new plantings that are not established yet. (See November for more information on protecting plants from frost.)

BULBS

Fall-blooming bulbs like *Lycoris* or *Belladonna* lilies (a.k.a. "naked ladies") can be divided now that their foliage will have died back. Refrain from watering the dormant bulbs until they sprout again in the late summer.

Spring-flowering bulbs that have already bloomed should be tidied up. Remove the spent flower stalk, but leave the foliage in place. You can tie the leaves into bundles with bits of string or raffia for a neater look. Don't remove the foliage until it has completely died back as it's needed to continue photosynthesizing to feed the bulb for next year's flower.

Bulbs that were forced cannot be forced again the following year, but with a little post-bloom care, you can usually coax out another year of blooms in the garden. To do that, move the plants outdoors and keep the foliage growing as long as possible in order to feed the bulbs while they're forming the next year's flower. Apply a water-soluble fertilizer every three to four weeks. After the foliage dies back completely, you can replant the bulbs in the garden or store them for later planting.

EDIBLES

Keep harvesting cool-season crops and when the harvests are finally done, be sure to clear out the plants and any debris they leave behind. Turning over the soil after the plants have been pulled helps to break the cycle of any pests that may have survived the winter.

Asparagus plants should be about ready to harvest at this time. The first year following planting the plants should be left to build a root mass, so there will be no harvest. The second year you can harvest spears by cutting the spears at a 45-degree angle to the soil. After four to six weeks of harvesting, just let the plants grow. The third year, you can harvest for eight to ten weeks. At the end of each harvest apply additional compost or fertilizer and water deeply. By harvesting in this way, the plant is able to continue to build a healthy, substantial root mass, which will enable it to be productive for many more years.

Onions that were planted from seed in November should be mature enough to harvest now (110 to 125 days after planting). Allow harvested onions to dry and cure before storing.

HOUSEPLANTS

Any tender plants that you've overwintered indoors can now be moved back outside. Follow the same process described in the "Plant, Annuals" section for hardening off seedlings.

LAWNS

Nothing spoils the look of a lawn more than an invasion of weeds. Annual weeds like crabgrass, goosegrass, California burclover, and spurge are just a few of the most likely culprits you may find taking over your lawn. To keep them in check, follow a plan of action that keeps your lawn in good health, takes out most seed heads before the seeds are released, and suppresses the growth of those seeds that do reach the ground.

The best way to keep your lawn weed-free is to keep it healthy, well watered, and disease-free.

■ *Remove weeds like crabgrass before they go to seed.*

A stressed lawn has a way of hanging out a welcome sign to weeds. They sense the opportunity to move in and take over, and they always take advantage of it. Determine your lawn's particular water needs and make sure it gets what it needs. Watch for signs of soil compaction and aerate as needed. (See the June Problem-Solve section for guidance on fixing lawn compaction problems.) Be careful not to overfertilize—doing so only provides more nutrients for weeds.

With annual weeds, you really don't even have to remove the entire plant. Just removing seedheads can keep the weed population in check. Just one crabgrass plant can produce more than 100,000 seeds. If you successfully remove any seed heads from that plant at the end of the year, it will die on its own without having released those 100,000 seeds to germinate in your lawn. Set your mowing height low enough to cut off the seedheads every time you mow.

If seeds are produced, you can still prevent them from putting down roots. An inexpensive, easy way to do this is to apply corn gluten meal (see earlier in this section). (See November for more information on common lawn weeds.)

PERENNIALS

Well-established bamboos are best divided or thinned at this time. The steps are more or less the same for dividing either the running form of bamboo or the clumping form. You don't have to dig up the entire plant in either case, but depending on how big and dense the bamboo is and what your soil is like, it may require some significant energy on your part to cut or saw through the rhizomes and dig out sections. In any case, be sure to include some mature culms (the jointed, hollow stems) with any division, not just new buds, which are less likely to survive the division and transplant.

With running bamboos, find a section that has two or more established culms and shows some new buds emerging. Using a saw, spade, or loppers, separate the rhizomes attached to that section from the original bamboo patch, leaving at least a couple of nodes of the rhizomes to it. Dig up the new section.

With clumping bamboos, you can actually slice through the entire clump to separate any size section you want as long as it includes three or four mature culms and some new buds. You can use a pruning saw to cut through the clump, but really dense clumps may require the use of an electric saw.

Once you've divided and dug up any new divisions, cut the mature culms to about half their height. (This allows them to survive the transplant shock easier.) Plant them in new ground or a container with fresh potting soil. The section may benefit from staking so it doesn't fall over with the wind. Water well and keep it moist until it is well established. Wait at least a month to apply a fertilizer.

Spring hailstorms can scar and damage succulent plants. Protect them by keeping them sheltered under eaves or other structures or be prepared to tent them or cover them with upturned pots when hail is predicted.

ROSES

As roses begin blooming you can thin or "disbud" rosebuds in order to develop larger flowers. Deadhead faded roses as needed. Keeping up with this practice will promote more blooms in re-blooming roses; however, don't deadhead roses that you want to develop hips.

SHRUBS

Prune winter-flowering shrubs like camellias (*Camellia japonica*) as soon as their bloom period ends. Camellias tend to develop long shoots in the summer months, which can be removed to maintain the shrub's shape without losing future flowers, since these shoots usually don't develop buds. If the shrub is very young, you may need to do a only bit of pinching, removing new growth at the tips of branches to encourage the plant to fill out. More mature shrubs may need a combination of thinning cuts (cutting an entire branch back to the larger branch it sprouted from) and heading cuts (removing just a section of the branch, cutting it back to just above a node). Thinning cuts allow for light and air to penetrate through the shrub and heading cuts promote bushiness, so

■ *There are two main types of pruning: heading back (left) and thinning (right).*

■ *Now is the time to prune* Hydrangea macrophylla.

think about what you want to accomplish before you choose your cuts. If the shrub has been unpruned for a few years and is overgrown, don't try to prune it back to the shape and size you want all at once. Focus on the lower two-thirds of the shrub the first year and leave the top third alone. The next year bring the height of the shrub down to the desired size and lightly clean up the lower portion that will have grown back. Never remove more than one-third of a shrub at any single pruning.

Hydrangeas are another shrub that may be pruned at this time, depending on the type of hydrangea and whether it blooms on new wood or old wood. As a general rule of thumb, if a hydrangea blooms on new wood, you should prune it now, late in the shrub's dormant season. *Hydrangea arborescens*, *H. aspera*, and some cultivars of *H. macrophylla* (the more common "mophead" variety) fall in this category. On the other hand, with hydrangeas that bloom on the previous year's wood, you should prune right after the bloom period finishes. This includes *H. 'Preziosa'* and *H. serrata*, and again, some cultivars of *H. macrophylla*. To make it a bit more complicated, some other cultivars of *H. macrophylla* bloom on both old *and* new wood; in those cases, when new growth starts to emerge in the spring you should thin out any dead wood, then wait until after the bloom period finishes to do the heavier pruning and shaping. Yet another special case is *H. paniculata*, with more conically shaped flower heads. In that case, remove the spent flowers in late fall and wait to do the shaping in the late dormant season—in other words, now. If you're in doubt about which variety of hydrangea you have, it's safest to prune only stems that have already bloomed. And remember, the more stems you leave, the more flowers you'll have, but they'll be smaller. If you want bigger flowers, leave fewer stems on the bush.

VINES & GROUNDCOVERS

Prune bougainvillea vines as soon as danger of frost has passed. The vines bloom on new wood each year, so pruning at this time will produce a better bloom season. Unless you have a thornless variety, be sure to wear long, heavy-duty gloves, such as rose gloves, when pruning. The thorns on bougainvillea can be wicked!

WATER

BULBS

Bulbs do best when they have even moisture throughout the growing season, so if you're experiencing dry spring conditions, provide supplemental water for spring-flowering bulbs from the time the first buds appear until the foliage has died back.

EDIBLES

To give newly planted warm-season crops the best start, deliver a consistent amount of water right to the roots of the plants. If you don't have a drip irrigation system installed, try using soaker hoses in your edible garden. They are a cheap but effective way to water with the least waste.

FERTILIZE

BULBS

Fertilize spring-blooming bulbs only until they blossom, and then stop.

EDIBLES

Feed blueberry shrubs with a fertilizer formulated for acid-loving plants, such as the kind used for azaleas and rhododendrons.

PERENNIALS

Succulents need little fertilization and, depending on the soil, often do well with no additional amendment. If you are going to fertilize succulents, however, now is the time to do it. Use an all-purpose fertilizer at half-strength.

ROSES

Feed any roses that have already been winter-pruned. Start with a side-dressing of compost and then continue with a monthly feeding of a water-soluble fertilizer.

Camellias, azaleas, and rhododendrons can all use feeding with a fertilizer formulated for acid-loving plants.

TREES

In interior parts of the state, it's now time to start feeding citrus and avocado trees with a fertilizer that includes iron. Citrus trees are particularly susceptible to iron deficiencies that will manifest as yellowing leaves (called chlorosis). Water-soluble fertilizers formulated for citrus can be sprayed on and absorbed directly into the foliage.

Feed other trees a high-nitrogen fertilizer such as a 20-10-10 formula. Apply the fertilizer throughout the entire area under the tree canopy and water it in well.

PROBLEM-SOLVE

ALL

In March many gardeners will have to wage a battle in earnest against snails and slugs. The combination of moist conditions from spring rains and lots of tender, green growth is irresistible to them, and they will slowly but determinedly make their slimy way through your garden, munching as they go.

As with all pests, your objective should be to manage and minimize damage, not completely eradicate. Here are a few methods you can try:

- Diatomaceous earth (DE) is a product composed of ground-up fossilized sea creatures. Sprinkle it around wherever snails and slugs are likely to be and they will avoid crossing over it. The reason? The jagged edges of the DE tear up the undersides of anything crawling over it, leaving the pests vulnerable to death by dehydration. Be sure to use food-grade DE, which is safe to use around pets and kids.

- Beer traps are a time-honored means of attracting and drowning snails and slugs. Pour beer in a shallow dish (an aluminum pie plate works well) and set it out. The snails will crawl in for a drink and drown. You'll need to keep emptying and refilling the trap, and you'll need to make sure the rain doesn't dilute the beer. (I've heard it rumored that Coors is their beer of choice, but perhaps your garden snails and slugs have a more refined palate.)

- Coffee grounds sprinkled liberally will deter snails and slugs and are an excellent soil amendment as well.

- If you have chickens and ducks, they will love having an opportunity to feast on the snails and slugs in your garden. They are a healthy addition to the birds' diets, so there's no reason to discourage their hunting and gathering. Ditto for any other birds that pass through your garden—they're more than happy to help keep the snail population in check.

■ *Snails are voracious eaters of many garden plants, including salad leaves.*

HERE'S HOW

TO CONTROL APHIDS

Aphids are another pest that really starts to make its presence felt at this time of year. You may see them clustered thickly on rosebuds or any other tender new growth that they can suck the juice from. Here are some suggestions for controlling aphids:

- For immediate but temporary relief, try blasting heavily infested foliage or buds with a strong jet of water from the hose.

- Introduce more beneficial insects into your garden. Good predators of aphids include ladybugs, praying mantises, lacewings, and parasitic wasps. The complaint you often hear with this tactic is that the beneficials you buy and release don't necessarily stay in your garden, and that's often true. But if you don't spray chemical pesticides and have enough aphids to support a population of beneficial insects, they will be drawn to your garden and stay there as long as the food supply lasts.

- Commercial products containing insecticidal soap or parasitic fungi provide organic control for a number of insect pests, including aphids.

- If you have a problem with ants, you're more likely to have a problem with aphids since the ants "farm" the aphids to get the "honeydew" that the aphids secrete. By controlling the ants, you can usually reduce the aphid population as well.

ANNUALS AND EDIBLES

If you go out to your garden one morning to discover your tender new seedlings have been mowed down at the soil line and are laying mortally wounded on the ground, you can be certain that the villains were cutworms working in the dead of night. Cutworms, which are the larvae of gray moths, are common in most gardens. While the adult moths cause no harm, cutworms can be a major nuisance when you're sowing new crops.

Because they do their dirty work at night and spend the daytime below ground, you're not likely to come across cutworms unless you're digging or cultivating. They are 1 to 2 inches in length and can be gray, green, brown, yellow, or striped, but you'll likely recognize them from the way they curl into the shape of a "C" when touched or

disturbed. In addition to attacking plant stems, some may feed on roots or climb up the plants to feed on buds, fruit, or foliage. Different kinds of cutworms will feed on many different kinds of plants, but beans, tomatoes, corn, peppers, cosmos, snapdragons, and sunflowers are among the plants most often attacked.

The best way to get ahead of cutworms and prevent their damage is to keep your planting area free of debris, which provides cover for the moths to lay their eggs that will hatch into cutworms, and weeds, which serve as a food source for them. Then, a couple of weeks before planting new seedlings, turn the soil, leaving the cutworms exposed to predators such as birds that will make a quick snack of them. When you plant the seedlings, protect each with a collar-like barrier of paper, cardboard, or aluminum foil around each plant. Paper cups or cardboard toilet paper tubes are perfect for the job. Submerge the barrier at least 1 inch below the soil surface, leaving several inches extending above the soil.

For additional controls, you can spray seedlings with insecticidal soap or Neem oil, or release parasitic wasps or parasitic nematodes in the garden. See April for information on using parasitic nematodes.

BULBS

If you had trouble with your daffodils or other spring-blooming bulbs budding but never flowering, you've experienced a condition called "bud blast." You will see healthy-looking foliage but the buds are papery, brown, dried-up—and so disappointing.

There can be a number of causes for bud blast, including lack of nutrition, insufficient sun exposure, unseasonable heat waves or excessive rain during the time the bulb was forming the next flower, or overcrowding if the bulbs have been in place for more than a few years. Viruses may also cause bud blast, but if the bulbs flowered well in previous years, that is less likely to be the problem.

If your bulbs experienced bud blast, take the following steps to improve your chances of getting healthy blooms next year:

1. Apply a low-nitrogen, high-phosphorus and potassium fertilizer now while the bulb is getting ready to produce the bloom for next year. (The American Daffodil Society recommends a 5-10-10 fertilizer.)

2. Allow the leaves and stems to die back naturally. If the dying foliage really bothers you, you can tie it into neat bundles with string or rafia, but it's really best to leave them alone.

3. After the foliage has died back completely, dig up all the bulbs and check them for signs of disease or decomposition. Toss any bulbs that appear mushy or damaged. Divide the remaining healthy bulbs as needed and store them somewhere cool and dry until it's time to replant them in the fall. I use those plastic mesh bags that onions and other veggies are packaged in at grocery stores to store my bulbs; they keep the bulbs together and allow good air circulation.

4. When you replant the bulbs in the fall be sure to site them where they will get at least a half-day of sun and feed them at the time of planting.

Performing this intervention should give your bulbs a good start in forming the next round of flowers and prevent future cases of the dreaded bud blast.

ROSES

If there are any signs that mice or other rodents are nibbling at your rose canes, try sprinkling bloodmeal over the mulch around the base of the bush to deter them.

■ *Brown, dried-up buds on spring-blooming bulbs is a condition called "bud blast."*

April

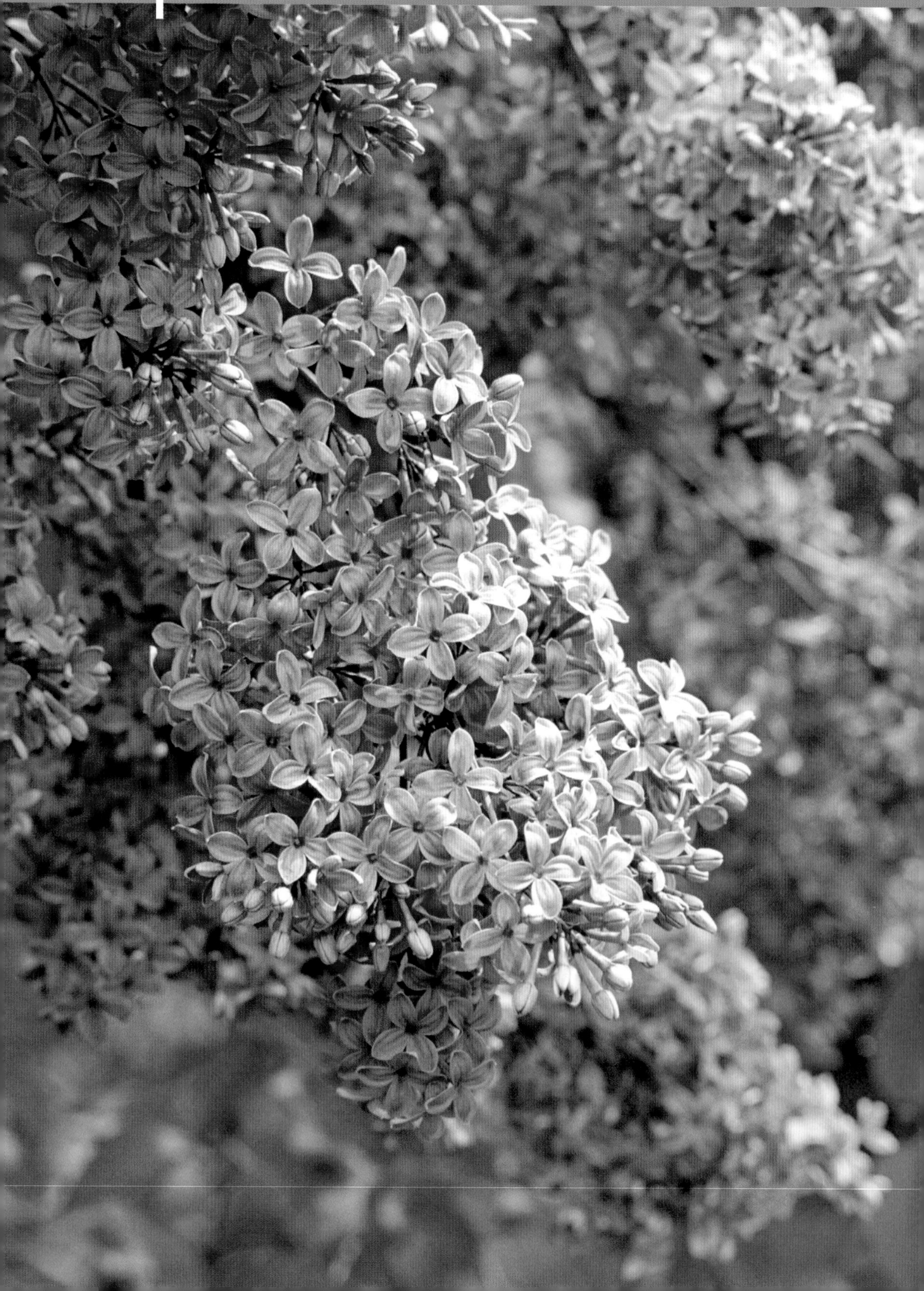

A lilac bush grows in my Bay Area garden and it has bloomed reliably each April since the third year it was in the ground. This is significant in only one respect: It's not supposed to grow here. My zone 10a garden is not supposed to have enough chill hours to set flowers on the common lilac (Syringa Vulgaris), but a lilac grew and bloomed in the garden of my childhood home, just about a mile away from where I garden now, so several years ago I thumbed my nose at the USDA Plant Hardiness Zone system and planted a lilac anyway. Each spring when I can cut a vase full of its fragrant purple flowers, I'm so glad that in this particular instance I didn't play by the rules.

I have planted other things not suited for my climate and they've sometimes died. I've planted things perfectly suited for my climate and sometimes *they've* died too. And that's the thing about gardening. No living thing comes with a guaranteed lifespan. Sometimes things just die. And sometimes plants will thrive in a spot they have no business growing in. In California, the land of countless microclimates, this seems to be even truer.

But before you plant, make a point this month, when we're still fluctuating between warm spring days and cold spring storms, of noting the microclimates in your own garden—the south-facing fence that retains heat, the lower terrace where cold air hovers, the space under the eaves of the house that is shielded from frost. These are the spots where you may find success with risky plant choices that require more heat or chill or frost protection than your garden generally offers.

It's okay to take some risks once in a while and take on the challenge of growing a plant not meant for your zone. That's part of the joy (and the challenge) of gardening here. Sometimes we just have to make up our own rules, play the game as best we can, and accept the consequences.

PLAN

ALL

In most areas, April is the month with the most garden tours. Touring other people's gardens is a great way to get ideas for future projects, lists of resources, and introductions to new plants. To find out what garden tours are planned, check with local garden clubs and nurseries. They're usually aware of all the dates and often are familiar with the kinds of gardens that different tours focus on. When you go on a tour, wear comfortable walking shoes with good treads that won't slip on wet pathways and bring a hat or some kind of sun protection. And don't forget your camera and a little notebook. Later on when you're trying to recall where you saw a beautifully designed water garden or a particular variety of Japanese maple, you'll be glad to have photos and notes to refer back to.

EDIBLES

If your edible garden is already feeling crowded, think about expanding it to the front yard. There are many fruits, vegetables, and herbs you can grow in a predominantly ornamental landscape in front of your house without making it look like a farm. Strawberries make an attractive groundcover. Colorful bunches of Swiss chard can be tucked into a flower bed. Herbs like basil, thyme, and sage add texture, color, and surprising wafts of scent. Not only will you gain more planting ground for your edibles, but you should also find that mixing flowers and fruit will lead to better pollination and consequently bigger yields of both.

Check to see if your city or homeowners association has ordinances governing front yard landscaping; you may be limited in terms of what you can plant, but more and more city agencies and homeowner associations are revising their views on edible landscaping. You should also consider how to protect your front-yard edibles from neighborhood dogs and cats that can create sanitation problems.

For ideas and inspiration on how to create a beautiful front yard with edible plants, see

■ *Many edibles can be incorporated into a flower garden.*

HERE'S HOW

TO BUILD A SIMPLE RAISED BED

1   Cut the wood and assemble the frame upside down on a flat surface. Drive deck screws through pilot holes at the corners.

2   Reinforce the corners by nailing metal corner brace hardware. Use galvanized joist hanger nails to fasten the braces.

3   Position the bed frame in your garden location. Bury the bottom at least 2 inches below grade.

4   Fill the bed with a suitable planting soil and rake smooth. The surface of the soil should be at least an inch or two below the top edges of the frame.

the Resources section for some books on that topic.

Want to really keep track of how productive your edible garden is this year? Invest in an accurate food scale and keep a running tally of your harvests. Weigh everything you pick, and perhaps even track where it goes—how much ends up on the family table, how much is frozen or canned, and how much is given away. You may be astonished at how many pounds of food can come out of your garden. Plus, at the end of the season you'll have a useful picture of which crops were worth the effort and which ones not so much. Then you can make next year's growing decisions based on reliable data rather than foggy memories or just planting the same crops you always plant. Information is power!

PERENNIALS, SHRUBS, AND TREES

Think now about what your garden will look like in fall and winter. Will there be colorful foliage? A variety of different textures? Cool-season blossoms? How different would your fall garden be with the orange flame of a persimmon tree, the scarlet explosion of an *Erica* shrub, or the understated elegance of the hellebore's blushing blooms? Maybe you need more evergreens or more succulents to provide some structural interest.

Although fall is a great time to plant, whatever you plant then will not have much time to get established, and summer is the worst time to plant. So that means planning and planting those perennials, shrubs, and trees in the next couple of months and making sure they get all the water and care they'll need to settle in during the summer. Then, come autumn and winter, you'll be rewarded with as much visual interest in the garden as you had in spring and summer.

PLANT

ALL

When installing new plants, whether ornamental or edible, it's always a good idea to keep the principles of hydrozoning in mind. *Hydrozoning* is the practice of clustering plants with similar water needs in close proximity. It allows for more efficient watering and minimizes the risk of over- or underwatering plants simply because they're in the neighborhood of a plant with drastically different water needs. Although it's a useful practice to employ at any time, it is particularly helpful in times of water rationing because it allows you to withhold water from sections of your garden with drought-tolerant plants while directing water to the areas where plants are thirstier. If you have a large garden without an irrigation system, you may also want to use hydrozoning to place the plants that you'll water less frequently farthest from the water source, meaning you'll have to haul a hose the length of the garden a little less often.

ANNUALS

As deciduous trees and shrubs have leafed out again, your garden may have developed more shady spots. Look to impatiens, lobelia, begonias, and coleus as good candidates for understory plantings to quickly fill in shady beds.

If you want to be able to harvest flowers for arrangements throughout the bloom season, plant a variety of flowers that have a good "vase life" and stagger the planting to keep the blooms coming. Good choices for a cutting garden include asters, baby's breath, calendula, celosia, cosmos, dianthus, larkspur, rudbeckia, scabiosa, snapdragons, statice, stock, sunflowers, and zinnias. You'll find six-packs of most of these in the nurseries now, but for the widest selection of varieties, you have to plant from seed. Many can be easily direct-seeded outdoors, allowing you to skip playing nursemaid to them in your house. It's crazy how easy some of these are to grow, and if you leave a few flowers on the plants, some of them will reseed themselves and keep the line going. Also, by mixing some cut-flower annuals in with your edible crops, you'll find that your plants will attract more pollinators, resulting in higher yields of both flowers and fruit.

EDIBLES

Brambleberries, a broad term for blackberries and raspberries, can be planted now in any region that is past any danger of frost. Blackberries can be grown in zones 5 to 9. Raspberries, which can be red, black, purple, or yellow, are generally hardier and can grow in zones 3 to 10.

HERE'S HOW

TO PLAN OR MAKEOVER A FOUNDATION BED

If you're thinking of establishing a new foundation bed or making over an old one, draw up a plan before you start digging, clearing, or planting.

While the style of your garden doesn't have to match the style of your home exactly, the two shouldn't fight each other. Will a Japanese-style Zen garden really blend well with your old Victorian house? Instead, plan a foundation bed that complements your home and leads seamlessly into it. Similarly, scale matters—a lot. A large house with a narrow foundation bed of small plants looks out of proportion. And a large, fast-growing tree will quickly dwarf a small house and become a potential hazard. Keep the size of the bed and plantings at maturity in proportion to the size of your home. The shape of the bed also plays a part. Houses may be all straight lines, but garden beds are more attractive with curves. Experiment by laying out a hose or rope until you find a shape that works.

Think of the bed in terms of layers. The tallest plants will go in the back of the bed, against the house. After establishing where the trees and tall shrubs will go, plot out where to place small shrubs and perennials. Be careful not to block windows or other architectural elements that you don't want to hide, but also consider the view when you're inside the house looking out. Last, fill in the bed with annuals and plants for seasonal interest, including bulbs and small deciduous shrubs.

With your plan in mind, you can create your plant list. Put the largest plants at the top of the list, noting what size you intend to buy. (Keep in mind that 1-gallon or 5-gallon plants will often become better established than bigger and more expensive plants.) Then add the smaller plants. Be sure to list alternatives in case you're not able to find the exact cultivars you want. And don't forget to add in other non-plant necessities, such as mulch, stakes, or other support structures, stones, and ornaments. When your list is complete, you'll be ready to start shopping and planting.

■ *Blackberries and raspberries can be planted as soon as danger of frost has passed.*

There are a number of viruses that can plague brambleberries so it's best to plant only certified virus-free plants. Red raspberries tend to be more disease-resistant (and have better flavor) than the black or yellow varieties. For red raspberries, good summer-bearing varieties include 'Cascade Delight', 'Chilcotin', and 'Tulameen'. For an everbearing variety, try 'Autumn Bliss', 'Bababerry', 'Caroline', and 'Fallred'. Good blackberry varieties to try are 'Apache', 'Black Satin', 'Ollalie', and 'Triple Crown'. All except 'Ollalie' are thornless.

Plant in full sun or afternoon shade in hot-summer areas. Brambleberries of all types must have well-drained soil or they can easily develop root rot. In areas with heavy clay soil, it is best to plant in a raised bed. Soil should be acidic (pH 6 to 6.5) and heavily amended with organic matter.

Before planting, work lots of composted manure into the soil. Space plants 2 to 12 feet apart, depending on the variety. Cut off the top growth on the four or five primary canes to encourage lateral branching. For blackberries and red and

yellow raspberries, train the five or six best canes on a trellis or some other support. Black and purple raspberries form clumps with arching canes and do not require additional support. Mulch heavily with compost or leaves.

Rhubarb is an edible plant that is attractive enough to fit in anywhere, even among ornamentals. With its large green leaves atop tall red or light green leafstalks, it's an easy-to-grow herbaceous perennial that will last for years, providing crop after crop of sweet-tasting stems to cook for pies, jams, sauces, even wine.

Container plants, and possibly bare-root rhizomes, are available in nurseries for planting now in zones 2 through 8. (In hotter regions, rhubarb can be planted in fall for harvest in winter and spring.) Rhubarb can be grown from seed, but it will not necessarily retain the same characteristics of the parent plant. To get the exact variety you want, you should plant root divisions or container plants. 'Victoria' is probably the most common variety of rhubarb grown. It is a heavy producer and has either red or green stalks. 'Crimson Red', 'Strawberry', 'Valentine', and 'McDonald' are also favored varieties with bright red stalks.

Plant rhubarb in full sun or in partial shade in the desert climates. Rhubarb prefers slightly acidic (pH 6.0 to 6.8), well-draining soil that is rich in organic matter. To plant divisions, dig holes 8 to 10 inches deep about 3 to 4 feet apart. Mix the soil that you've removed with an equal part of compost or composted manure. If your soil does not have good drainage, add in an equal amount of sand. Refill the holes with soil mix, burying the roots with the tops set right at the soil line. Water well and mulch. (See April's Care section for information on harvesting rhubarb.)

■ *Plant tomatoes deep in your garden.*

■ *Rhubarb is an edible plant that's attractive enough to include among ornamentals.*

In the warmest parts of the state, it's *finally* tomato time! Hardened-off seedlings (those that have already been acclimated to outdoor conditions) can be planted outdoors as soon as all danger of frost has passed and nighttime temperatures are consistently above 50 degrees Fahrenheit. Tomatoes can be grown throughout California, but finding the variety best-suited for your climate is key. (See Here's How to Select the Best Tomato Variety for Your Garden.)

Plant tomatoes in full sun (six hours minimum per day) in well-drained soil that is rich in organic matter. Work compost into the bed and plant the tomatoes 2 to 3 feet apart, burying the stems up to the bottom leaves. If plants are leggy, you can bury them even deeper. More roots will develop along the buried stem and the plant will be fuller and stronger. Water well and mulch.

Make sure that plants have sufficient support with stakes or wire cages. Otherwise, branches will break off and you'll lose tomatoes before they're ripe. It's best to set up the support at the time of planting. I recommend that you not bother with the funnel-shaped wire tomato supports that are commonly sold in hardware stores and garden centers. Except for the smallest tomato plants, they provide completely inadequate support and are a waste of money. Opt instead for big, round cages constructed of heavy-duty wire fencing, at least

HERE'S HOW

TO SELECT THE BEST TOMATO VARIETY FOR YOUR GARDEN

When selecting tomato varieties, keep in mind that the bigger the fruit, the more heat you need for ripening. Without a lot of heat, larger tomatoes may grow but not develop great flavor. That means cooler regions will have a harder time growing beefsteak tomatoes but may do fine with cherry tomatoes. In addition to climate concerns, you should also pay attention to whether the plants are determinate or indeterminate. *Determinate* varieties are bushier, more limited in height, and can usually get by without staking or other support. If you want to grow tomatoes in containers, determinate varieties are your best option. *Indeterminate* varieties are more like vines and grow to 6 or 7 feet with the proper support. Indeterminate plants are typically more productive, bearing over a longer period of time.

For areas with cool or short growing seasons, recommended varieties include 'San Francisco Fog', 'Early Girl', 'Fourth of July', 'Siberia', 'Stupice', 'Gold Nugget', 'Legend', 'Oregon Spring', 'Oregon Pride', and 'Siletz'. Smaller tomatoes (cherry, grape, or currant) tend to do well in cooler areas as well. Some of the favorites of the small tomatoes include 'Sun Gold', 'Supersweet 100', 'Sweet 100', 'Sweet Million', and 'Juliet'.

■ *'Green Zebra'*

4 feet high. Another option is to insert four strong stakes at least a foot deep in the ground around the plant, then wrap twine around the stakes at several levels to keep heavy fruit-laden branches from breaking or bending to the ground.

Keep adding more warm-season crops (see March), repeating plantings of your favorites every two to three weeks so you can extend the harvest over a longer period. Warmer parts of the state can add corn to the list of edibles. (See June for information on growing corn.)

You can set out transplants of leeks this month. (See November for more information on growing leeks.)

In hot-summer areas (mostly Southern California and the Central Valley, but you know if you live in a hot area), try 'Creole', 'Eva Purple Ball', 'Ozark Pink', 'Solar Set', 'Tropic', and 'Viva Italia'. Large beefsteak tomatoes do better in these regions as well; recommended hybrids include 'Beefsteak', 'Beefmaster', 'Big Beef', and 'Delicious'.

Heirloom varieties gain more fans every year, but they do have some challenges in terms of their susceptibility to disease. For tomato lovers, the flavor of heirlooms may be worth the risk. Some favorite heirloom varieties include 'Brandywine', 'Mortgage Lifter', 'Green Zebra', 'Black Krim', 'Cherokee Purple', 'Marvel Stripe', and 'Principe Borghese'.

Be on the lookout for grafted tomatoes, which are appearing on the market more frequently. By grafting heirloom varieties onto hybrid rootstocks that are more vigorous and disease-resistant, growers have created plants that offer the flavor and variety of heirlooms without so many of the problems. Only a few growers are doing this so far, and the plants are more expensive than typical tomato plants, but they tend to be high-yielding and some people even report getting a second year of tomatoes from the plants.

■ *'Black Krim'*

GROWING FLOWERS FOR FLAVOR

There's more to growing edibles than just fruits, vegetables, herbs, and nuts. Don't forget flowers. Some of the blossoms you already have growing could easily find their way into your lunchtime salad or decorate your favorite dessert. Here are some common flowers that you can grow to cook with or to safely garnish a dish:

- Bachelor's button/cornflower (*Centaurea cyanus*)
- Bee balm/bergamot (*Monarda didyma*)
- Borage (*Borago officinalis*)
- Breadseed poppy (*Papaver* spp.)
- Calendula (*Calendula officinalis*)

- Carnation/Sweet William (*Dianthus*)
- Chamomile (*Matricaria recutita*)
- Chrysanthemum (*Chrysanthemum*)
- Daisy (*Bellis perennis*)
- Dandelion (*Taraxacum officinale*)
- Daylilies (*Hemerocallis*)

■ *Nasturtium flowers and leaves are a spicy addition to salads.*

PERENNIALS

Tropical plants are best planted now when they are out of danger of frost but have a little time to get established before the hot, dry weather sets in. This includes bamboos, birds of paradise, cannas, crotons, hibiscus, orchids, palms, and many others. When siting a new tropical plant in a garden that gets even occasional frosts, be sure to consider what means of protection you'll use to avoid frost damage. Planting near the foundation of the house where a plant may be shielded under the eaves or against a south-facing wall may be all the protection a tropical plant will need in a light frost. In zones 7 and below, planting in containers that can be moved indoors or to a more sheltered area outdoors is often the best option.

This is also a good time to take cuttings of most succulents to propagate new plants. Allow the

- Hibiscus (*Hibiscus rosa-sinensis*)
- Lavender (*Lavendula*)
- Lilac (*Syringa vulgaris*)
- Marigold (*Tagetes tenuifolia*)
- Nasturtium (*Tropaeolum majus*)
- Pansy (*Viola × wittrockiana*)
- Rose (*Rosa*)
- Scented geranium (*Pelargonium*)
- Sunflower (*Helianthus annuus*)
- Sweet violet (*Viola odorata*)
- Tuberous begonias (*Begonia × tuberosa*)

Some of the flowers can be eaten in their entirety; others have only edible petals. For some, like the breadseed poppy and the sunflower, it's the seeds that are edible. Roses not only have edible petals, but the rose hips (seedpods) can be used for jellies, teas, or other dishes.

It is important to note that any flowers used in food *must not be treated with pesticides.* Also, *never* eat flowers you find growing on the side of the road—who knows what car emissions and other toxins they may have absorbed. Some people can have allergic reactions, particularly to the pollen of some flowers. Because plants may have some parts that are edible and other parts that are highly poisonous, you should research any flower you use in food to make sure you are using only the edible parts.

cuttings to sit in a dry, cool space for a few days to callous over before planting.

ROSES

You can still plant bare-root roses (if you can find them) in zones 1 through 7, but it's more likely that you'll find container-grown roses in the nurseries now. They can be planted in all zones in the state.

TREES

Few plants can establish a "Mediterranean" feel in a garden more than an olive tree, and now is the time to plant one. Most olive trees can grow in zones 9 to 11, but a few are hardy to zones 7 or 8. Fruiting varieties generally require long periods of high heat and some winter chill but no late frosts that can kill blossoms. They are hardy to 15 degrees Fahrenheit. If you're not concerned about harvesting fruits, or if you just want to avoid the messiness that the fruiting trees can create, look for an ornamental variety. Fruiting varieties include 'Arquebina', 'Mission', and 'Picholine'. All three varieties are considered self-fruitful (meaning no separate pollinator is needed) but will produce a better crop with another tree for cross-pollination. Ornamental, or nonfruiting, varieties include 'Majestic Beauty' and the dwarf 'Little Ollie'.

Plant olive trees in full sun in deep, well-drained neutral (pH 7) soil. They can also be grown in large containers or espaliered against a fence or wall. Avoid planting fruiting trees near patios or driveways where the fallen fruit can leave dark stains. Olive trees are evergreen, but some drop more litter than others, so be sure to inquire about leaf drop on the variety you buy.

Olive trees are shallow-rooted and the roots should be handled with some care. Plant the tree in a hole as deep as the rootball and twice as wide. If it is at all rootbound, gently loosen or trim away circular roots. Fill the hole with loose soil and mulch heavily, keeping the mulch several inches away from the base of the trunk. Water deeply and mulch.

Pomegranate trees are also appropriate for Mediterranean gardens—or any garden that wants an evergreen, drought-tolerant plant and delicious fruit. Pomegranates do best in climates with cool winters and hot, dry summers, such as in zones 7 to 10. As with olives, pomegranates come in fruiting and nonfruiting varieties. The most commonly planted fruiting pomegranate in California is 'Wonderful', but other varieties to try are 'Utah Sweet', 'Granada', and 'Eversweet', which does better in cooler climates than 'Wonderful'. Nonfruiting varieties include 'Variegata', 'Mme. Legrelle', 'Taysho', and the dwarf 'Chico'.

Plant in full sun; in partial shade fruiting trees may grow and flower but not set fruit. Pomegranates prefer well-drained, slightly acidic soil (pH 5.5 to 7.0) but can do well enough in alkaline soil. They can be grown in containers, particularly in areas where frost protection is needed.

Plant in a hole twice as wide but no deeper than the rootball. Make sure that soil does not come up higher on the trunk than it was in the container. Take care that roots do not dry out before planting and water well once planted.

VINES & GROUNDCOVERS

Wisteria is one of the most popular choices of vines to grow in California and it's little wonder when you consider what a spectacular display they put on each spring. They are not difficult to grow; in fact, they are vigorous growers, but they require some patience since they will not bloom for several years after planting (two or more years for grafted plants or as many as ten to fifteen years for seed-grown plants).

The best time to plant wisteria is now or in the fall. When you purchase your plant, be sure to ask if the plant was grafted or grown from seed and how long you'll need to wait for blooms. There are basically three kinds of wisteria available: Chinese (*Wisteria sinensis*), Japanese (*W. floribunda*), or American (*W. frutescens*). In California, you'll most likely find Chinese or Japanese varieties; the American variety is native to the southeastern United States and is preferred there because the Chinese and Japanese varieties can be invasive.

Wisteria can be grown as a climbing vine, a groundcover, or a free-standing or espaliered tree, so consider the form you want when choosing where to plant. It requires six to eight hours of full sun and well-draining soil. To plant, dig a hole as deep as the rootball and two to three times as wide. Place the plant in the hole and fill up halfway. Water well and allow the water to drain away, then fill the hole the rest of the way and water again. Top with a couple of inches of compost and then a couple of inches of mulch. If growing as a vine, make sure that you have a sturdy support structure in place to attach it to. If growing as a free-standing tree, you will need to stake it until it has completely established itself.

Another spectacular vine to plant now is the passion flower vine (*Passiflora*), as well as its edible versions, the passion fruit vine (*Passiflora edulis*). While the passion fruit vine is evergreen or semi-evergreen, the passion flower vine has deciduous cultivars as well. Passiflora can grow to 30 feet high and produce intricate flowers (also called maypops) that for some people symbolize the passion of Christ. Most flowers are in shades of white and lavender, with a few varieties having red or yellow flowers. The vines bloom in warm weather, which can mean year-round in some parts of the state. The fruiting varieties ripen in summer and fall.

Passion fruit vines can be grown in zones 8 to 10. Passion flower vines can be grown in zones 6 to 11, depending on the variety. All varieties need well-drained soil that is rich in organic matter and low in salt. Ideal soil is pH 6.5 to 7.5 but it can adapt to a wide range of soils types. The vine must be planted where it will have a trellis or other support to grow on and protection from the wind.

Most of the commercially sold passion fruit vines are hybrids grafted onto rootstock for greater resistance to root disease. Grafted plants are also much hardier and longer-lived. Plant the grafted vine in a hole as deep and twice as wide as the rootball, taking care not to cover the graft union. Mulch and water well.

Although it is not the preferred method, you can also grow the plants from seed. If you use seed taken directly from the fruit, they will usually germinate in two to three weeks. Older seeds will germinate more slowly, although you can speed germination by nicking the seed with a nail file or rubbing it with sandpaper before planting.

CARE

ALL

Any plants that appear to have been damaged by frost during the winter months can now be cleaned up. Branches that have no sign of budding and appear dead can be removed, trimming back until you find healthy live wood.

BULBS

Remove dead flowers and seedheads immediately after blooming has finished in order to channel the bulb's energy into producing new and bigger bulbs. Leave the foliage in place to die back naturally and if the bulbs appear to have grown too crowded, mark the area or note in your garden journal that they will need to be divided. (Spring bulbs can be divided any time after the foliage has died back through the fall.) Last, lay down a 3- to 4-inch layer of mulch over any bulbs you have planted. The mulch will help retain moisture during the hotter months to come and keep the bulbs from drying out while the next year's flowers are forming.

EDIBLES

Rhubarb plants need to grow for two full seasons without harvesting stalks. In the third season, you can harvest stalks for four to five weeks in the spring. In subsequent springs, you can stretch the harvest time to eight weeks. Do not cut the stalks; instead, grasp them at the base, pulling sideways and outward. Never harvest all the stalks from a plant. After harvesting, water and feed the plant with a balanced fertilizer. If any blossom stalks appear, cut them out. *Just remember:* Rhubarb leaves contain oxalates, which are poisonous and can be lethal when consumed in large enough quantities. Be sure to cook and eat only the stems, not the leaves!

PERENNIALS

Plants overwintered indoors get tender. Even semi-hardy succulents can become susceptible to sunburn and windburn. When moving plants back outdoors, situate them first in shade or part shade, then over a period of weeks move them to a spot with the proper amount of sun exposure.

ROSES

Cold-winter regions should finish any pruning that remains to be done. Early spring is a good time throughout the state for pruning Knockout roses and other landscape-type roses. Remove all broken or dead canes, take out a few interior canes to improve air circulation through the bush, and cut it back to about one-third of its height.

Many people seem to think that you can't grow roses without spraying lots of chemicals, but in fact you can, especially if you've taken the important steps of selecting and planting disease-resistant varieties and keeping them pruned to promote good air circulation. I spray my roses only in the years when they really seem to be struggling with pest or disease damage, and when I do spray, I use only organic controls, such as Neem oil. If your roses do develop a problem that requires spraying, be sure to spray the plant completely, from the top down to the soil, including the undersides of leaves.

Keep weeding around roses and use a pre-emergent herbicide like corn gluten meal to keep weed seeds from germinating. Apply or freshen up mulch to a depth of 3 to 4 inches. Keep deadheading spent blossoms or disbudding for larger flowers, and keep the ground surrounding the shrub clear of dead foliage and flowers.

SHRUBS

Spring is a good time to prune both broad-leafed and thin-leafed evergreens before their new growth appears. Most evergreens need only minimal shaping and removal of the three Ds: dead, damaged, or diseased wood, which can be (and should be) pruned out at any time of year. There's no benefit to leaving a bad branch on a shrub or tree. If it breaks off, it can leave a bigger wound on the trunk and possibly lead to other breakage of surrounding branches. If the wood is infected, leaving it on can allow the infection to spread to other parts of the tree or to other plants.

For all other woody plants, there are two questions to ask yourself before pruning: Does this plant bloom in spring or summer, and does it bloom on new wood or old wood? If it blooms in spring, wait until after the blooms have faded to prune. If it blooms in summer and it blooms on new wood, prune in early spring so that the new wood will have time to grow. If it blooms in summer on old wood, wait until the fall to prune.

TREES

Once any danger of frost has passed, it's safe to prune citrus trees. Trim leggy branches and pinch out new growth to shape as desired. If the tree is getting too dense, you can thin the canopy to allow for more sunlight to get to the fruit.

Most other fruit trees should be pruned before bud break while the tree is still dormant. If you missed this window of opportunity, it is best to wait until summer and then prune only enough to shape the tree and maintain good air circulation without sacrificing too much fruit.

Thin the fruits of the early-fruiting varieties of fruit trees as soon as they are about the size of dime. Some people hate to thin fruit, thinking that it reduces the crop size. It's true that you'll get fewer fruits, but thinning will not only make a significant difference in the size and quality of the fruit, it will also result in fewer pest and disease problems.

As trees fill in with new growth, take note of the branches that may be susceptible to sunburn in the heat of summer. Sometimes pruning trees to allow for good air circulation through the canopy means that sunlight can beat down onto exposed branches or the crotch of the tree and burn the bark, in much the same way that our skin can sunburn. And just as sunburn turns skin a bright red, one of the primary signs of sunburn on a tree is discoloration of the bark. Sunburn generally

won't kill a tree, or even a whole branch, but it can inhibit its ability to take up water and nutrients from the roots throughout the branches, weakening it and making it vulnerable to pests and pathogens.

Following are some tips to help prevent sunburn on trees:

- Most important, be sure that you plant trees where they will get the correct sun exposure for their needs. Shade-loving trees will not do well in full sun no matter what precautions you may take.

- Keep trees properly watered, especially when they're young. With appropriate hydration, trees can develop healthier bark to resist sunburn.

- Spread a layer of mulch around the base of the tree, making sure to avoid piling the mulch up around the base of the trunk where it can cause rot. The mulch will help to deflect some light away from the tree and also help to hold moisture in the soil for the tree's roots.

- On very young trees leave any small branches and foliage growing out of the trunk in place. They not only shield the trunk from scorching

■ *Thin fruit early in the season to get better quality fruit later.*

■ *Over-pruning can leave branches and trunk exposed and susceptible to sunburn.*

sunlight but also help to feed the tree's roots. Remove unwanted branches from the trunk only when they are about the diameter of a thick pencil.

- Avoid severely pruning an established tree all at once. If you need to rejuvenate an overgrown tree, spread the pruning over two or three years so that you won't take away too much of the canopy at one time, exposing too much naked branch to the sunlight.

- If you do have exposed branches that are vulnerable, you can apply a coat of diluted white latex paint to them. Pay particular attention to the parts of the tree facing south or southwest, as they will absorb the harshest sunlight. The paint will wash away over time so you may need to reapply.

VINES & GROUNDCOVERS

Pruning clematis vines can seem rather complicated because different cultivars fall into three categories, depending upon when they bloom and whether they bloom on old or new wood. To keep it simple, you can follow these more general guidelines for all types of clematis. In the first year following planting, cut back all clematis vines, leaving only two sets of leaf buds on each stem. This will limit the blooms for that year, but it will redirect the plant's energy into developing a more vigorous root system. In subsequent years, leave the previous year's growth in place until you see leaf buds sprouting in mid-spring. At that time you can cut out dead or weak stems and cut some of the remaining stems back to just a few buds to control the size and shape of the vine.

WATER

ALL

Although it's true a drip-emitter irrigation system is the best and most efficient method of watering plants, sometimes that's just not an option. If hand-watering is your regular means of watering, be sure that you're doing it correctly. Water early in the morning so that wet foliage has a chance to dry in the sun during the day. For most plants, but particularly for ones prone to fungal diseases, aiming the water spray directly at the soil rather than over the entire plant will help to minimize the spread of disease pathogens. Invest in a good quality hose that doesn't kink easily. (Hint: All hoses kink. Some are just worse than others.) The right watering attachment makes a difference as well. The best choice is a wand that delivers a good volume of water at a low pressure. Unlike the trigger or other type of attachments, wands allow you to easily water hanging plants or container plants at all levels.

■ *Drip irrigation is the most efficient method of watering your garden.*

■ *When watering by hand, be sure to water at the base of the plant.*

Whatever method of watering you use, keep in mind that deep watering always beats more frequent but shallow watering, and the sandier your soil is, the more frequently you should be watering. Also, if you recycle water from your household (grey water), do not use it on your edible plants. Use the grey water on ornamental plants and lawns and save the fresh water for your fruits and vegetables. Ditto for well water, unless you've had it tested and know it to be free of contaminants and toxins.

Keep these guidelines in mind and you should be able to keep your garden properly hydrated as the warm, dry season sets in.

HOUSEPLANTS
Begin to withhold water from potted poinsettias, allowing the plant to dry out gradually. Once it's dry, store it in a cool, well-ventilated area (but not below 60 degrees Fahrenheit).

LAWNS
When April showers are a little hit or miss, it can be difficult to determine if your lawn is getting a consistent amount of water. Here's a quick-and-easy test to see if your lawn needs watering: Step on it. If the grass doesn't spring back up after you lift up your foot, it needs water. If you don't trust the foot test, go back to the best test of all—the finger test. Stick your finger in the soil as deep as possible. If the soil at the tip of your finger (which is about as far down as grass roots go) is moist, you can wait to water.

ROSES
Roses, whether newly planted or well-established, require a consistent amount of water—about 1 inch of water a week, in one or two applications, depending on how fast-draining your soil is. As a rule, it's best to water at root level with drip emitters or soaker hoses to keep fungal diseases from setting in and spreading. However, if you hand-water, do it early in the day and completely wash the whole plant, top to bottom. This allows the water spray to wash off fungal spores and pests like aphids, and the water has time to dry on the foliage before nightfall.

FERTILIZE

ALL
Now that most things are actively growing and need some kind of supplemental nutrition, get organized this month about fertilizing. Keep track of what plants you feed, what kind of fertilizer you give them, and how much. If you give them a timed-release fertilizer, which slowly releases nutrients for up to six months, there's no need to feed them monthly. Similarly, if you apply a

HERE'S HOW

TO USE MANURE IN THE GARDEN

One of the most nutrient-rich amendments you can add to the garden is something that most people think of only as sewer-worthy: manure. Many types of animal manure are rich in the nutrients all plants need—nitrogen, phosphorus, and potassium—plus microbes that are great for healthy soil. There are, however, some disadvantages and concerns involved with using manure in home gardens.

■ *To be composted, manure must be heated to 145 degrees Fahrenheit.*

First, it's important to understand the stages that manure goes through. Fresh manure is high in nitrogen compounds and ammonia that can burn plants and initially inhibit seed germination. Aged manure has been stored for at least six months, allowing some of that nitrogen and ammonia to break down. It's still nutrient-rich but can also still burn plants. To be considered "composted," manure must be heated to 145 degrees Fahrenheit and turned enough so that the entire pile has heated through.

While manure can be a great source of nutrients, it does also have some drawbacks. While we tend to think of manure as organic matter, if it comes from non-organic farms or other sources, it may contain residue of pesticides, antibiotics, or other medications that were given to the animals. In addition, it may carry harmful pathogens like E. coli, listeria, or salmonella, which can be particularly dangerous for children. And manure is notorious for being a source of spreading weed seeds, which can turn your garden beds into a weed patch.

In spite of the drawbacks, manure can be a useful addition to your soil if you practice a few simple tips:

- Never use raw manure of any kind in your home garden.

- Don't use manure from cats, dogs, or other meat-eating animals in the garden. They can contain harmful pathogens. And (need I really say this?) *never* use human manure in the garden.

- If you use aged manure, it should be aged for a minimum of six months, and you should wait at least one month following application before planting.

- If you use composted manure, apply it at a rate of 40 pounds per 100 square feet, and work it into the soil to a depth of 6 to 9 inches.

- If you want to obtain fresh manure for composting, the best sources are local farms, zoos, or stables. Manure composts best when it is mixed with bedding materials like straw. Be sure to wear gloves and washable rubber boots when handling fresh manure, and wash your hands carefully afterward.

- Want to know which animal produces the most nutrient-rich manure? Rabbits! Next on the list are chickens, followed (in order) by sheep, horses, cattle, ducks, and pigs.

■ *To test your soil's drainage, dig a 1-foot deep hole. Fill it with water, and let it drain. Fill it again, measure the water depth with a ruler, and let it drain for fifteen minutes. Measure the water depth again, and multiply by four. Less than 1 is slow-draining soil; a rate from 1 to 6 inches is good; more than 6 is a fast-draining soil.*

foliar feeding, it may not be wise to amend the soil soon after. Overfeeding can do as much damage as underfeeding—more even, if you consider that excess fertilizer runoff ends up in our open water systems.

It's also important not to fertilize a stressed plant. It's tempting when a plant looks sickly from too little or too much water, for example, to think that a shot of fertilizer will perk the plant right up. Wrong! Drought-stressed or overwatered plants are not prepared to process a rush of nutrients, and the result will usually be fertilizer burn or even death of the plant.

Fertilizer "burn" occurs when excess fertilizer raises the salt content of the soil. There is a higher risk of burn with synthetic fertilizers than with organic amendments because organic fertilizers, like timed-release synthetic fertilizers, tend to break down more slowly in the soil. Fertilizer burn can begin to show within days of fertilizer application and will appear as brown or discolored foliage, which, if severe enough, can kill a plant. If you suspect that your plants have fertilizer burn, your only recourse is to try to flush the salts out of the soil with water. Soak the plant well, allow the water to be absorbed, then water some more. Keep repeating until the soil literally can't absorb more water. This will move the salts through the soil, away from a plant's roots. The excess water can take a toll on the plant as well, but this is the only way to clear the soil of the excess fertilizer.

LAWNS

Most lawns are ready for a booster shot of fertilizer in spring, but fertilizing done haphazardly can do more damage than not fertilizing at all. Refer to Here's How to Fertilize Lawn Without Waste or Overkill for guidelines to help you feed your lawn efficiently and sustainably.

PERENNIALS

Feed most spring- and summer-blooming perennials now with a sidedressing of compost or an application of a timed-release fertilizer for flowering plants.

Daylilies can receive a sidedressing of compost now; unless the soil is very poor, they will not need any more fertilization for the rest of the year. Additional feedings would just encourage more green growth, not more blooms.

It's not really necessary to fertilize succulents in the ground, but you can feed succulents in containers with a liquid fertilizer diluted to half strength.

HERE'S HOW

TO FERTILIZE LAWN WITHOUT WASTE OR OVERKILL

1. Timing matters. It's important that you don't feed your lawn too soon in the spring. If you live in an area where there is snowfall, wait until the lawn starts to green up; in other areas, make sure the lawn is growing, indicating that the roots are healthy enough to take in the nutrients you're about to provide. If you fertilize before then, the fertilizer that isn't absorbed by the roots will wash away.

2. Rake the lawn well to remove debris and leaves so the fertilizer will be able to reach the soil. Also, remove obvious weeds like dandelions. There's no reason to give them a nutrient boost.

3. Don't think "more is better" when it comes to fertilizer; apply the right amount and no more. Plan on applying a ½ pound of nitrogen per 1,000 square feet, using a spreader to distribute it evenly. There is no advantage to adding more than that amount. It will only contribute to fertilizer runoff that ends up in water systems or excessive growth that requires more mowing.

4. Take into account the amount of recent and forecasted rainfall. Make sure the lawn is not drought-stressed when you fertilize. If the weather has been dry, water the day before applying the fertilizer and then again after the application. If there is a stretch of wet weather in the forecast, it's best to delay fertilizing until the storms have passed. Excessive rainfall will just wash the nutrients away before the grass roots can absorb them.

ROSES

Feed all roses. Use a fertilizer especially formulated for roses, or do a foliar feeding with fish or kelp emulsion.

VINES & GROUNDCOVERS

Wisteria plants are generally not heavy feeders, but juvenile plants (those not old enough to bloom yet) benefit from feeding once each spring. Apply a sidedressing of compost or a balanced fertilizer and water it in well. Mature wisteria should only be fertilized if it's showing signs of nutrient deficiency, namely yellowing foliage or new growth that's insufficient or stunted.

PROBLEM-SOLVE

ALL

Remain vigilant for snails, slugs, and aphids. The snails and slugs will be prevalent as long as wetter conditions prevail, and the aphids will be feasting as long as there is tender new growth—until enough predators show up to keep their population in check. (See March for details.)

LAWNS

If your lawn is pockmarked with unsightly brown patches, you may be having a problem with sod webworms. A telltale sign is moths flying close to the lawn at dusk, but to confirm the diagnosis, soak the suspected area with a solution of 1 tablespoon dishwashing liquid in 1 gallon of water. If the webworms are present, they'll float to the surface. More than fifteen per square yard means you'll need to treat the lawn with parasitic nematodes (tiny beneficial roundworms that kill pests with a bacterium). (See Here's How to Control Pests with Parasitic Nematodes, opposite, for more information.)

Sometimes, however, the biggest offenders against lawns are the furry, four-legged kind. The ammonia in dog urine can leave brown spots in even the healthiest grasses. To avoid the problem, you can designate a particular, hidden spot in the garden for your dog to use, but if the brown patches continue to appear, sprinkle the area with horticultural lime and water it in well. A regularly watered lawn will generally be less susceptible to damage from dog urine.

■ *Dogs can be some of the main causes of lawn troubles as this dog urine mark shows.*

HERE'S HOW

TO CONTROL PESTS WITH PARASITIC NEMATODES

Parasitic nematodes (also referred to as predatory or beneficial nematodes) are an effective method of control for insects that live in the soil during the larval stage, including sod webworms, white grubs, cutworms, slugs, snails, earwigs, fungus gnats, squash vine borers, thrips, and a number of types of beetles. The nematodes live in the soil for months after application and work by infecting their prey with a bacterium that kills them within days of infection, but without harming plant roots.

Follow these steps to apply the nematodes:

1. Choose the appropriate brand of nematode treatment depending on what pests you want to control:

PEST	NEMATODE	BRAND NAME
Sod webworms, grubs, beetles, and thrips	*Heterorhabditis bacteriophora*	NemaSeek, Heteromask, and Terranem
Fungus gnats	*Steinernema feltiae*	NemAttack, NemaShield, Scanmask, and Entonem
Snails and slugs	*Phasmarhabditis hermaphrodita*	Nemaslug
Caterpillars, fungus gnats, some larvae	*Steinernema carpocapsae*	Capsanem

   These products are available either as a spray solution or in sponges that you soak in water and then spray the solution on the soil.

2. Apply to the soil on a cool, cloudy day or in the evening so that the nematodes will be able to burrow down into the soil before they get dried out. The nematodes will die if they are exposed to hot, dry conditions or UV light such as sunlight.

3. Re-apply the solution every six weeks for continuous protection.

4. For container plants that have received a nematode treatment, be sure to water the container from the bottom because overhead watering will flush the nematodes out of the soil.

SHRUBS & TREES

You may be noticing a lot of ants trekking up and down the woody plants in your garden. They are likely busy farming aphids, which will be sucking all the juices out of your plants' new foliage. You can control the ants, and thereby help control the aphids, by washing the shrub or tree with an insecticidal soap and then applying a product that leaves a sticky barrier all the way around the base of the trunk, just above the ground. Be sure to remove any low branches that hang to the ground, or the ants will simply use them as a way of bypassing the barrier.

WATER GARDENS

If raccoons are tearing up plants in your water garden, it's more likely that they're searching for snails, slugs, or fish. Moving the potted plants in your pond away from shallow ledges and into the deepest part or the center of the pond may help since raccoons don't really like stepping into water that is more than 6 or 8 inches deep. Netting laid over the surface of the pond may help protect the fish, but raccoons have nimble little paws and they may be able to tear the netting off. (See June for ideas on making raccoons feel unwelcome in your garden.)

May

May is the month most often associated with roses, in spite of the fact that in California you can find many roses in bloom from early spring all the way through fall. I know that May is usually the time when I'm starting to wish that I had planted more roses in my garden. The ones I do have are typically blooming so magnificently at this point, sweetly perfuming the air, that I can only wish for more. The best thing about roses is their scent, but the second best thing is that they are amazingly hardy plants.

It was a surprise to me when I started gardening to discover just how resilient roses are—how they can survive bad pruning or even no pruning, how they can hold their own against a plague of aphids, and how they can tough it out through a drought. It was a surprise because people tend to think that roses are delicate and fussy and difficult to grow. It's unfair how much roses are thought of as garden divas, especially given the newer hybrids with greater disease resistance and repeating bloom periods.

There are quite a few plants out there that have been similarly labeled "difficult," often in an equally undeserved fashion. Usually, a "fussy" plant is just a plant in the wrong place. Move it to the right place, give it the conditions it needs, and its fussiness disappears—the garden diva becomes a contented member of the chorus. Sometimes the right place just doesn't exist in your garden. That's OK. Dig it up and adopt it out to someone who can provide the right place (or in the really dire cases, send it to the compost bin), then look for another plant that's better suited to that spot.

This is a good month to take another look at your fussiest plants because any plant that isn't thriving in May could really be in dire shape in August. Find out what the plants really need that they're not getting, and decide whether they would do better somewhere else. Make "right plant, right place" your gardening mantra and no plant—not roses, not orchids, not Japanese maples—will be too fussy. Then *you* can be the sole diva in your garden.

PLAN

ALL

Look ahead to the summer months and note any garden-centered celebrations you'll be hosting. A graduation party or wedding reception? A Fourth of July barbecue? Or maybe just an alfresco brunch for two? How could your garden be better prepared for entertaining? Make sure there is ample shade for relaxing and that pathways are clear enough for foot traffic. If they've been overgrown by shrubbery, plan now for getting the brush pruned and cleaned up. Map out where you could set up a table for eating or serving drinks and where you could set up additional chairs if needed. And of course, give any garden furniture that's been in storage or that's been outside through the cold weather a good cleaning so that it's ready for even the drop-in garden visitor.

Planning any vacations this summer? If so, look around now to line up someone to care for your garden. That may include watering, mowing the lawn, or bringing in any ripening fruits and vegetables. If you don't know anyone to call on, check with local nurseries, garden clubs, or the horticulture department of a nearby community college. They may have contacts they can refer or a bulletin board where you can post a "help wanted" ad.

If you haven't already invested in one, this is a good time to think about purchasing a good garden cart or wheelbarrow. Even if you already have your spring garden set up, there's always more compost, mulch, and plants to haul around, and you'll be even more glad to have it on hand when cleanup time rolls around in the fall. Look for one that is sturdy, maneuverable, with good cargo capacity, and designed for easy dumping.

ROSES

Check out some local rose gardens this month. They'll be at peak bloom and you will likely find some varieties you've never seen before that you may want to include in your garden. If you get a chance to speak to the gardener in charge, you may be able to get some useful information about which ones grow well in your area and have the best disease resistance.

PLANT

ANNUALS

If you want to easily multiply the annuals in your garden, plant the ones that will self-sow their seeds. All you have to do then is not deadhead them, and they will set seeds that will fall to the ground and send up a wave of new plants. The list of self-sowers includes alyssum, bachelor's buttons, calendula, California poppy, candytuft, clarkia, coreopsis, cosmos, flax, larkspur, love-in-a-mist, lupine, and nasturtium.

EDIBLES

Tomatoes can now be planted throughout the state. (See April for information on planting tomatoes and choosing the best varieties for your region.)

■ *A good wheelbarrow is a great help in the garden.*

Plan ahead for your Thanksgiving dinner and plant some sweet potatoes now. There are two kinds of sweet potatoes: Those with sweet, orange-yellow flesh and those with firmer, drier white flesh. The orange-flesh type is the kind you see sold in supermarkets as yams. Recommended varieties of this type include 'Centennial', 'Jewel', 'Kona-B', 'Vineless Puerto Rico', 'Nancy Hall', and 'Vardaman'. Favored white-flesh varieties include 'Onokeo', 'Waimanalo Red', and 'Yellow Jersey'.

Sweet potatoes can be planted as soon as danger of frost has passed *and* the soil temperature has reached 70 degrees Fahrenheit. They can be grown throughout California, but a long, hot growing season is required to produce a good crop. Plant in full sun in well-drained, slightly acidic soil (pH 5.0 to 6.5).

The most important part of planting sweet potatoes is what you plant. Use only certified disease-free slips, which are rooted pieces of tuber. You can buy organic sweet potatoes and root them yourself by cutting them in half and placing them on a bed of moist potting soil. Cover with a few inches more of potting soil and keep them moist and warm until shoots and leaves appear. In about six weeks, they will be ready to dig up, cut into pieces, and replant. The problem with this is that you must keep the tubers really warm to get the slips started, which usually requires a heating mat or some other heat source. It's just much easier to buy your slips from a trusted seed supplier.

Before planting the slips, apply a fertilizer that is low in nitrogen and high in phosphorous and potassium (such as 0-5-5 or 0-10-10) and work it into the soil several inches deep. Plant the slips so that just the tips of the stems and leaves are exposed. Space them 1 foot apart in rows 3 feet apart. Use ditches between the rows to ensure good drainage. Keep the bed consistently moist until the plants are established and growing. Once established, the plants require less water.

If you added fertilizer to the soil at the time of planting, additional feeding isn't needed and will just increase the foliage without improving the tubers. Using row covers will help to keep the bed warmer and will also prevent pests like flea beetles, cucumber beetles, and wireworms from getting access. Nematodes can still be a problem; the best way to combat that is to rotate crops so that you never grow sweet potatoes in the same bed two years in a row. Sweet potatoes are ready to harvest approximately three months after planting. (See August for information on harvesting.)

ROSES

You can still plant container-grown roses throughout the state, but you can plant bare-root roses now only in the coldest regions (zones 1 to 4). If you want to have blooms this year, be sure you select a variety that is a repeat bloomer; the once-a-year bloomers will be finished or almost finished blooming this month.

TREES

Pineapple guava (*Feijoa sellowiana*) is about as accommodating as a plant can be, both in the garden and in the kitchen. An evergreen shrub that can be trained as a tree, it has gray-green leaves, pink-red blossoms, and green, egg-shaped fruits that drop at your feet when they're ready to be eaten. It can be left in all its shrubby fullness, pruned to a hedge, espaliered against a fence, or grown in a container. You can nibble its blossoms in the spring and its fruit in the fall, and it will adapt to just about any soil type or level of maintenance you care to provide.

Pineapple guavas grow in zones 8 to 11, but crops will be disappointing if there are not at least 50 hours of winter chill. (See December for more on winter chilling.) Plant trees in full sun or in partial shade in the hottest regions. In colder regions, it can be grown in containers and brought indoors in the winter. 'Nikita' (a dwarf), 'Coolidge', 'Pineapple Gem', 'Beechwood', 'Mammoth', 'Nazemetz', and 'Trask' are all self-fruitful, but planting a cross-pollinizer will result in a heavier crop.

Plant young trees after danger of frost has passed. In areas without frosts, pineapple guavas can be planted at any time. (They can also be grown from seed, but the fruit will not necessarily be true to type.) Plant in a hole twice as wide as, but no deeper than, the rootball. Make sure that soil does not come up higher on the trunk than it was in the container. Take care that roots do not dry

■ *Water hyacinths are easy to grow—so easy they can become invasive.*

out before planting, and water well and mulch once planted. Although pineapple guavas are very drought-tolerant, you should see that your tree gets fairly regular watering to get the best fruit quality.

Pineapple guava flowers, appearing in the spring, are edible, sweet-tasting, and fragrant. They can be used in salads or to make jams and jellies. The fruit ripens in the fall and will drop off the tree when it is fully ripe and at its peak flavor.

VINES & GROUNDCOVERS

Even if you have no interest in home-brewing, a hops vine (*Humulus lupulus*) can be a great addition to your garden. These fast-growing vines are a striking ornamental and the flowers not only can be used to flavor beer, they also are an eye-catching and unusual addition to cut-flower bouquets.

Hops vines are grown from rhizomes, which may be found in the spring in some nurseries, but you'll find them more readily available online. Rhizomes should be planted this month at the latest; later planting may not allow enough time for flowering.

Plant hops in full sun and rich, well-draining soil that is slightly acidic (pH 6.2 to 6.5). Hops vines are extreme climbers, reaching 20 to 25 feet in a season, so you need to make sure they have ample support. Plant rhizomes 3 to 5 feet apart and 6 to 10 inches deep and mulch well. They do best with short, frequent watering the first year, then deep, less frequent watering in subsequent years. The vines will grow like mad, but don't expect many flowers the first year. After harvest in the fall, the vines will die back to the ground each year.

WATER GARDENS

For an easy way to add plants to your water garden, look to floating plants like water hyacinths and water lettuce. These plants act as natural water filters by floating freely on the surface with their roots trailing along in the water below, absorbing excess nutrients that can lead to algae growth and pollutants. Water hyacinths are frost-sensitive, but if you get them established in the pond now, they'll have time to produce lavender or pink flowers in the summer.

These plants multiply rapidly and you will need to thin them as they grow, so don't add too many. But "planting" couldn't be easier: you just toss them into the pond and they float on their merry way.

(Note: Although water hyacinths are being used in sewage treatment plants in Southern California, the plants can double in volume in a matter of a few weeks and are therefore extremely invasive in open water systems. When you thin or remove water hyacinths from your water garden, you should compost or dispose of the plants in the trash. Never release water hyacinth plants into water systems or gardens other than your own pond or fountain.)

CARE

ALL

Do some spring cleaning in the garden this month. Keep walkways swept and clear of overgrown branches. Make sure all plants are properly staked and supported to keep them from falling over and breaking. Label all your new plantings or note them in a garden journal. If you're finished sowing seeds for a while, clean up and sterilize your seed trays and store them for next fall or spring. Be sure to properly store your stash of leftover seeds in airtight containers in a cool, dry place like the refrigerator.

BULBS

Dead foliage can be removed from spring-blooming bulbs, and the bulbs can be dug up and moved or divided now.

EDIBLES

Continue thinning fruit on fruit trees as soon as they are the size of a dime. As you thin, keep an eye out for signs of pest damage or disease.

If you planted potatoes back in March, you should be able to harvest as early as this month. The growing time for potatoes runs anywhere from two to four months. You can begin to harvest early

■ *Harvest new potatoes carefully and you'll have more later in the season.*

potatoes ("new potatoes") when plants begin to bloom. By inserting your hand into the loose soil, you can harvest new potatoes without pulling up the whole plant, leaving it to develop more mature tubers for a later harvest. For mature potatoes, wait until the plants die down, then use a garden fork to carefully dig the potatoes from the ground. If you planted in towers, you can just push the soil and mulch aside to see if they're ready for harvest and pull them out.

Prune woody herbs like lavender, sage, rosemary, thyme, marjoram, and oregano now. Thin out branches to allow sunlight to penetrate to the center of the shrub; otherwise, they will develop new foliage at the branch ends but grow hollow in the middle. Don't trim branches all the way back to the trunk. Instead leave a few nodes of foliage on each branch so the plant will fill out. Be sure to save your trimmings for use in the kitchen or as fragrant kindling for your grill.

Install floating row covers over low-growing crops to prevent or minimize problems with pests or heat damage. Sheets of spun-bonded polypropylene or polyester allow air, water, and a certain percentage of sunlight to penetrate to plants below but block many insects and other pests. The fabric comes in various weights, and in addition to providing some heat protection, they can also be used in the winter for some frost protection. Lightweight fabrics allow up to 90 percent light transmission but also tear more easily so they have a shorter life span. Heavyweight fabrics provide the most frost protection but also block 50 to 70 percent of the light, so plants will grow more slowly and may get leggy from lack of light. Medium-weight fabrics are the most common choice for floating row covers, allowing up to 85 percent light penetration and frost protection down to 28 degrees Fahrenheit.

Choose a fabric width that will cover the full planting bed, with allowance for the full potential height of the plants, and enough extra fabric on each side to secure the cover to the ground. Insert hoops, which you purchase at garden supply centers or create out of 9-gauge wire or flexible PVC tubing, into the ground over the bed of plants and drape the fabric over the hoops to make a tunnel. Use bricks or other weights to hold the fabric in place all the way around the base of the tunnel and secure the fabric to the hoops with clamps.

■ *Floating row covers can minimize damage from pests or heat.*

Install row covers before you see any evidence of insect pests. Root crops like carrots and onions can grow the full season under row covers. Other crops do better when the row covers are removed to allow direct sun once the plants are well established and the threat of pest damage is less severe. Crops that require insect pollination, such as squash and tomatoes, will either have to be hand-pollinated or have the row covers removed as soon as the flowers appear.

While the row cover fabric can block enough light to prevent sun damage on really hot days, enough heat can build up inside a row-cover tunnel to cause wilt. On days of extreme heat, open the ends of the tunnel to allow hot air to escape.

As your crops begin to mature it's a good idea to save some seeds from the best plants to replant later in the season for a second harvest or next year. As the warmer weather causes lettuces and greens to bolt, you can leave some to set seed that you can collect and save. Farmers have been saving seeds since the earliest days of agriculture, but we've learned a thing or two along the way to make the process more efficient. There are good reasons for saving seeds, first of which is the money it saves. Instead of having to purchase new seed year after year for your favorite crops, often at $1.50 or more a pack, you can save the seed of the plants you know you were able to grow successfully. Even the best seed companies have occasional crop failures, and saving your own seeds will ensure that you'll have the seeds you want each year.

Another reason to save seeds is to be able to participate in seed exchanges. These seed swaps are becoming more and more common and you can find them through gardening groups, on the Internet, or maybe even your local library. My city library recently started a seed library where you can take out seeds contributed by other gardeners and deposit seeds that you have saved. As with seeds saved from your own garden, you can be fairly confident that seeds from a local seed exchange will grow well in your garden.

Check out Here's How to Save Seeds for instructions on collecting, cleaning, and storing seeds.

■ *Power aerating your lawn creates openings for air and nutrients to get deep into the root system. Fill the holes with a light compost by raking it in.*

HOUSEPLANTS

Plants that have been near south- or west-facing windows through the winter and early spring should now be moved to a north- or east-facing window, where they'll be less likely to get stressed from the more intense summer light.

For poinsettias that you are trying to rebloom, cut the stems back to 4 inches above the soil in mid-May and repot the plant in fresh potting mix. Water well and return it to the same light and temperature conditions it had when in flower.

LAWNS

If you did not aerate your lawn in February as part of the dethatching process, this is a good time to do it. Aerating will allow for better penetration of water to the grass roots so the lawn will hold up better in the hotter days ahead. You can rent an aerator to run across your lawn to pull out plugs of grass, roots, and soil. Rake up the soil plugs; you can shake out the loose soil and compost the rest of the plugs. Fill the holes left behind with a light compost to feed the soil and allow better drainage.

HERE'S HOW

TO SAVE SEEDS

Saving seeds is a great way to keep the success stories in your garden ongoing. With your own saved seeds, you'll know that you're planting not only your favorite crops, but also the ones that have performed well in your soil and climate and been spared the pesticide contamination that most commercial seeds have been subjected to. You'll know exactly what you're planting and what you can expect from it.

- To collect seeds, you have to be willing to sacrifice the fruit or seedpods on one or two plants. Select your healthiest and most vigorous plants to save seeds from; after all, you want to carry on the genetic characteristics of the best of the crop. After the fruit or seedpods have fully matured, open them up and collect the seeds. Wash the seeds well to make sure all of the flesh surrounding the seeds has been removed.

- One of my favorite ways to wash seeds is to put them in the bottom few inches of the foot of an old pair of pantyhose. Tie the leg of the pantyhose in a knot to hold the seeds in place at the toe, then hang them over the

edge of a toilet tank so that the seeds are immersed and the top end of the pantyhose is held in place by the lid of the toilet tank. Every time the toilet is flushed the water rushing over the seeds will clean them a bit more, carrying away the naturally occurring germination inhibitors that often surround seeds in the fruit.

- Many gardeners prefer to clean some seeds such as tomato seeds by fermenting them. This process basically follows the same fermenting process that occurs in nature when the fruit drops to the ground and rots. Scoop out the seeds from the fruit and place them in a jar or bowl with twice the amount of water as the volume of the seeds. Cover with a lid or plastic wrap and let them sit at room temperature. Shake or stir the contents of the container a couple times a day for several days. You'll see the good seeds sink to the bottom and bad seeds and other debris will float to the surface. A layer of mold will start to form on top of the water. When the mold covers the entire surface, add more water, stir, then let it rest. When the contents have

HERE'S HOW

TO USE A POWER CORE AERATOR

■ *Water the entire yard lightly a few hours before you aerate to ensure that the soil is moist, but don't overwater or you will bog down the machine in mud.*

■ *Flag all sprinkler heads, shallow sprinkler lines, and shallow buried cables, wires, and utility lines. Clear the lawn of other debris such as small tree branches.*

settled, pour off the top layer of water and debris. Add more water and repeat until only the good, clean seeds are left.

- However you clean the seeds, once they are completely clean spread them out in a single layer on paper towels on a cookie sheet or plate. Put the seeds somewhere out of direct light but with good air circulation and let them dry *completely*. When you think the seed is dry, spread them out on a fresh paper towel and dry them another day just to make sure. When they really are completely dry, package them for storage.

- Ultimately, seeds should be stored in an airtight container, but you can package the different varieties in envelopes, plastic containers, or zip-top bags, and then store those labeled packages together in an airtight container. (If you want to get fancy, you can do a Google search for "seed pack templates" and find all kinds of designs for seed envelopes to download and print from your computer.) Once the seeds are all packed, store the container in your refrigerator (not

the freezer!). Heat and sunlight can damage seeds, so the refrigerator provides the best, most consistent climate for seed storage.

- Assuming they are properly stored, you can expect corn, leeks, rhubarb, parsnip, and parsley seeds to last a couple of years. Asparagus, beans, Brussels sprouts, cabbage, carrots, cauliflower, celery, kale, lettuce, okra, peas, peppers, radish, spinach, turnip, and watermelon can last two to three years, and tomatoes, eggplant, and cucumber might last three to five years. (See February for information on testing the viability of seeds that have been stored.)

A word of warning about saving seeds: Many plants, such as apples, for example, do not grow true from seed. You can plant the seed and grow an apple tree from it, but the fruit you'll get from it will not be a genetic match to the fruit the seed came from and will most likely be inferior to that original fruit (the parent plant). If you want a dependable fruit tree, you need to buy a grafted variety from a nursery or learn to graft one yourself.

■ *Set the depth gauge on the coring machine to maximum. Run the machine across the lawn, back and forth in one direction. Then run it again, perpendicular to the original direction.*

■ *Allow the cores pulled up by the aerator to dry for a day, then gently rake across them to break them up so that they decompose more quickly.*

PERENNIALS

Cut back ornamental grasses now. If the plant has not yet sent out new leaves, you can cut most types to 4 inches high. If new growth has already started you can still cut them back by about one-third. You can use pruners or hedge shears to do this, but you don't have to be terribly gentle about this—even a weed-whacker will handle the job. Every five to seven years you should divide grass clumps. After digging up the clump, separate it into smaller clumps using a garden spade, ax, or sharp knife. Replant the newly divided sections immediately or the fine roots will dry out and die.

Evergreen "grasses" like yucca, cordyline, and flax are not technically grasses and should be pruned differently than ornamental grasses. For these plants, clean up the foliage by cutting out brown or damaged leaves at the base. If you need to reduce the size of the plant overall, you can trim out as much as two-thirds of the plant this way. If you need to cut it back even more severely, you can shear off all the foliage at the base, leaving either a

bare mound or trunk. If the trunk is tall, you can cut it by half (in colder areas where these plants are not always hardy, cut the trunk back no more than one-third). New foliage will resprout from the base or from just below the cut on the trunk fairly quickly and the plant will start to look normal again in about four months.

Some succulents are winter growers that then go more or less dormant from May to August. The list of summer-dormant succulents includes aeoniums, aloes, dudleyas, kalanchoes, sedums, and senecios. Some dormant succulents, such as aeoniums, may start to defoliate, leading you to think that they're dying. They're not; they'll start growing again in September.

ROSES

For an optimum rose display, be prepared to deadhead repeat-blooming roses throughout the entire bloom season. Prune one-time bloomers as soon as the bloom period is finished. Cutting back 'Lady Banks' roses hard after blooming may

■ *Cut back ornamental grasses to a few inches high.*

HERE'S HOW

TO DIVIDE AND REPOT CYMBIDIUM ORCHIDS

Cymbidium orchids are winter bloomers that may start blooming in December or January but the flower spikes may last into April when left on the plant. By sometime in May, they're usually finished blooming and you can now divide or repot ones that have outgrown their containers. Cymbidiums grow from pseudobulbs, which are bulb-like forms that grow above the ground. Each pseudobulb flowers just once, but even after they are past flowering they aid the plant by storing food. The productive pseudobulbs are at the front of the plant and the unproductive ones are at the back. When dividing the plant, it's best to keep four or five back bulbs with every three productive pseudobulbs.

■ *Orchid potting medium*

1. Make sure the plant is well watered before dividing and repotting.

2. Remove the plant from the old container; you may need to use a knife or can-cutter to do this.

3. Remove all old potting medium, especially at the center of the rootball.

4. Trim away any roots that are not healthy. Healthy roots should be fat and white; roots that are brown, shriveled, or mushy must be removed.

5. If you are dividing the plant, use a sharp, sterile knife to cut cleanly between the pseudobulbs and down through the roots.

6. Repot each division in a clean plastic pot with enough holes to allow for excellent drainage.

   Cymbidiums like to be a bit crowded in their pots so choose containers that are no more than 1 or 2 inches bigger in diameter than the rootball. Sit each division in the new container with the bottom of the pseudobulbs level with the top of the pot. Add fresh potting medium (small-chipped redwood bark is best) to the pot to fill in around the roots and securely hold the plant in the pot, but leave the pseudobulbs above the soil level.

7. Water well and allow the water to drain away.

8. Place the newly divided cymbidiums in a protected area with semishade and wait until the following month to resume fertilizing.

If you repot in May and begin fertilizing again in June, new divisions will usually bloom the following winter.

stimulate a second, lighter bloom period, but it's necessary mainly to keep the plant manageable and produce new wood for next year's blooms.

Keep suckers on all roses pruned back as well, cutting them all the way back to the trunk or to the roots, if they're growing from below the soil. Letting them grow will only sap energy from the plant and the suckers will never produce quality blooms.

TREES

Prune conifers other than pines now. The conifers that can be pruned now are those of indeterminate growth with random branching (as opposed to the whorled branching of pines); these include cypress, redwood, dawn redwood, bald cypress, yew, juniper, and hemlock. These trees should not be shaped in a way that interferes with their natural growth habit. Never *top* a conifer (pruning large upright branches between nodes) because it stunts the tree in a way that can never be corrected. You should also be careful not to remove too many lower branches at once; if you do, you'll end up with a big conifer lollipop. Instead, remove just a few low branches each year as the tree is growing.

WATER

ALL

Rainfall in May can be erratic, so you'll need to ensure that plants get a consistent amount of water, generally about an inch each week. It helps to give your irrigation system a check-up to make sure it's running correctly and meeting your plants' water needs. Follow these steps:

1. Begin by turning the system on and walking around your yard. Make note of any place where a sprinkler head or drip emitter isn't functioning correctly. Look for plants that appear to be suffering from over- or underwatering and note their locations to make adjustments.

2. Check the system's timer. If it's set to run for 10-minute intervals, time it to see that it's actually running for that amount of time.

3. Measure the water flow in inches. Put a small container such as a tuna can near a sprinkler head or directly under a drip emitter and measure the amount of water it collects in the set time. You may need to adjust the number of minutes the water is on or the frequency at which it runs in order to get just the right amount of water to your plants.

4. If any sprinkler heads or drip emitters have broken, it's generally easy to remove them and attach replacements. Sometimes they just get clogged by mineral deposits and can be flushed clean with a blast from the hose. Some systems have disposable filters that need to be replaced.

■ *A sprinkler system is a good way to keep your lawn and gardens consistently watered.*

5. Clear the area surrounding the sprinkler heads so they aren't choked by weeds or other plant growth. Make sure the heads are accurately aimed or that drip emitters are not in direct contact with the trunks of any shrubs or trees, which can lead to crown rot.

6. Make sure the controller (clock) accurately reflects the current time and day, then reprogram the system for the watering frequency and duration required for the season.

7. Test the system by turning it on again and rechecking the trouble spots to make sure the problems have been fixed.

BULBS

Summer-blooming bulbs such as lilies and gladioli need regular water now until the bulbs begin their dormancy with the first frost. Water them less often but more deeply than you would water your lawn to establish a healthy root system.

PERENNIALS

Water dormant succulents such as aeoniums, aloes, dudleyas, kalanchoes, sedums, and senecios more lightly than summer-growing varieties, particularly if they are in beds or containers with less-than-ideal drainage.

TREES

Withhold supplemental water from oak and other native trees that are well adapted to our dry summers. Be particularly careful of oak trees that are surrounded by lawn or other thirsty plantings; watering under the tree canopy now (and through the summer) could be detrimental to the health of the tree.

FERTILIZE

BULBS

Start feeding summer-blooming bulbs such as lilies and gladioli as soon as they start to sprout. Some bulbs may have more specialized needs, but in general, a once-a-month application of a balanced fertilizer (such as a 10-10-10 or 8-8-8 fertilizer) at a rate of 3 to 4 pounds per 100 square feet will do well.

EDIBLES

Continue adding a monthly sidedressing of compost to warm-season crops. Blueberries will benefit from a fertilizer for acid-loving plants. Blackberries and raspberries, on the other hand, should not be fed anything other than compost; too much nitrogen will only produce more green growth, not more berries. Grape vines need a balanced fertilizer. Artichokes will benefit from feeding now before the buds are ready for harvest.

HOUSEPLANTS

Resume regular fertilizing for most houseplants. A liquid or water-soluble balanced fertilizer will do well for most indoor plants, but for African violets and other blooming houseplants, it's best to use a fertilizer specially formulated for flowering plants, which will have a higher ratio of phosphorus to stimulate bloom.

Fertilize potted poinsettias every couple of weeks with a complete liquid fertilizer.

SHRUBS

Feed azaleas, camellias, and rhododendrons with a fertilizer formulated for acid-loving plants right after they finish blooming.

PROBLEM-SOLVE

ALL

A common problem in many gardens is the fungal disease known as powdery mildew. There are actually many species of powdery mildew, each affecting a different type of plant, but they all have the common appearance of a white or gray powder occurring on foliage, stems, and fruit. And while the powdery mildew that attacks your strawberries may not be the same as the powdery mildew that affects your squash plants, the infections are spread the same way and in the same conditions. The fungal spores are airborne, often carried on wind, but can also be passed by humans or pets carrying the spores. The spores will lie dormant in plant debris through the winter until the environmental conditions are just right for it to attack. The ideal conditions for it are moderate to high humidity, low light, a slightly acidic surface, and temperatures of more

To prevent or limit the spread of powdery mildew, it is best to water early in the day at the soil level. Space plants and keep them pruned to allow for good air circulation. Practice good garden sanitation and keep plant debris cleared from the ground. When plants are infected, quarantine them if possible. If only a few leaves or branches are affected, try removing them without spreading the fungal spores by tying a plastic bag over the foliage and then cutting off the branch. Dispose of infected foliage in the trash, not in a compost bin. Controls like Neem or horticultural oil can be sprayed on plants in the early stages of infection as well.

If you live anywhere other than a decidedly urban setting, you may find your biggest garden pests at this time are hungry deer. As people have set up homes or entire housing developments in areas that used to be wild, deer have taken to garden foraging with what can only be described as enthusiasm and perseverance. Although I've never lived and gardened in an area where deer were a problem, I've listened sympathetically to other gardeners who have related long lists of the plants they've lost to invading deer. Aside from the plants that are eaten completely, deer will leave behind damage to trees and other shrubs up to about 6 feet high from their chewing and tearing at foliage and bark, trampled low-growing plants, and piles of droppings.

Deer can be a problem at almost any time of year, but your garden may be even more tempting to them when there is as much tender new growth as there is now. While there are many commercial products and home remedies that purport to repel deer, the only deterrent I've heard of that reliably keeps deer away is a sturdy fence that is 6 to 8 feet tall. Deer are amazingly adaptive so that motion-detector devices designed to scare them away work for only a short time before the deer catch on, and scent-based repellents are effective temporarily if at all. Fencing that is tall enough to block a deer's high jump can be a significant investment, especially for a large garden. But when you consider the cost of all the plants that you're likely to lose to deer over a period of years, it's probably an investment worth making.

■ *Powdery mildew is primarily a cosmetic problem in home gardens. It is rarely severe enough to kill a plant.*

than 60 but less than 85 degrees Fahrenheit—conditions which are most common in spring and fall.

With the ideal conditions present, powdery mildew will strike new growth first, then spread to the rest of the plant. In home gardens, powdery mildew is primarily a cosmetic problem; it is rarely fatal to the plant but it is unattractive. It is more likely to attack stressed plants, such as those suffering from drought or annual plants that are reaching the end of their life cycles.

A deer fence must be at least 6 feet tall.

EDIBLES

As tomato plants grow you'll need to keep a sharp eye out for the number-one most-hated pest of tomato growers: the tomato hornworm. Up to 4½ inches long and ½ to ¾ inches in diameter, these bright green larvae with white chevron-shaped markings down their sides and a black horn at the end of their body will develop into gray or brown hornworm moths. While the moths themselves are harmless, feeding only on nectar, the larvae are ravenous feeders on leaves, stems, and fruit of any plant in the nightshade (Solanaceae) family, including eggplant, pepper, potato, tobacco, tomato, or tomatillo. One or two hornworms can defoliate a plant in a matter of days.

To control tomato hornworms, check your tomato plants (and other nightshade plants) daily for signs the hornworms are present—either the hornworms themselves, the dark green pellets of excrement they leave behind, or the disappearing foliage they've consumed. The easiest strategy is to handpick the hornworms and destroy them. If you have many plants that they would feed on, a more effective approach would be to release parasitic wasps. These tiny wasps lay eggs that look like white grains of rice on the bodies of the hornworms. When the larvae hatch out of the eggs, they feed on the hornworms until they die. It is also helpful to till the soil where nightshade plants have grown following the final harvest. This will

Parasitic wasps attack a hornworm.

help to kill or expose to predators any hornworm pupae that would overwinter in the soil and hatch the following spring. Rotating crops (not just individual crops but plant families) from year to year also helps to break the cycle. (See September for more information on rotating crops.)

ROSES

One of the problems that most often plagues rose-growers is the fungal disease blackspot (*Diplocarpon rosae*). It thrives in warm weather (75 to 85 degrees Fahrenheit) when conditions are wet and causes black splotches to appear on leaves and canes. Affected leaves will turn yellow and drop, allowing the fungal spores to lurk in the soil, where they can be splashed back on other foliage by rain or watering, continuing the disease cycle.

There is no real cure for blackspot so the best course is to try to prevent it or to break the disease cycle once it occurs. The best way to prevent it is to plant roses that are resistant to the blackspot fungus. Hundreds of hybrids have been developed with this resistance and there

SUDDEN OAK DEATH

There is a killing disease sweeping through the forests as well as the urban areas of California that gardeners should be aware of: Sudden Oak Death (SOD). Caused by the fungus-like pathogen *Phytophthora ramorum*, SOD has been responsible for the deaths of millions of tanoak and oak trees in the state since the mid-1990s. It has been most prevalent in the wet, cool climates of the coastal counties from Monterey to Humboldt (and up into southwest Oregon).

In addition to oak and tanoak trees, many common garden plants are susceptible to the SOD pathogen (although not necessarily to the extent of being fatal), including camellia, lilac, rhododendron, and viburnum. California bay laurel trees are not killed by the infection, but they seem to harbor the pathogen and are thought to have played a significant role in the spread of the disease.

There are two main symptoms of the disease. In oak and tanoak trees, cankers appear on the trunk. In other plants the most likely symptoms are leaf spots and dying shoots. The cankers are the more serious issue because they can significantly weaken a tree, making it susceptible to boring insects that can finish it off. Oaks and tanoaks that have been infected can become a serious hazard in urban and suburban settings where falling branches could result in injury to passersby or damage to property.

If you think you might have an infected tree or shrub in your garden, go to www.suddenoakdeath.org to see if your plant is on the list of host plants, compare your plant to the photos of symptoms, and see if you are in an infested area. If you still think SOD is likely, contact your local county agricultural commissioner to determine how to have a tissue sample taken, which is necessary to confirm the diagnosis. An infected plant may not necessarily have to be removed, but if a large tree is infected and must be removed, be aware that the structural integrity of the tree may be compromised by the infection and it may be advisable to hire a professional tree removal service to do the job safely. (Note: You should never remove a tree without checking local ordinances first. Trees may be protected based on species, trunk diameter, height, or other issues.)

There is only one preventative treatment recommended for susceptible trees and that is a phosphonate fungicide called Agri-Fos. It cannot cure a tree once it has been infected, but it can help uninfected trees resist infection and suppress the progress of the disease in very early cases of infection. It can be injected into a healthy tree or sprayed onto the trunk, followed by booster treatments every one to two years. Since California bay laurel is known to be a major player in the spread of SOD, you may want to treat healthy trees in close proximity to California bay laurel when there are known infections within 150 to 1000 feet.

Prune bushes in an open-vase form and trim as needed throughout the growing season to keep good air circulation through the foliage.

If blackspot has occurred in the past on a bush, you can treat it by spraying weekly with Neem oil; however, do not apply Neem when the temperature is more than 80 degrees Fahrenheit or within two weeks of using any product containing sulfur.

WATER GARDENS

Warmer spring weather will often bring about an algae bloom in water gardens and fountains, turning the water the color of pea soup and creating an unhealthy environment for fish and plants. To control algae, skim the surface with a stick, rake, or brush to remove filamentous algae. For algae that clings to rocks and other surfaces, let the algae dry and then brush it off. On surfaces that can't be dried, spray the algae with hydrogen peroxide, which will kill the algae without affecting plants and fish. The algae will turn white and then can be scraped off. It is essential that all dead algae be removed from in or around the pond because its decomposition will release gases that can be harmful to fish and plants.

To keep algae growth in check, add algae-eating pond snails or floating plants that help keep algae in check, or install a biological filter or UV filter.

■ *Blackspot is best prevented by choosing disease-resistant varieties and practicing good garden sanitation.*

is always the old favorite, *Rosa rugosa*, which is naturally resistant.

Sanitation is key to blackspot prevention. Keep fallen leaves and other debris picked up from the ground surrounding the bush as well.

Keep the foliage dry by using drip irrigation or soaker hoses. If you must use overhead watering, water early in the morning so that the leaves have time to dry in the sun. Avoid handling the foliage when it is wet.

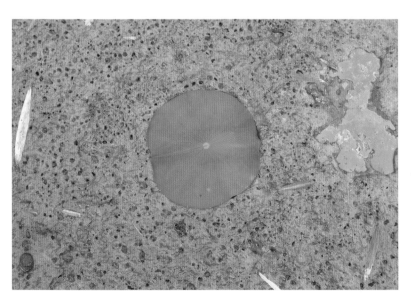

■ *Pond snails or floating plants will help keep pond algae from getting out of control.*

June

Summertime and the living is easy. *Or so the song goes. But do you ever take it easy in your garden? Certainly, there are tasks to be tackled this month—plants to be pruned, watered, fed; flowers to be cut; fruits to be harvested. But more than a to-do list, a garden is a place "to be." When you allow yourself a chance to rest and refuel in your garden, those tasks seem less like a chore and more like a rite, a way to bless this piece of land and everything in it.*

Sometimes we get so carried away with planting and pruning and feeding and watering that we forget to take the time to enjoy our gardens. To sit and reflect on the beauty instead of just considering what needs to be done. To invite our friends into it, so they too can enjoy our personal slice of nature. To marvel at the complexity that exists within any garden, no matter how small or simple. To just rest in its peace and quiet.

This month, as the bustle and activity of spring shifts into a more low-key period of maintenance, take some time to just sit. Find a comfortable new chair or dust off an old bench and place it where you'll have a good view of the garden, then plant yourself there for a little while. Give yourself a chance to admire the garden as it is and remember what it looked like when you started gardening. Take some time to dream about the plants you'd like to add and the changes you'd like to make, but mostly just appreciate it for what it is right now.

Then have some friends and family over. It doesn't have to be a big soiree, *a la* Martha Stewart. Just invite them in and enjoy them enjoying the garden. Without these moments to just be in the garden, without our tools, without getting our hands dirty, "garden" is only a verb, never a noun.

What could be easier?

PLAN

ALL

As summer vacation begins, make sure that your garden is child-ready. That means not only that the garden is free of clutter and safe for children to play in, but also ready for children to garden in. Plan fun activities for the children to participate in that center around the garden itself, or give them a patch of the garden to plant and be solely responsible for. Many California schools have made school gardens part of the regular curriculum, allowing children to learn about planting and routine care of plants. You may be surprised at how much they already know about gardening—and how much you can learn from them.

If there is one time this month when you really might want to make sure your garden is well watered, it's right before the Fourth of July, especially if you or your neighbors will be setting off any fireworks. Clear out any dry brush or dead woody material that could catch fire from an errant spark. Be especially careful around plants that are known to contain highly combustible oils, like eucalyptus. (See October for more information on making your garden fire-safe.)

ANNUALS & PERENNIALS

If you expect to host a Fourth of July gathering or just want to dress your garden in patriotic colors for the holiday, shop now for six-packs of annuals and perennials in red, white, and blue. Quick-growing choices include petunias, lobelia, verbena, pansies, and bachelor's buttons. Pot them up now and they should be full and heavy with blooms by the Fourth.

Impatiens have long been a popular choice for these types of displays because they fill in quickly, provide a lot of color, and work well in shade or partial shade. However, many parts of the country have been experiencing problems with downy mildew attacking the tender perennial *Impatiens walleriana*. Downy mildew is a fungal disease that spreads by spores carried on water splash. Once in your garden, downy mildew can establish itself in the soil and carry over season after season, attacking new plants. To avoid the problem, select other shade-loving plants such as New Guinea impatiens, begonias, coleus, or caladium.

BULBS

Place orders for autumn-flowering bulbs like autumn-flowering crocus (*Crocus speciosus*) and spider lilies (*Lycoris*). Other options to look for include nerines and sternbergia. When planted in July, they'll deliver some beautiful blooms through the fall.

EDIBLES

Be prepared for the harvests to come, especially the ones that will come fast and heavy, like strawberries, stone fruits, and tomatoes. If you plan to can some of your fruits or vegetables, make sure you have enough jars, lids, and rings on hand as well as all the other supplies necessary, including recipes and canning instructions. If you are freezing foods, stock up on freezer bags and containers. Investing in a food dehydrator gives you another way to preserve the harvest, although some foods can be dried in the oven or sun-dried. The National Center for Home Food Preservation (http://nchfp.uga.edu/) has a lot of information and publications on safe food-preservation methods. Ball's Fresh

■ *Canning is a good way to preserve your harvest for the winter months.*

Preserving website (www.freshpreserving.com) is a good source of information for canning recipes and other information.

If you plan to share your bounty with friends and family, let them know in advance that you expect to have produce for them so they can plan too. And if you have more than you and yours can handle, remember that there are always those in need. Go to the Ample Harvest website (www.ampleharvest.org) to find out what food pantries in your community will happily accept your excess fruits and vegetables.

PLANT

ALL

As we enter what is typically the dry season in California, it's best to get any planting out of the way early in the month. Even drought-tolerant plants generally require regular watering until they are well established. For annuals that may mean the first few months; for perennials, it's more like a full year. Newly planted trees often require more than a year to establish themselves. Anything planted in the summer will need special attention throughout the dry season—and even with that, they may struggle to survive. Coastal areas that experience "June gloom" have a little bit more of a grace period for planting, but don't push your luck. Get new plants in the ground ASAP.

ANNUALS

What would summer be without sunflowers? Although you could have started sunflower seeds indoors anytime from midspring until now, this is the best time for direct planting outside. The warmer soil temperatures speed up germination, and the longer days provide the sunlight needed to produce tall stems and big flowers.

To sow sunflower seeds, prepare a planting space that is free of weeds with loose soil with at least six hours of sun daily. Insert the seeds about ½ inch deep and 4 to 5 inches apart. Press down firmly to make sure the seeds have good contact with the soil and water well. It's a good idea to cover the newly planted seeds with upside-down plastic berry baskets in order to keep them from being raided

■ *Sunflower varieties are available in a wide range of sizes and colors.*

by the birds. Keep the area evenly moist. Most varieties will germinate in eight to fourteen days. To get a longer bloom period, sow seeds every 10 days or so throughout the month. When seedlings are about 3 inches high, thin to 12 inches apart for the smaller varieties, 18 inches apart for the larger plants. Plants will flower in summer and into the fall.

There are so many varieties of sunflowers now, you can choose tall flowers with large, single flower heads, branching varieties with somewhat smaller blooms, and dwarf varieties that grow only a couple of feet high and are suitable for container growing. Colors range from the traditional deep golden yellow to orange, pink, cream, and even chocolate-burgundy. If you are growing sunflowers in order to harvest the seeds for snacking, be sure to select a variety for that—some options include 'Sunseed', 'Snack Seed', and 'Sunzilla'.

EDIBLES

You can still plant warm-season veggies this month, and you may be ready for second plantings of some crops, such as beans, beets, carrots, chard, and scallions.

Corn is one edible that many people would like to grow but it really needs two things. It needs space (at least a 4-by-4-foot bed) because it is pollinated by the wind and therefore *must* be planted in blocks for the wind to be able to do its thing. And it needs heat for the kernels to develop properly. If you live in a cool-summer area, you may still be able to grow an early hybrid variety, but the space issue is non-negotiable. Plant a single row of corn and you'll likely end up with a single row of cornstalks—and that's all.

Sweet corn—those beautiful ears of yellow or white corn you see in the supermarket—are the most popular choice to grow, but even in that category there are standard, sugar-enhanced, and supersweet varieties. These last two types are sweeter when picked and also maintain their sweetness longer after picking. Besides sweet corn, there is baby corn, popcorn, and ornamental corn, which may or may not be good for eating.

You can begin sowing seeds as early as two weeks after the average last frost date through June. To stretch out the harvest, sow seeds three or four times at two-week intervals. Another way to prolong the harvest is to plant early, midseason, and late varieties at the same time.

Corn can be grown throughout California. Plant in rich, well-drained soil in full sun. Before planting, work compost into the soil. Because it is pollinated by the wind, corn should be planted in blocks of four rows or more. This best allows for the breeze to carry the pollen from the silks of one ear to the silks of another. Space the rows 3 feet apart and sow a couple of seeds 1 inch deep and 1 foot apart. Corn seeds should germinate in seven to ten days. If some of the seeds don't germinate, replace with new seeds and the seedlings should catch up quickly. When the seedlings come up, thin to the best plant every foot. Another plan is to plant in hills 3 feet apart on all sides. Sow six to seven seeds in each hill and thin to the three strongest

■ *Large seeds such as corn, beans, and peas are easy to space out in rows.*

■ *Plants with tiny seeds, like carrots and lettuces, are often easier to sow scattered in wide rows. You can get a lot more food per square foot in wide rows.*

■ *Warm-season crops such as melons and squashes are often sown three to five seeds at a time in hills. The hill has better air exposure so the soil warms sooner.*

HERE'S HOW

TO PLANT A "THREE SISTERS" GARDEN

If you have enough space, you may want to try a planting scheme called "The Three Sisters." This is a companion planting technique used by Native Americans that groups corn, pole beans, and squash together, and not only does it speak to heritage planting, but it's a good example of dense planting. The corn provides the pole for the beans to grow on, the beans fix nitrogen into the soil, and the squash acts as a mulch to shade out weeds. Begin by creating soil mounds 18 inches across and 5 feet apart from each other. Plant four corn seeds in a 6-inch square in the center of each mound. When the corn seedlings reach 4 inches in height, plant four beans, each 3 inches from each corn plant. At the same time, create mounds in the rows between the corn mounds and plant three squash seeds 4 inches apart from each other in each of the new mounds. When the squash seedlings come up, thin to two plants per mound. Keep the area weeded until the squash plants fill out enough to keep the weeds down.

seedlings in each. For baby corn, plant 1 inch deep, 1–2 inches apart and thin to 4 inches apart.

Unless the seed packet says differently, do not plant popcorn and sweet corn or supersweet and standard sweet corn near each other; cross-pollination between these types can have negative effects on the corn.

PERENNIALS

While the general rule of thumb is that fall is the best time for planting permanent landscape plants, palms are a definite exception to the rule. Although frequently thought of as trees or shrubs, palms are really grasses—and tropical grasses at that. As tropical plants that are sensitive to frosts, planting in fall leaves palms vulnerable to the winter chills before they've had a chance to really get established. Better to plant palms in late spring or early summer so they have a few more months of warm weather to help them settle in.

Before planting a palm, it may be beneficial to tie up the fronds to prevent breakage during planting. Then prepare a hole the same depth as the rootball and a little wider. There is no need to amend the soil unless your soil has poor drainage. In that case you might add horticultural sand to the backfill soil. Keeping the palm well watered through the summer and fall until the rainy season begins is essential. Because palms are relatively shallow-rooted, regular watering matters more than deep watering, so water at least once a week and more often in very hot weather or when the palm looks stressed.

Some large palms to consider are the native California fan palm (*Washingtonia filifera*), which grows to 60 feet and is hardy to 18 degrees Fahrenheit; the Canary Island date palm (*Phoenix canariensis*), which grows to 45 feet and is hardy to 20 degrees; and the queen palm (*Syagrus romanzoffiana*), which grows to 50 feet and is hardy to 25 degrees.

Smaller palms include the triangle palm (*Dypsis decaryi*), growing to 20 feet tall and very drought-tolerant; the umbrella palm (*Hedyscepe canterburyana*), growing to 30 feet and hardy to 28 degrees Fahrenheit; and the MacArthur palm (*Ptychosperma macarthuri*), a multi-trunked palm growing 10 to 25 feet tall and suitable for container growing.

■ *Look for disease-resistant rose varieties, such as the beautiful 'Julia Child'.*

ROSES

You can continue to plant container-grown roses. Check the plant carefully for signs of disease before buying and check on the cultivar's disease resistance. Some terrific options for disease-resistant roses include climbers 'Altissimo' and 'Fourth of July'; floribundas 'Betty Boop', 'Julia Child', and 'Hot Cocoa'; and grandifloras 'Sunshine Daydream' and 'About Face'.

Knock Out landscape roses have become popular partly for their disease resistance, but it now appears they are vulnerable to one rose disease—rose rosette disease, a particularly devastating virus that is spread by mites. Knock Out roses are not any more susceptible to this disease than other roses, but because they are often planted *en masse*, the disease can spread more easily and quickly

HERE'S HOW

TO PLANT A CONTAINER-GROWN ROSE OR SHRUB

Dig a planting hole twice as wide as the rootball, but no deeper. The plant should sit at the same place it was growing in the container or maybe an inch or so above the surrounding soil to allow for settling. Place the container on its side and roll it on the ground while tapping it to loosen the roots. Upend the container and gently pull it off of the plant roots. Do not pull the plant by the stem.

Use your fingers to loosen any roots that may be matted, gently untangling them. Roots that are tightly coiled should be cut apart and loosened. Gently spread the roots wide so they are pointing outward as much as possible. Set the shrub into the hole. Backfill the hole with the original soil. Mound the soil to create a ridge around the plant to hold water. Water well and cover the soil with organic mulch, keeping it a few inches from the shrub.

among them. Aside from rose rosette disease, Knock Out roses are still among the most disease-resistant roses available.

CARE

ALL

Apply a 3- to 4-inch layer of mulch throughout the garden to keep moisture in the soil instead of evaporating into the air and to discourage weeds. Not all mulches are created the same, however. For some guidance in selecting the best mulch material for your garden, refer to Here's How to Choose a Mulch.

ANNUALS

Continue to deadhead annual flowers to encourage more blooms. If plants are getting leggy, pinch them back hard. With adequate water and fertilizer, they'll fill out with lots of new growth and blossoms.

BULBS

Prevent droopy and damaged blooms on summer bulbs, particularly those that have large flowers on weak stems, such as oriental lilies. Stake the plants before the buds open, but take care to avoid hitting the bulb when driving the stake into the ground.

EDIBLES

Pull weeds when they're young before they can set seed or send out runners. Regular weeding will allow your vegetable plants to grow without having to compete for every drop of water. Weeds can also quickly overwhelm low-growing vegetables and block out much-needed sunshine.

Lightly prune tomato plants to prevent branches from breaking under excessive weight, encourage the plant's energy to go into fruit production rather than green growth, and improve air circulation around the plant, which can help avoid disease. Pruning also gives you an opportunity to check closely for pest damage. Determinate tomato plants require less pruning than indeterminate plants but can still benefit from some trimming of long branches. You should also remove suckers, the smaller branches that sprout from the crotch between a larger branch and the main stem. For larger tomato types, such as beefsteaks, thinning the fruit will result in bigger tomatoes.

While you have the pruners out, clip off any runners that your strawberry plants have put out. Letting them run will give you a fuller groundcover of strawberry plants, but removing the runners will give you more strawberries. For June-bearing varieties, you can let runners grow after the harvest,

■ *Remove the entire root system or rhizome of a weed, but be careful not to uproot neighboring plants. Use a weeding tool to get leverage, if needed.*

HERE'S HOW

TO CHOOSE A MULCH

Visit any garden center or nursery and you'll quickly discover that there are numerous options when it comes to choosing a mulch. Before making your selection, consider what you want a mulch to do. A good mulch should do all of the following:

- Minimize evaporation in the soil
- Suppress weeds
- Moderate soil temperatures
- Reduce soil erosion
- Improve a garden's appearance
- Be readily available at a reasonable cost

In addition, organic mulches will improve the soil structure and add nutrients to the soil as they decompose. The most common choices for mulch all have pros and cons. Consider these options for your garden:

- **Bark or wood chips:** Among the most commonly used mulches, bark and wood chips are easily available in bags from garden centers but can also be obtained (sometimes for free) from tree services that are happy to unload truckfuls of chips of trees they've pruned or cut down rather than pay to dump them. Wood chips can be slow to deteriorate, but they can bind up nitrogen in the soil as they do, which robs nearby plants of needed nutrition. Bark chips can also be toxic to plants if they are too fresh.

■ *Pine straw mulch*

- **Straw:** Straw mulch can be hard to find in urban and suburban areas but is readily available in rural areas. Rice straw adds nutrients to the soil and doesn't have seeds, but it deteriorates quickly. Wheat or oat straw lasts longer but you have to deal with the seeds first by soaking the straw before spreading it out and allowing the seeds to sprout and die. Straw is not expensive and is good at holding moisture in the soil but allowing air to pass through.

- **Alfalfa hay or pellets:** This is a more expensive option but a good source of nitrogen for the soil. It is seedless and long-lasting compared to rice straw. Since it is pelletized and bagged, it is easier to transport than bales of straw.

- **Shredded redwood "hair":** Shredded redwood can make a very attractive mulch, but it's lightweight and can blow around. Also, weed seeds and other debris can get caught in the finely shredded fibers, making it messy.

- **Cocoa bean hulls:** This mulch gained a lot of popularity primarily for its fragrance. It smells like chocolate. The downside is the fragrance doesn't last long, it's expensive, and it's lightweight enough to blow away. It can also be toxic for dogs if they should eat it.

- **Grape seed mulch or compost:** This is California, after all, and all that winery waste has to go somewhere. Grape seed

■ *Bark mulch*

compost makes a really dark (almost black) mulch that is long lasting and will feed the soil as it decomposes. It's not as readily available as other mulches but nurseries and soil suppliers may be able to hook you up. Depending on the source, you may need to screen or filter it before spreading it out to remove bits of vine and other debris.

- **Yard waste (grass clippings or leaves):** Using your own yard waste as a mulch is one cost-saving option. Grass clippings and dead leaves make an effective, if not the prettiest, mulch and will feed the soil as they decompose. It's recommended that you run the waste though a chipper first.

- **Gravel:** Used as mulch, gravel's greatest benefit is that it doesn't decompose, so as long as you lay down landscape fabric first, it stays on top of the soil. It's heavy enough not to blow away, but it does tend to migrate and you'll find pieces of gravel popping up all over the place, including in the lawn where it can be caught by the lawn mower and thrown, potentially causing injury. Realistically, gravel only works as mulch in areas where you won't be doing any future digging, so that limits its use to walkways, driveways, and permanently planted shrub beds.

- **Sawdust:** Sawdust can be effective at lowering the pH level of soil as it

decomposes so it is sometimes used as a mulch for acid-loving plants. It's not very long-lasting as a mulch, however, and it's also important that the sawdust not include particles from chemically treated woods if you are going to use it around edible plants.

- **Pine needles:** If you have a good source for pine needles, you have a gardener's goldmine. Pine needles make a terrific, acidifying mulch. They're long-lasting and don't compact too much.

- **Landscape fabric:** Frequently used underneath other mulch materials, landscape fabric is purported to suppress weeds while allowing water to penetrate through to the soil. The fact is, however, that it does a poor job of both. Weed seeds can get caught in the weave of the fabric and germinate and most fabrics allow little if any water to permeate. Some professional grade landscape fabrics may do a better job than the fabrics commonly sold in garden centers, but before you lay landscape fabric in your garden, it's a good idea to test it to see if it is water-permeable.

- **Black plastic:** Although it's effective at suppressing weeds, black plastic is a poor choice of soil cover in home gardens. It prevents water and sunlight from penetrating to the soil below, which can create unhealthy soil conditions.

- **Cardboard:** If you are looking for a weed-suppressing material to put down underneath a layer of mulch, cardboard is your best bet. It is effective at blocking sunlight from weeds and weed seeds below, but it allows water to get through. It is recommended as an effective way to kill a lawn that you want to reseed or replace with other landscaping. You can use cut-up pieces of cardboard boxes (overlapping them for complete coverage) or you can purchase large rolls of cardboard that you can lay out in longer pieces and cover with wood chips or bark.

■ *Gravel mulch*

but for other varieties, only let runners grow if you want more plants more than you want fruit.

Keep picking fruit as it ripens. Leaving it on the plant long enough to rot can encourage disease spread and raiding rodents. If birds, squirrels, or other wildlife are beating you to the harvest,

use bird netting or floating row covers to protect your bounty.

Be ruthless about removing unproductive plants, which are a waste of valuable garden space and water. As each plant comes to the end of its production cycle and the yield tapers off, replace it

HERE'S HOW

TO HARVEST HERBS FOR DRYING

While it's great to use herbs freshly picked from your garden, you may want to dry some so that you'll have them ready for use well into the winter. For peak flavor and the best results in the drying process, harvest herbs in mid-morning after the sun has dried the dew on the leaves. Picking later in the day allows some of the plant's essential oils to dry in the sun, and with the oil goes the flavor. If you are harvesting the leaves,

■ *You can just tie and hang herbs to dry for future use.*

the flavor will be most intense before the plant starts to flower. If you are harvesting the flowers, try to pick them as soon as possible after they've fully opened. If you are harvesting the seeds, gather the seedpods when they've started to turn brown and crisp but before they're ready to burst open. As long as the herbs have been grown organically, it's not usually necessary to wash them before drying; just remove any dead leaves or debris and make sure no insects have been harvested along with the herbs.

There are several methods available for drying herbs, including solar drying, using a dehydrator, oven drying, and microwave drying, but the simplest method is also the most foolproof—air drying. To dry herb leaves like basil, thyme, and oregano, tie small branches and sprigs into little bundles using string or twist-ties. Place the bundles in muslin bags or paper bags with air holes cut in them, and tie the opening of the bag closed. Hang the bag somewhere cool, dark, and dry, checking on them periodically to determine when they've dried completely. For flowers and seeds, air drying is best done on a screen-covered frame. Spread a layer of cheesecloth over the screen, then lay out the flowers or seeds and top with another layer of cheesecloth.

Different herbs will dry at different rates and the temperature and humidity will also affect drying times. Keep checking every few days; most herbs will dry completely in less than fourteen days. When drying is complete, store the herbs in airtight containers. They should retain their flavor for six months to a year.

with a second planting or a new and different crop. By doing so, you can extend your garden's harvest well into autumn or beyond.

LAWNS

Taller lawns tolerate hot, dry days better than shorter lawns, so adjust the settings on your mower to one of the higher settings. Some types of grasses should be trimmed shorter than others; check this table for the ideal summer setting for your type of lawn:

3 inches	Bahiagrass
	Fescue
	Blue grama
	Buffalograss
2½ inches	St. Augustinegrass
	Kentucky bluegrass
2 inches	Ryegrass
	Centipedegrass
	Zoysiagrass
1½ inches	Bermudagrass
1 inch	Bentgrass

PERENNIALS

Lightly prune and shape perennials, especially the aggressive growers that can take over the entire bed such as bugleweed (*Ajuga reptans*), mint (*Mentha* spp.), bee balm (*Monarda didyma*), lamb's ear (*Stachys byzantina*), Japanese anemone (*Anemone × hybrid*), and horsetail reed (*Equisetum hyemale*). Thin out a few interior branches to keep air circulating through the plant and shorten the long, gangly branches that ruin the form. Deadhead flowering perennials to extend the bloom period.

ROSES

Continue to deadhead roses to keep repeat bloomers blooming. Even landscape roses that are not supposed to need deadheading, such as Knock Out roses, benefit from occasional deadheading, which will stimulate not only repeat flowering but overall plant growth. If you'd like to have larger roses, you can also practice "disbudding," a practice of reducing the number of buds so that the remaining buds will get more food and light. For hybrid tea roses, remove the smaller side buds so the central bud on the stem will be larger. For floribunda roses, remove the bud in the middle of a cluster, which will cause the rest of the cluster to open at the same time for a more striking display.

Prune climbing roses that are one-time bloomers in spring or early summer right after the bloom period has ended. (See January for information on how to prune climbing roses.) Climbers that bloom into summer or have a second bloom period later should be pruned in the winter.

■ *Some flowering shrubs, such as shrub roses, benefit from deadheading to remove the spent blossoms. In some cases it encourages repeat bloom or improves the next season's bloom. It can also make the shrub look nicer. Removing spent flowers is not essential to the health of a shrub, so it is purely optional.*

WATER

ALL

You may notice a white crust forming on the top of the soil in your container plants. That crust is made up of mineral salts that accumulate from water and fertilizers and could be extremely damaging to some plants, causing reduced or stunted growth, brown leaf tips, dropping leaves, dead root tips, or wilting. Some plants can tolerate salts better than others, but it's advisable to leach the salts from container plants every four to six months. First scrape off the white crust on the top of the soil down to about ¼ inch. Unless the plant is very shallow-rooted you probably won't need to replace the topsoil. With the soil surface cleared, water the plant, allowing the water to run out of the container rather than accumulate in a saucer. It generally takes an amount of water twice the volume of the container to flush the excess salts out of the soil. Keep in mind that if the plant has not been repotted with fresh soil in more than a year or two, it may be beneficial to completely repot it rather than flushing the soil.

EDIBLES

As fruiting plants are kicking into high gear, they depend on regular watering, preferably directed right to the plants' roots. Irregular watering can stress plants and lead to lower yields and problems such as blossom-end rot in tomatoes. Plan for a minimum of 1 inch of water per plant, more in times of extreme heat. Overhead watering can encourage the spread of fungal diseases, so use drip irrigation or soaker hoses wherever possible.

Some edibles, such as corn, require more than the weekly 1 inch of water. Expect to provide at least 1½ inch of water per week for corn. When the tassels emerge from the end of the ears, it's time to deeply water corn plants, making sure that the entire root zone is completely saturated. Do this again when the silks form.

WATER GARDENS

Keep a close eye on the water level of ponds and other water features throughout the warm-weather months. In fish-stocked ponds, in particular, even a 1-inch drop of water level from evaporation can

HERE'S HOW

TO WATER (OR NOT WATER) CALIFORNIA NATIVES

Most California native plants are adapted to summers that are warm and dry. To provide ideal conditions for them, you should withhold supplemental water from most native plants from June through October. Some natives are more flexible than others, but the most sensitive ones can develop root or crown rot if watered regularly at this time, particularly if they're in poorly draining soil. This can be difficult to accommodate if they are interplanted with nonnatives that do require watering. Hydrozoning (grouping plants according to their water needs) is the best way to handle these differing watering requirements.

If you can't relocate plants at this time to prevent over- or underwatering, try directing water specifically only to the plants that need it. If you have drip irrigation installed, you can adjust or block drip emitters. If you hand-water, you can use an overhead spray to wash off native plants occasionally, but direct the most water to the nonnative plants that need the water.

California natives benefit greatly from having a 2-inch layer of mulch (as long as the mulch doesn't bury the base of the stem where it can encourage rotting). For the first year after planting, they need regular moisture to get established, but you should water only when the soil a couple of inches below the surface is dry. After the first year, a plant that is native to your region should be able to survive without supplemental watering. Native plants that are from a different part of California that is significantly wetter or cooler than your region may need occasional watering at the driest times of the year. (But then, a plant from a region that has that different a climate isn't exactly "native," is it?)

TO WATER SUCCULENTS IN THE DRY SEASON

Although succulents have adapted to dry periods by storing water in their leaves and stems, most still need some supplemental water in the dry summer months. Most succulents are shallow-rooted so frequency of watering generally matters more than deep watering. Water early in the day so water doesn't sit on the leaves and stems overnight, which can lead to rotting.

1. Water in-ground succulents every ten to fourteen days, more if it has been windy or temperatures are above 80 degrees Fahrenheit.

2. Water container succulents once a week or more, depending on the size of the container (the smaller the container, the more frequently it needs watering). Do not let containers sit in water-filled saucers, even in hot weather.

alter the chemical balance enough to be harmful to fish and other aquatic animals. When you do have to add more water, place the hose at the bottom of the pond so that the temperature and pH change will be mild and won't shock the fish. If adding water from a municipal source that treats the water with chlorine or chloramines, be sure to treat the water with a conditioner to keep it from becoming toxic for the fish.

FERTILIZE

ANNUALS AND PERENNIALS

Keep feeding summer-blooming annuals and perennials. A fertilizer formulated for flowering plants will contain more phosphorus (and have a higher middle number in the N-P-K code), which will help extend the bloom period.

EDIBLES

Keep up a regular fertilizing schedule or add a sidedressing of compost monthly. Be sure not to fertilize when plants are drought-stressed. Water them well first, then apply the fertilizer a couple days later.

■ *Apply a sidedressing of compost, manure, or granular fertilizer to give vegetables a midseason boost.*

Take special care with the bigger plants like corn, which tend to be heavy feeders. Apply a high-nitrogen fertilizer when the plants are 12 to 15 inches high and again when they are 2 to 2½ feet high.

HOUSEPLANTS

While most houseplants should be fed from spring through fall, bromeliads really need regular feeding only through the summer months. Dilute a complete liquid plant food to half strength and spray the leaves and center "tank" area of the plant where water accumulates, allowing some of the spray to fall on the soil as well. Repeat every two to three weeks through September. To encourage the bromeliad to flower, add a pinch of Epsom salts to its regular watering.

PERENNIALS

Resume feeding cymbidium orchids that were repotted in May. (See January for more information on feeding orchids.)

ROSES

In all parts of the state, roses should continue to get monthly feedings.

PROBLEM-SOLVE

EDIBLES

Fruiting plants may not be the only things that will entice raccoons and possums into your garden, but they are among the most irresistible garden features for these adorable but annoying and potentially dangerous pests. Even in urban suburban gardens, raccoons and—to a lesser degree—possums have becoming a bigger and bigger problem, and they can be frustratingly difficult to deter.

To protect your harvest, as well other plants, pets, and even your home, there are a few methods of deterring these pests, but the results tend to be mixed and not necessarily long-term. Motion-activated sprinkler devices can be installed to shoot a jet of water that will (for a while, at least) scare away the predators. Low-voltage electric fencing installed about 6 inches above the ground will probably be more effective, but that can be costly and a bit of a headache to have to work around.

■ *A motion-activated sprinkler is an effective way to keep small animals out of your garden.*

Most scent-based deterrents, such as mothballs or pheromone-based products, don't seem to deter raccoons at all, but one low-cost, low-tech solution I've used with pretty good results is to soak rags in rubbing alcohol or ammonia and lay the rags along the paths that raccoons are using to enter your garden. I placed these along fences and gates and even draped a few of the soaked rags over branches of the plum tree that was their current target. I didn't have problems with raccoons in the garden for the rest of the season.

LAWNS

If your lawn has lost its vibrancy and is losing the fight to weeds, the problem may be soil

HERE'S HOW

TO SOLARIZE YOUR SOIL

What do you do when really invasive weeds, diseases, or pests take hold in your garden and the usual controls aren't gaining the upper hand? Sometimes desperate times call for desperate measures.

One option is to *solarize* the soil using sheets of plastic to raise the temperature of the soil, killing weeds, weed seeds, pathogens, and pests. There are some drawbacks to this process: It can kill beneficial organisms in the soil as well as the weeds, although earthworms and other beneficials usually seem to either move deeper into the soil to escape the heat or recolonize the soil quickly after the solarization process is over. Solarization also works better on some weeds than on others. While it's quite effective against annual weeds, perennial weeds with stolons, such as Bermudagrass, are more likely to survive or rebound following solarization.

To solarize your soil, follow these steps:

1. Clear the soil of plants, rocks, and debris. A clean, clear, and smooth surface will make tighter contact with the plastic covering.

2. Wet the soil to a depth of 12 inches. Wet soil conducts heat better than dry soil, so the deeper you irrigate, the deeper the heat will travel through the soil.

3. Cover the area with clear plastic sheeting that is 1 to 4 mils thick. The thinner the plastic, the better it heats, but thinner plastic is also more susceptible to tearing. Rolls of plastic used for painting jobs can be found in hardware stores and will work well for solarizing.

4. Weigh down the plastic around the edges, making sure that good contact is made between the soil and the plastic. If there is too much air in between, the soil will not heat up as much.

5. To achieve the full effects of solarization, the soil needs to reach a temperature between 110 and 125 degrees Fahrenheit to a depth of 6 inches. During the warmest times of the year (June through August in most parts of the state), weeds, pathogens, and pests will be killed in four to six weeks at this temperature. In cooler periods, it may take six to eight weeks. In the Central Valley and desert regions, a four-week period between June and September will probably be sufficient.

6. After the solarization period is complete, remove the plastic. You can plant immediately, but it's best not to till deeply or disturb the soil more than necessary so as not to bring up weed seeds that may still be viable. Plants grown in solarized soil will often grow faster due to the lack of competition with weeds and because the rapid decomposition of organic matter due to the heat of the soil increases the available nutrients in the soil.

compaction. Compaction generally occurs in areas where there is a lot of foot traffic or heavy equipment being moved. Some soils are more susceptible than others to compaction, depending on the soil structure. When soil becomes compacted, the particles that make up the soil are closer together, leaving less room for oxygen and water to get to plants' roots.

How do you know if your soil is compacted? One easy test is the shovel test. If it's difficult to insert a shovel into the ground, then the soil is compacted. Easier still is the walking test. When you walk across your lawn, the ground should feel springy beneath your step. If there's no spring in your step, then compaction is the problem. But one dead giveaway is the presence of many weeds in your lawn. Weeds adapt to the adverse conditions of compacted soil in a way that grasses can't. They simply out-compete your lawn for what little air and water filters through the compacted ground.

If your soil is compacted, it's best to treat it now so that it will be better able to withstand the hot weather to come. Treating your lawn for soil compaction is a four-step process of aerating and amending the soil:

1. Mow the lawn one-third shorter than usual.

2. Water deeply at least twice a few days before you plan to aerate.

3. Aerate the soil using a punch core aerator, not a spike aerator. A punch core aerator actually removes plugs of soil from the ground, leaving a small hole for water and nutrients to enter. When done, rake to clear away the soil plugs.

4. Topdress the lawn with organic matter and rake it in evenly. This can include a lightweight compost, composted manure, or even coffee grounds. The organic supplements

■ *Aerate your lawn before the worst heat of summer sets in.*

Poison oak may be growing in your garden. Remove it by hand if you're not allergic to it, or spray with an herbicide if you are.

not only provide nutrients to the roots of the lawn, they also encourage earthworms, which loosen the soil and leave castings to feed it even more.

With regular watering and mowing, your lawn should regain its usual health and vigor.

PERENNIALS

Be on the lookout for poison oak (*Toxicodendron diversilobum*) popping up in the garden, particularly in rural and suburban woody areas. Remember that old rhyme: "Leaves of three, leave it be." That refers to the three-leaflet leaves of the poison oak plant and the allergic reaction you may get if you come in contact with it. Based on the number of work hours lost each year due to dermatitis caused by poison oak, it is considered the most hazardous plant in California. If you come in contact with the leaves, you should immediately pour isopropyl alcohol on the affected area, then wash it with cold water and mild soap. Avoid using warm water on the irritated area because that makes the plant's oil penetrate deeper into the skin.

If poison oak should creep into your garden, the best way to remove it is by hand if you don't have a sensitivity to the plant. If you do, or if you don't want to find out if you do, the best recourse is application of the herbicide glyphosate (contained in the commercial herbicide Roundup®). Timing is crucial when it comes to spraying. You must apply the herbicide after the fruit has formed in the spring but before the leaves turn yellow or red in the late summer and fall. Follow the directions carefully when applying any chemical control such as glyphosate, and take precautions to keep it from drifting to other plants.

TREES

At this time of year, fruit trees, particularly apples and pears, will experience a lightening of the load that's often called "June drop." Essentially, the tree will thin its current crop by dropping what may seem like a significant number of fruits to the ground. It's easy for a gardener to despair when seeing half the crop of immature fruit rotting on the ground, but this is a normal and necessary process for the tree to go through. In most years fruit trees set more fruit than is actually needed for a good crop. By dropping some of the fruit, the tree reduces the strain on its resources and helps ensure that the remaining fruit will develop well.

Drops may occur at other times of the year as well. Early-season drops occur when the tree releases fruits that were not properly pollinated, and late-season drops can happen when fruit has gotten wormy and ripened too early. Sudden weather changes can also cause fruit drop at any time during the season.

June drop, or any naturally occurring fruit drop, should not keep you from thinning fruits. Thinning results in larger, healthier fruits with fewer pest problems and blemishes. Fruits should be thinned when they are about the size of a dime. For apples, for example, reduce each cluster to just one fruit and keep the fruits spaced about 6 to 8 inches apart on the branch. Thin other fruits in a similar way to reduce the load on branches and create a healthier environment for the fruit to ripen.

July

Welcome to the dry garden. One of the ways that gardening in California has changed in recent years is that many Californians have accepted the fact that water is a limited resource and filling our gardens with thirsty plants may be a lesson in endless frustration. Many gardeners have embraced xeriscaping, the practice of gardening in ways that reduce or eliminate the need for supplemental water. In the dry days of July xeriscaping makes obvious sense, but the truth is we need to be water-conscious all year long.

As more of us turn away from the traditional garden style that was dominated by large, water-hogging lawns, this new way of gardening represents a sea change in the type of gardens we have. You are just as likely to see front yards dominated by drought-tolerant Mediterranean plants and succulents now as you are green lawns.

But today's dry garden doesn't necessarily look dry. It's brimming with native plants that flower throughout the year. It can be a mosaic of succulents in shades of blue, green, gray, or even gold. It attracts a multitude of bees, hummingbirds, and other pollinators that come to drink from the nectar-rich blossoms.

You may not be ready to embrace a completely dry garden, but there are ways to utilize dry-garden techniques in any garden. You can create no- or low-water zones that are planted only with drought-resistant, hardy plants and that use other water-saving practices like mulching. You can reduce or replace your lawn with low-water plants or even with artificial turf. You can install a grey-water system to divert water to your ornamental plants instead of into the sewer system.

Check with your local water utility for information on how you can make your garden a more successful dry garden. Some utilities even offer rebate programs for getting rid of your lawn to reduce your water usage. Local Master Gardeners will also have helpful information on the drought-tolerant and native plants you can use in your garden.

You don't have to look far to see that a dry garden needn't be a dull garden.

PLAN

EDIBLES

When fruit ripens, it's time to harvest and harvests don't wait. If you have a large fruit tree that will be ready to pick soon, get the necessary equipment ready now. Depending on the tree(s), you may need a tall ladder, tarps, bushel baskets, and a long-handled fruit picker. If you don't own these tools, check to see if your local public library has a tool-lending library where you can borrow the items for the short time you'll need them. You may also want to line up some family and friends to help—extra sets of hands make quicker work of even a large harvest.

■ *Be ready with ladders, tarps, and long-handled fruit pickers when your fruit starts to ripen on the trees.*

PLANT

EDIBLES

Plant peas now through August for an early-autumn harvest. There are three broad categories of peas: Shelling peas, which are harvested for the seeds inside the pods; edible-pod peas, which are harvested before the seeds have matured; and peas that are a combination of the two. Peas can be grown in bush form or on vines that climb up to 6 feet by curling tendrils (which are also edible).

Peas can tolerate light frosts but hot weather can lead to mildew problems and low yields. Plant in full sun in cool-summer areas, or in afternoon shade in the hottest regions. Peas prefer well-draining soil that's been amended with compost and bone meal or rock phosphate.

Soaking seeds overnight prior to planting speeds up germination. Sow seeds 2 inches deep in light (sandy) soil and ½ to 1 inch deep in heavy (clay) soil. For bush peas, space the rows 2 feet apart. For vines, allow 5 feet between rows. Water the ground before planting, then withhold supplemental water until seedlings begin to emerge, which should occur in as few as six or as many as thirty-six days.

As the seedlings grow, keep evenly moist but not soggy. Overhead watering can often lead to mildew problems, so drip irrigation or soaker hoses are recommended.

Peas are vulnerable to pea weevils, aphids, and thrips. Neem oil can usually keep infestations under control. Disease problems include powdery mildew (particularly in hot weather), fusarium wilt, and pea enation mosaic virus. Planting disease-resistant varieties is really the only way to combat the last two.

Peas will generally be ready for harvest sixty to seventy days after planting, or three weeks after the blossoms appear. Pick all the pods that are ready because if seeds are left on the vine to ripen, the plant will stop producing. For shelling peas, harvest when the pods swell up but before their bright green color begins to fade. For edible-podded peas, harvest when the pods are 2 to 3 inches long but before the seeds swell. Harvest time lasts two to six

■ *Peas sprouting*

■ *Peas growing*

■ *Peas flowering*

■ *Peas fruiting*

weeks from one planting, and vining peas can be expected to have the longest harvesting period. A typical yield would be 2 to 3 pounds of peas from a 15-foot row over a one-week period.

For shelling peas, recommended varieties include 'Mr. Big', 'Green Arrow', 'Maestro', 'Alderman', 'Garden Sweet', 'Survivor', 'Thomas Laxton', and 'Wando'. Also favored are the smaller, French variety of shelling peas known as *petits pois*. The varieties include 'Waverex' and 'Precovelle'.

For edible-podded peas (sugar or snow peas), try 'Mammoth Melting Sugar', 'Oregon Giant', 'Oregon Sugar Pod II', and 'Snow Wind'. There are also varieties that are a combination of shelling and edible-pod peas. These include 'Super Sugar Snap', 'Sugar Ann', and 'Sugar Lace'.

Growing your own carrots means you're not limited to the traditional orange varieties. These fast and easy-to-grow vegetables come in a rainbow of colors and shapes ranging from long and tapered to short and round. The long, tapered orange roots that we usually see in the grocery stores are called Imperator varieties and they include 'Sugarsnax 54', 'Purple Haze' (purple skin with an orange core), 'Red Samurai' (red), 'Rainbow' (a multicolor mix), and 'Deep Purple' (purple). Nantes carrots are fast-growing cylindrical roots 6 to 7 inches long. Varieties include 'Bolero', 'Nelson', 'Napa',

'Touchon', 'Parano', and 'White Satin' (white). Chantenay carrots are short and stocky and grow sweeter in cooler soil. Favorite varieties are 'Hercules' and 'Royal Chantenay'. Mini carrots are baby and radish-style roots, such as 'Babette' and 'Romeo'.

For a fall crop, sow seeds at least 10 to 12 weeks before the first frost date. Once they're growing, carrots can usually withstand a light frost but not a hard freeze. Plant in full sun in light-textured, well-draining soil. Work compost into the soil before planting and make sure the soil is fine and loose to a depth of 12 inches. Rocks and clods of hard soil can cause carrots to fork and grow in misshapen forms. In areas with heavy clay soil, plant miniature varieties of carrots in containers.

Sprinkle the seeds thinly and cover with fine garden soil. Sow seeds in rows 1 foot apart or broadcast the seeds over a prepared area. When the carrot tops are 1 to 2 inches high, thin the seedlings to 1½ to 2 inches apart. After thinning, run a thin row of a balanced fertilizer down the row of carrots about 2 inches from the seedlings. Don't be heavy-handed with the fertilizer. It will just cause too much green growth on top and misshapen roots below. Thin again in another couple of weeks if they look crowded. (The thinned seedlings are edible.)

HERE'S HOW

TO SOW SEEDS OUTSIDE

Some plants, particularly root vegetables like radishes, beets, and carrots, prefer not to be moved, so you should plant their seeds directly into the garden.

Water the plants by directing the watering wand or hose nozzle at the base of the plant. Count to ten while watering each plant and then go back and repeat the process. If you have the time and money, put soaker hoses around your vegetable garden beds. It will be much easier to water; you can just turn on the hoses and let them run while you do something else.

Sprinkle the seeds in the row according to spacing instructions on the seed package. Some seed packets will advise you to sow the seeds "thickly." That means to sprinkle a lot of seeds in one area because the

Keep the rows weeded and evenly moist. Uneven watering can cause the roots to split. Row covers will help to prevent damage from pests like carrot fly as well as rabbits, mice, and moles.

You can begin harvesting when carrots reach finger size, usually 30 to 40 days after sowing. They will reach full maturity 60 to 70 days after sowing. Mark the expected harvest date in your garden journal.

HOUSEPLANTS

One category of houseplants that has become popular is a group called *epiphytes*. Epiphytes are plants that grow on other plants, but they are not parasites. They take their moisture and nutrition from the air and the rain without robbing the plants they dwell on of any nutrients. For that reason, epiphytes are often called "air plants" and can be "planted" on just about anything. You'll often see epiphyte arrangements attached to driftwood or shells, or even hung directly on a wall. Some common epiphytes include orchids, bromeliads, anthuriums, philodendrons, staghorn ferns, and Spanish moss. Epiphytes can live perfectly happily outdoors, under the right conditions, but their soilless state and ability to grow on just about anything make them a natural choice for a houseplant.

Don't let the term "air plant" mislead you, however. Epiphytes can't survive in your home on just

seeds don't sprout consistently. You can always snip off seedlings at the soil line to make room if more seeds than you need sprout and grow too close together.

Sprinkle seed-starting mix over the seeds. While you can cover seeds outdoors with regular garden soil, seeds sprout more easily when they're covered with the lightweight seed-starting mix. After covering the seeds, water them. Do not let the soil dry out until you see the seeds starting to sprout. If the seeds dry out while they're sprouting, they'll die.

Label the rows where you've planted seeds. Seed leaves can look similar to one another when they're sprouting, and you don't want to forget what you planted, where.

Tillandsia is a type of epiphytic plant, which doesn't grow in soil.

air. Once or twice a week, epiphytes should be submerged in water for up to three or four hours. You can use municipal tap water on them, but they'll appreciate rain water, bottled water, or well water even more and will likely bloom more quickly with it. For nutrition, you can mix a half-strength dose of orchid food into the bathwater once a month.

The right lighting is also important. They want bright indirect light, just like they'd find if they were perched high in a dense canopy of a tree. Midday sunlight hitting them directly could dry them out too much.

Dry air can also be problematic, so during the summer months if your home is either very hot or very air-conditioned, give epiphytes a spritz of water every couple of days in between soakings.

PERENNIALS

This dry time of year is a good time to root succulent cuttings as long as you have a spot in bright shade to keep the cuttings while they root. Succulents are some of the easiest plants to root from cuttings—it's very nearly foolproof.

For shrub-type succulents like sedums, you can just snip off cuttings a few inches long with several rows of leaves. Strip away the bottom few rows and set them somewhere dry and cool out of direct sunlight for a few days. The cut areas will seal off, forming a callus. You can then insert the cuttings into a pot or flat of a well-draining potting mix. (I like to mix equal parts of a commercial potting mix and perlite for rooting cuttings. The perlite ensures good drainage while the potting mix holds just enough moisture to keep the cuttings from drying out too much.) Make sure the callused areas have good contact with the soil mix. Keep the soil mix barely moist and set it somewhere dry and shady. Roots will begin to emerge from the nodes where the leaves were within just a few days.

Succulents that have a rosette form without a stem usually form small plants (offsets) that are attached to the parent plant. Those offsets can be cut off with a sharp knife, callused over, and just laid on top of the potting mix to root. Rosette-shaped succulents, like aeoniums, that sit atop a stem can get leggy and top-heavy. When that happens, you can cut off the entire rosette top. Not only will the original rosette callus and set roots, but little baby rosettes will form along the leaf nodes of the headless trunk. Those new rosettes can then be harvested and rooted the same way.

Other succulents such as agaves or aloes also form baby plants called "pups," which are attached to the parent by rhizomes. Those can also be cut off with some of the rhizome attached and rooted.

You can quickly create a multitude of new succulent plants by harvesting and rooting cuttings in this way. As I said, it's almost foolproof!

CARE

ALL

Container plants needs special attention in the heat of summer, and sometimes making sure they're getting adequate water just isn't enough. If you have plants that have outgrown their containers or that have been in the same soil in their containers for more than a couple of years, rejuvenate them by repotting them in fresh soil and, if necessary, in a larger container so they can grow again. Before repotting, trim away any roots that look dead or diseased. If the roots are girdled (growing in a tight

■ *Get melons off the ground with a string support structure.*

circle) it's important to slice through the rootball to break the girdling habit and stimulate new root growth outward. After repotting with fresh potting soil, be sure to keep the plant well watered for the next few weeks to avoid shock. The plants should respond with a flush of new growth and more vigor overall.

EDIBLES

After harvesting artichoke buds, cut the plants down to the ground. In the Central Coast region, the plants will grow back and produce a second crop in the fall.

Keep pruning tomato plants to remove suckers and ensure good air circulation, and make sure that branches with fruit have enough support to hold the fruit. You can thin fruit to allow tomatoes to grow larger and to avoid branches breaking under the weight of too many fruits.

■ *Root-bound plants like this spider plant need to be repotted in larger containers. Be sure to slice through the roots before repotting.*

Melons, some squashes, and cucumbers may need extra support to keep heavy fruits from breaking branches as well. Long strips cut from old pantyhose work great to create a sling that you can tie to a trellis to hold up the fruit and keep it from pulling off the branch.

Make regular passes through all the edibles to hand pick pests off of the plants.

LAWNS

Mow higher and more often. Taller grass is more drought-tolerant and shades the ground more, which helps to minimize evaporation and discourages weed seed germination. (See June for the proper mower setting for your type of lawn.)

PERENNIALS

In the hottest parts of the state, you'll need to move or shelter container-grown succulents to protect them from sunburn. In long periods of intense heat and sun exposure, many succulents will turn reddish orange. If actual sunburn develops, they'll show beige patches that will not heal. Take care that containers don't dry out excessively, which will make it harder for the plants to tolerate the extreme heat.

ROSES

Deadhead roses to encourage repeat blooming. In order to achieve larger blooms, you can *disbud* by removing side buds on hybrid tea roses or pinching out the center bud of a cluster on floribunda roses. Keep the rose bed weeded and remove fallen petals and leaves to discourage the spread of diseases.

SHRUBS AND TREES

Prune woody plants this month to control size and appearance. For fruit trees that have already been harvested, prune out the branches that were unproductive and thin the canopy to improve air circulation. For trees that are still bearing fruit, prune more lightly. It may be best to sacrifice some fruit if the canopy is too dense and needs to be thinned. You can remove dead, diseased, or damaged wood at any time. You should also remove suckers that grow up from the base of the trunk and the spindly vertical branches known as water sprouts. These will only produce lateral branches that make it look like little trees growing within the larger tree.

WATER SPROUTS

■ *Water sprouts appear on tree limbs or trunks. These weak shoots interfere with the growth and appearance of the tree and should be removed promptly.*

Water sprouts, which are particularly common in pear and apple trees, are not productive and in addition to spoiling the look of the tree, they can make the canopy too dense. Cut water sprouts back to the lateral branches they're growing from.

VINES & GROUNDCOVERS

Trim spring-blooming groundcovers now to remove spent blooms and encourage new growth. Simple mowing can cut some groundcovers back. Lantana, African daisy, and coyote bush are a few that respond well to mowing. The woodier the stems, the less likely it is that they can be trimmed by mowing.

Many vines, such as wisteria and jasmine, can use a bit of trimming now too. The summer heat causes them to send out long, wispy branches that look untidy. Cut them back to maintain the vine's shape and control the spread.

WATER

ALL

Water early, deeply, and less frequently. By watering in the early morning, there is time for the water to seep in with less evaporation and roots will be revitalized before the heat of the day sets in. Deep but less frequent watering encourages drought-tolerant roots. One inch of water once or twice a week is probably adequate in mild weather, but hotter spells call for more frequent watering.

Beyond having a regular watering schedule, there are a few extra things you can do to help your plants make the most of the available water.

- **Mulch:** A 3- to 4-inch layer of organic mulch (wood chips, compost, straw, pine needles, newspaper, cardboard, and so forth) minimizes evaporation, keeping more of the water in the ground where it can get to the roots. Mulching is one of the single most effective things you can do to keep your garden healthy.

- **Vigilance:** Be vigilant about weeds, which rob your plants of water and nutrients. Pull weeds as soon as you see them and use mulch to help suppress them. One added benefit of using drip irrigation rather than using a sprinkler to water everything indiscriminately is that you're not encouraging more weed growth. Instead the water goes directly to the roots of your plants.

- **Hydrozoning:** Use hydrozoning, a system of grouping plants together by their water needs. If all the plants that need heavy watering are grouped in one area and all the ones who need infrequent deep watering are in another, you can give each group just the water they need and no more. Also, make sure you water the whole root area. For trees, that means watering the entire space within the drip line of the tree, not just immediately surrounding the trunk.

- **Irrigation:** If you have an irrigation system installed, make sure it's operating at peak efficiency. Check drip emitters or sprinkler heads to make sure they aren't clogged and they are properly aimed so the water goes to the plants, not the sidewalk. Use the system's timer to water early in the morning and for the proper interval. Some of the newer, more advanced irrigation control systems even download satellite weather information to adjust the watering schedule to what your garden really needs.

One of the simplest, most inexpensive, and most environmentally responsible ways to water a lawn is by tapping a system such as a rain barrel that collects rainwater and stores it for controlled irrigation.

Container plants that get completely dehydrated in the summer heat may be hard to rehydrate again. The soil may contract so that water runs down the sides of the soil surrounding the rootball without penetrating to the roots inside. To correct the problem, completely immerse the container in a bucket of water until bubbles stop flowing to the surface (it may take an hour or more). Then remove the container from the water and place it in a sunny location to dry and

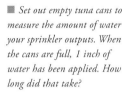

■ *Set out empty tuna cans to measure the amount of water your sprinkler outputs. When the cans are full, 1 inch of water has been applied. How long did that take?*

drain completely. For containers that are too large to immerse, the only option is to apply water in small, continuous amounts until the soil is finally saturated.

FERTILIZE

ALL
Having a large and healthy compost pile will pay off at this time year when so much of the garden is actively growing and requires feeding. You can start composting at any time of year, but there's no time like the present. See Here's How to Start and Maintain a Compost Pile to learn how to turn your garden and kitchen waste into black gold.

ANNUALS, PERENNIALS, ROSES, & SHRUBS
Feed all plants that are in flower or in bud. Make sure that plants are not drought-stressed at the time of feeding or they may burn. In those cases, water well first and fertilize a week later.

EDIBLES
Continue to feed warm-season crops with sidedressings of compost or applications of an organic high-phosphorus fertilizer for the fruiting crops. Avoid high-nitrogen fertilizers that will encourage spurts of green growth, which will attract insect pests.

In the coastal parts of the state, after the last artichokes have been harvested, feed the plants once more to encourage a second crop.

VINES & GROUNDCOVERS
Feed groundcovers that have been trimmed or mowed with a fertilizer at a rate of 1 to 2 pounds of nitrogen per 1,000 square feet. Water well before and after application.

PROBLEM-SOLVE

ALL
If you're noticing discolored damage on leaves of plants, you may have an infestation of thrips or whiteflies. They often begin in the spring but can hang on through the summer. Both of these insects can suck the sap out of leaves, causing them to look scraped or scarred with whitish, silvery, or yellow patches. The damage may not look that significant but if left uncontrolled, thrips or whiteflies can damage enough leaves on a plant to kill it. Both thrips and whiteflies feed on a large

HERE'S HOW

TO WATER VERTICAL GARDENS

Vertical gardening can take many forms from hanging baskets to wreaths to wall-mounted planting systems. Magazines are filled with pages of small gardens looking lush, colorful, and densely packed, but keeping a vertical garden looking that way month after month takes special attention, especially when it comes to watering. If you just water the hanging garden in place, directing a spray of water from the top to the bottom, you will probably find that the plants at the top grow at a different rate than the ones at the bottom. The top plants may get too little water and the ones at the bottom that catch all the runoff may be drowned. Consider these tips when you water your plants that are growing up:

- For living wreaths, which are often planted with succulents, the best approach is to take the wreath off the wall, completely submerse it in water, and let it soak for about an hour. After the soaking, allow the wreath to drain for a while before rehanging. Soak the wreath this way every three to four weeks, and more often in summer.

- For succulents or other plants growing in vertically mounted boxes or frames, remove the box from the wall and lay it flat to water. Water it slowly and lightly—just enough to completely moisten the soil and roots without excess water collecting at the bottom or draining out. Do this every two to three weeks for succulents, more often for other kinds of plants.

- Hanging baskets can be watered in place as long as drainage is not a problem. Ideally, use a long-handled water wand that allows you to direct a light spray directly downward onto the soil. The frequency of watering varies greatly, depending on the size of the container and the type of plant. The best way to determine a hanging basket's water needs is with the good, old-fashioned finger test—stick your finger all the way into the soil around the roots. If it feels dry, it's time to water.

- Woolly Pockets and other wall-mounted planting systems may or may not contain their own irrigation systems, but even with an irrigation system you need to monitor the plants' water needs closely. Frankly, some planting systems work better than others, depending on where and how it's mounted and what plants are used. Where possible, use the finger test to ensure that the plants' roots are not drying out, and water or adjust the irrigation schedule as needed.

It's tempting to mist wall gardens with water in between watering to keep them looking fresh, but this is generally not a good idea. Shallow watering like you get from a spray bottle encourages shallow root growth and even though vertically growing plants may not have deep containers, you want to encourage the roots to grow down, not close to the surface.

TO START AND MAINTAIN A COMPOST PILE

To start a compost pile, find an area in your garden that is convenient to access but preferably out of view. You don't have to have any kind of container to hold your compost pile, you can just pile it up. If you do want to keep it contained, you can use plastic trash containers, wood pallets, or wire fencing to construct a structure to hold the pile.

Compost is created from a mix of "brown" materials such as dead leaves and flowers, straw, sawdust, and shredded newspaper, and "green" materials such as grass clippings, plant trimmings, vegetable and fruit scraps from the kitchen, and manure from herbivore animals such as rabbits and chickens. These materials are layered at a ratio of three parts brown materials to one part green materials, with a shovelful or two of garden soil in between the layers. Do not include meat scraps or waste from meat-eating animals like cats and dogs; these materials can add pathogens that will then end up in your soil.

As you build the pile a few layers at a time, add water to moisten the compost but not make it soggy. The water helps the materials decompose. Too little or too much water slows the decomposition process. Every few weeks, use a garden fork to turn the materials over. As the materials break down, the pile heats up and then cools off as the decomposition slows down. Turning the materials puts more oxygen into the mix and gets the decomposition process revved up again.

If you keep the compost pile "cooking" well enough, it should break down to a nutrient-rich, crumbly brown medium that has no offensive odors. You can then apply that compost as a sidedressing or topdressing or use it as a mulch around your plants. If you have the room, it's helpful to keep more than one compost pile cooking so you have an ongoing supply.

■ *Whiteflies are sucking insects that can damage plants and transmit disease.*

variety of ornamental and edible plants and can act as a vector in the spread of viruses and other plant diseases.

Thrips in the adult stage are yellow to dark brown winged insects less than 0.06 inch long, barely large enough to be seen by the naked eye. The larvae are lighter in color and half the size of adults. Whitefly adults are smaller, about 0.04 inch long, with white, winged, soft bodies with a waxy coating. Before the adult stage they appear similar to scale, to which they are related. Thrips are usually found on the topsides of leaves; whiteflies are found on the undersides.

Whichever of these two pests you find to be doing the damage, the controls are generally the same. Yellow sticky traps are pretty good at attracting and trapping the flying adult insects. Neem or an insecticidal soap is effective against the insects in the immature stages. Garlic sprays are also useful. Thrips in the pupal stage fall off the leaves they've been feeding on and live in the soil, so a layer of diatomaceous earth spread underneath infested plants will kill the pupae. Similarly, a plastic barrier on top of the soil will prevent the pupae from burrowing into the soil where they can live and even overwinter until temperatures climb above 60 degrees Fahrenheit once again. (With indoor plants, thrips can be active all year long.)

Neither of these insects is likely to do significant damage unless their population explodes. The best way to prevent that from happening is to avoid

using broad-spectrum insecticides, which decimate beneficial insect populations as well as pests.

Another insect pest to watch for at this time is scale. There are two types of scale: soft and armored. Both appear as roundish bumps on stems, branches, and leaves of plants, but soft scale are brown or gray, more oval-shaped, and soft-bodied while armored also come in shades of white, yellow or even black, are more circular in shape, and hard-bodied. Both types are sucking insects that pierce the plant's tissue to suck out the sap. As with aphids, scale produce a kind of honeydew that draws ants. They can leave discolored blotches on the plant in the spots where they've been sucking, and extreme infestations can lead to leaf drop and even death of the plant.

Unlike aphids, scale can be hard to budge with the spray from a hose. For minor infestations, wipe down plants with cotton balls or paper towels soaked in alcohol. Neem, insecticidal soap, or horticultural oil used during the growing season will only be effective on soft scale, but a dormant-season horticultural oil will work on both types.

Scale can be as small as $\frac{1}{10}$ inch in diameter, so you may have to look closely, even with a magnifying glass, to distinguish it from the odd bump or brown spot on a stem. But scale can do enough damage that it's worth it to keep a close watch for this pest.

■ *A citrus plant infested by brown soft scale*

■ *Yellowing between the veining of leaves, as in this strawberry plant, is a sign of iron deficiency.*

Sometimes leaf discoloration is not due to pest damage at all but to a mineral deficiency (which can happen anytime of year, though summer is frequently when it's seen). Leaves showing signs of chlorosis (yellowing in between green veining) are often a sign of an iron deficiency, or sometimes a deficiency in iron, manganese, and zinc. All three of these nutrients become less available to plants in soils with a high pH level (7.0 or above). Areas where topsoil has been removed, or where the soil is lacking in organic matter, or where the soil is waterlogged are all potential problem spots for deficiencies in these minerals. Sometimes plants near the foundation of a house may suffer from these deficiencies because of lime leaching out of the concrete foundation, which raises the pH of the soil, making the nutrients unavailable. Iron, manganese, and zinc are essential in the photosynthesis process and zinc is also important in determining plant size and maturation.

Iron and manganese deficiencies are somewhat similar in appearance. New leaves are affected first and they appear yellowish in between the green veins. With manganese deficiency, the leaves will also have necrotic spots appearing in the yellow and the leaves will eventually develop a light gray or purple metallic sheen. With zinc deficiency, new growth will appear stunted with short sections between leaf nodes and the leaves will appear twisted and smaller in size. Older leaves will look pitted in the upper area between veining with yellowing that eventually turns brown. Flowers may also look twisted and distorted.

A simple soil test will confirm whether the soil is deficient in one or more of these minerals, or (more likely) the high pH level is keeping the plants from using the minerals already present. (See March for information on conducting a soil test.) If you need to raise the pH level of the soil, refer to March for guidance. Primarily, it's a matter of adding organic matter to the soil, but it will take time for the soil pH to change significantly. In the meantime, you should foliar-feed any plants showing signs of iron-manganese-zinc deficiency with a chelated fertilizer containing all three nutrients. Spraying the plants with a seaweed extract solution can also help.

EDIBLES

Another common problem showing up in edible gardens at this time of year is blossom-end rot, which occurs on tomatoes and other fruit. Blossom-end rot is not a disease but the result of calcium deficiency in the plant. That doesn't mean, however, that the soil is necessarily deficient in calcium. The calcium may be present, but the plant may not be able to access it. This is usually due to irregular watering. See Here's How to Control Blossom-End Rot for guidance on managing the problem.

LAWNS

Brown patches appearing in the lawn at this time of year may be the result of chinch bugs. These pests

■ *Chinch bugs may be the cause of brown patches in your lawn.*

may appear as grubs that curl into a "C" shape when exposed, or as black adults with white wings. Immature bugs may be red or orange and pink with white bands. Most prevalent in midsummer

to fall, they suck the juices from grasses and particularly attack St. Augustinegrass. As with most pests, they are best controlled by regularly watering the lawn and keeping it free of thatch.

HERE'S HOW

TO CONTROL BLOSSOM-END ROT

You may first notice the calcium deficiency that causes blossom-end rot from suspicious signs on the leaves and stems: Growth may appear stunted, foliage may be dark green, and there may be patches of brown, dead tissue along leaf edges and new growth. The dead-giveaways, however, are the sunken brown-black spots on the blossom end of the fruits.

To correct the problem causing blossom-end rot, it's best to determine if the soil is really calcium-deficient. The only way to do this is to run a soil test, as described in Here's How to Test Your Soil's

pH and Nutrient Level in March. The soil test from the lab at the University of Massachusetts at Amherst will clearly tell you whether or not you have a calcium problem. If you do, you can correct it by adding dolomitic limestone, calcium sulfate (also called "gypsum"), or calcium nitrate (available as a water-soluble fertilizer that can be sprayed on plants).

Without a clear indication that your soil is deficient in calcium, however, you can assume that the problem is that the plant hasn't been able to access the calcium that's already there. That may be because your watering schedule has been irregular, or because excessive rain has flushed the available calcium away from the root zone. Do what

you can to keep the watering schedule regular and apply at least 3 to 4 inches of mulch around the plants to keep the water from evaporating. As the watering schedule becomes more even, you should see fewer instances of blossom-end rot until it eventually stops completely. At that point, in addition to regular watering, monthly sidedressings of compost should keep the soil healthy enough, and if you add in ground eggshells, fish bones, or seashells it will definitely have an adequate supply of calcium.

August

They call these the dog days of summer. The ancient Romans considered the dog days an evil time, a time of fevers, tempers, and frenzies. But for us, the dog days needn't be dark. They can be as free and playful as the four-legged creatures that run 'round our gardens.

As the summer heat makes planting at this time unwise, August is mostly a time to clean, clear, and maintain the garden. And, we hope, enjoy it. How much more can we enjoy it if our pets are enjoying it along with us? For those of us with pets, whether they're dogs, cats, birds, fish, or reptiles, gardening is about creating a safe and welcoming place for our animals and for ourselves. Gardening with pets presents certain challenges. We need to keep the garden clean for them as well as clean up after them. We may need to avoid certain toxic plants and create space that's safe for them to run around in. They may require outdoor shelter and protection from predators.

But beyond the health and safety issues, we want our gardens to be a haven for our pets as much as for ourselves, a place to romp and frolic and have fun. You may not want your dog to have the run of the entire garden, but you can designate a part of the garden as dog-friendly and another part as no-dogs-allowed. Cats are a little more difficult to restrict, but I've found that planting catnip and creating little spots for them to find shelter encourages them to spend their time in the garden rather than roaming the neighborhood. Having places for your pet to lounge in the shade or chase a ball may mean the difference between a pet that's happy and content in the garden and one that's digging and chewing and getting into trouble.

With a few adjustments, you can turn your yard into a safe, fun refuge for your pet companions. Then you won't be the only happy puppy in your garden.

PLAN

ALL

Fall is just around the corner, which means it will soon be the prime time of the year for planting and landscaping. Get ready for it by cleaning up your potting area and restocking bags of potting soil, amendments, and fertilizers that you will need to have on hand. Wash and sterilize empty pots that you'll need for new plants and get your tools sharpened and in order. If you expect to be sowing seeds for any cool-season annuals in the fall, get your seed-starting gear clean and prepped. You'll be glad in the busy autumn days to come that you got these little tasks out of the way early.

BULBS

Bulb planting and forcing will begin in earnest in another month. Shop now for containers to put them in. Garage sales and thrift stores can be a great source of interesting containers like tins, vintage baking pans, and pieces of china or silverplate. You can also look for glass vases with a wide mouth and narrow neck that can hold hyacinth or narcissus bulbs to be rooted in water.

■ *Hyacinths can be grown in a variety of media, even in a glass of water!*

HERE'S HOW

TO GROW GRASS TO KEEP YOUR CAT HAPPY

Cats (and some dogs) love to nibble at grass, but you may not want to encourage them to chew on the lawn. Planting a pot of grasses especially for your pets will encourage them to leave other plants alone (particularly housecats that sometimes nibble out of boredom). You can sow seeds of just about any annual cereal grass, but many suppliers (see Resources) sell packets of grass mixes especially for cats. These combinations of rye, oats, barley, and wheat are very appealing to cats, especially when you fertilize them with a shot of fish emulsion.

Choose a wide, shallow pot, such as a bulb pot, to sow the seeds in. Fill it up to about an inch from the top with potting soil, then sprinkle the grass seeds over the top. Aim to space the seeds about ¼ inch apart. Sprinkle about ½ inch of potting mix over the seeds and press to get good contact between the soil and seeds. Water well and place where it will get at least a half-day of sun. Seeds should germinate within a week. Wait until the grass is a couple of inches high before giving it to your cats to nibble. Water regularly and feed with a fish emulsion solution every couple of weeks.

EDIBLES

Get ready for the final major harvests that are about to come. Have canning equipment or freezer bags on hand so that you can process your fruits and vegetables as soon as they're picked. You may want to clear out a space somewhere cool and dry, like a basement, to store winter squash or root vegetables where they won't be vulnerable to pests.

PLANT

EDIBLES

In mild-winter parts of the state, you can start planting most root vegetables, including beets, turnips, carrots, and potatoes. You can also sow

■ *Each beet "seed" is actually a cluster of seeds. Once they sprout, they will need to be thinned.*

radish seeds weekly to keep the harvest going through the fall and winter. Plant in full sun or, in the hottest regions, in light shade. Radishes like rich soil with lots of organic matter, so prepare the bed by working in composted manure before planting. Sow seeds ½ inch deep, 1 inch apart, in rows 1 to 1½ feet apart, or just broadcast the seed over the prepared bed. Seeds germinate in five to seven days. When seedlings reach 2 or 3 inches in height, thin out every other plant. If you didn't add compost before planting, feed the seedlings ten days after planting with a fish emulsion solution.

Consistent, even watering is important to achieve the best radish flavor. Keep the bed weeded; floating row covers may be necessary to keep birds and flea beetles from getting to the seedlings. For peak flavor, harvest and eat radishes as soon as the roots reach full size, which can be as early as three weeks or as long as two months. The longer they are left in the ground, the stronger the flavor will grow.

Home growers will find far more varieties available than they would ever find in the store. Round, white-fleshed varieties include 'Crimson Crunch' with bright red skin, 'Pink Punch' with magenta skin, and 'Easter Egg II', which has a mix of white, pink, red, and purple skins. So-called "breakfast radishes" are longer and cylindrical and sweeter in flavor. They include 'French Dressing', 'Red Flame', and 'Petit Dejeuner'. Asian varieties called 'Beauty Heart' and 'Misato Rose Flesh' have watermelon-like colors—light green on the outside and red on the inside.

But if you really favor the more traditional red-on-the-outside, white-on-the-inside radish, look for 'Cherry Belle' and 'Cherriette'. Like beets, radishes are a twofer vegetable: both the greens and the root are edible.

In coastal areas (zones 10 to 11) you can plant bananas now. (In inland areas, a better time to plant is March or April.) With dramatic leaves growing 5 to 9 feet long and colorful flowers (which are also edible) appearing on drooping stalks, bananas (*Musa acuminata*), and their relative, plantains, bring a heavy dose of the tropics to your garden. These herbaceous perennials are fast growers, but they can't tolerate frosts and they need heat to be productive.

■ *Banana plant,* Musa *'Lady Finger', grows in zones 10 and 11.*

While standard varieties can grow to 20 feet, dwarf varieties, topping out at 7 to 15 feet, are best for home gardens, and they can even be grown in large containers. Recommended dwarf varieties include 'Dwarf Cavendish', 'Dwarf Brazilian', 'Enana Gigante', 'Goldfinger', 'Ice Cream', 'Apple', 'Williams', 'Dwarf Red Jamaican', and 'Rajapuri'. Standard varieties, which grow 18 to 20 feet tall, include 'Red Jamaica', 'Lady Finger', and 'Lacatan'. The plantain called 'Orinoco' grows to 20 feet, but a dwarf version is also available.

Plant bananas near a warm, south-facing wall to protect them from wind and frosts. Most varieties require full sun, although some do well in partial shade. They prefer slightly acidic soil (pH 5.5–6.5) amended with lots of compost. Plant each rhizome in a 3-by-2-foot hole. If planting multiples, space dwarf varieties 10 feet apart and standard varieties 15 feet apart.

Bananas want to believe they're in the tropics even if they aren't, and that means rich soil, lots of moisture, and heavy feeding. Water regularly and mulch to keep them from drying out. Standing water will cause the roots to rot, but occasional deep watering is necessary to help leach excess salts from the soil. Fertilize monthly with a balanced fertilizer. Make sure they are protected in the winter. Bananas will freeze at 28 degrees Fahrenheit, although plantains are a bit hardier.

Banana plants spread by suckers and underground roots, forming clumps up to 10 feet wide if you don't control them. Only let one stalk grow the first year and in later years prune out all but one or two stalks. It takes twelve to eighteen months for a stalk to start flowering.

Scale, aphids, and sooty mold can be a problem but are best managed by controlling ants' access to the banana plant. The easiest way to do this is by applying a sticky barrier around the base of each stalk.

Bananas form in clusters called *hands*. After fruit has set, remove the spent flowers at the end of the bunch to lighten the weight on the stalk. In late summer or early fall (approximately seventy to one-hundred days after bloom) the fruit at the top of the cluster will start to turn yellow. Cut and remove the whole cluster to let them ripen inside at room temperature. If left on the tree, the fruit will split open and rot.

PERENNIALS

Plant bearded irises now through September for spring blooms. Bearded irises require a minimum of six hours of direct sun each day and do best when they have a bit more. They also require well-draining soil or the rhizomes can easily begin to rot. Plant bearded iris so that the top of the rhizome is just above the soil line and the roots are fanned out below. Space them about 16 inches apart and don't mulch directly over the rhizomes.

Hybridizers have released a lot of "reblooming" bearded iris varieties in recent years, which in most parts of California should bloom in both spring and fall. Not all rebloomers bloom on the same schedule, however, and not all will dependably rebloom in all environments. Some varieties may also not rebloom until after the first couple of years in the ground. On the whole, you should get more blooms from reblooming iris, but they also require a bit more attention—more water, more fertilizer, more frequent dividing. Some of the most popular reblooming varieties include 'Immortality', 'Autumn Tryst', and 'Sugar Blues'.

CARE

ALL

Take some time this month to do some cleanup around the garden. Rake up fallen fruit and other debris that otherwise makes a lovely campground for insect pests. Deadhead flowering plants and do light summer pruning to keep pathways clear and borders groomed. Hose down tall shrubs and small trees early on a hot day to wash away dust that might impair photosynthesis. (Do not hose down any plants that show signs of disease. The water splash will easily spread fungal spores and bacteria.)

BULBS

August is the best time to divide naturalizing bulbs, such as alliums, anemones, crocuses, irises,

In preparation to dividing irises, trim back the fans. After separating, let them dry a bit.

muscari, daffodils, and tulips. Dig them up with a trowel or shovel, taking care not to cut into the bulbs. Separate any bulbs that are full size or nearly full size. Smaller bulbs are best left attached to a larger bulb until they're big enough to flower. Check them over carefully for signs of damage or disease and toss out any that don't look healthy or feel heavy in your hand. Be sure to allow the bulbs to dry and store them some place cool and well-ventilated until you're ready to replant them.

EDIBLES

If you planted sweet potatoes in May, they should be ready to harvest any time now (110 to 120 days after planting). To harvest, dig carefully with a garden fork or shovel. Dry the roots in the sun until they are dry enough to brush off the dirt. They then need to be cured someplace that is warm (at least 85 degrees Fahrenheit) and humid for ten to fourteen days before storing in a cool, dry place (not below 55 degrees). The flavor will improve with storage. You can wait to harvest later but you should definitely bring them in before the first frost; if a sudden frost should kill the plants, harvest the tubers immediately.

PERENNIALS

Now through the end of summer is a good time to divide perennials such as bearded iris, cannas, lily of the valley, or any perennial that grows from a rhizome. Most of these perennials should be divided every three to four years. A good way to remember to do it is to do all the dividing each leap year. One exception is reblooming iris varieties, which grow faster and may need to be divided every two to three years.

Begin by digging out the full clump of plants with a garden fork or shovel, taking care not to pierce or slice into the roots and rhizomes. Brush away most of the dirt, then use a hose to wash off the remaining soil so you can clearly see all the rhizomes.

HERE'S HOW

TO CREATE A PET-FRIENDLY AND PET-SAFE GARDEN

It's not hard to make your garden a safe and fun place for dogs and cats, but it does take a little planning and maybe some training. Begin by taking the following steps and use positive reinforcement to keep your pet on his best behavior in your garden.

- Begin by creating a enclosed area that your pet will be allowed to enjoy. That means completely fencing the area to keep your pet in and predators out.

- Provide a shaded place for shelter from the sun. Whether it's a doghouse, a covered deck or porch, or a shady tree, it's essential that your pet have a place to retreat to when the sun becomes too intense.

- Always have clean water available. No pet should be kept outdoors without access to drinking water. Make sure it's clean, cool, and can't be knocked over.

- Be aware of the toxic plants that are in your garden. Most animals seem to know what plants are poisonous and when they do eat the wrong thing, they usually spit it back up in pretty short order. But it's a good idea to be aware of which plants are toxic so that you can either take steps to keep your pets away or at least know what signs to watch for in case of poisoning.

- There's a greater chance that your pet could be poisoned by fertilizers and soil amendments than by toxic plants, so take care to keep all containers of pesticides and fertilizers safely out of your pets' reach. Don't assume that organic products are any safer than synthetic ones. Amendments like bone meal, blood meal, fish emulsion, and cocoa bean hulls used as mulch can smell very appealing but can make an animal very sick.

- Use the carrot-and-stick- approach in selecting plant materials. That means using tall or thorny plants as barriers to keep animals out of certain areas and plants with appealing scents to lure them toward the areas that are pet-friendly. Cats dislike citrus scents but love catnip, catmint, and cat thyme. Dogs may be turned off by natural repellents like citronella grass (*Cymbopogon nardus*) or some scented geraniums like *Pelargonium* 'Citronella'.

- If you designate a particular place in your garden for your pet to use as a bathroom, it's less likely that you'll have to clean up messes all over the yard. You can provide an outdoor litter box for cats to use, and dogs can be trained to use one particular spot. It's essential that you keep the area clean or they won't continue to use it.

- Keep other animals safe from your pets. Adding a bell to your cat's collar can make it harder for him to attack songbirds. It may also be necessary to keep pet chickens in a separate part of the garden or install a barrier to a pond containing fish.

You should be able to break apart most of the rhizomes with just your fingers, but if you need to use a sharp knife to cut into any of them, be sure to disinfect the blade first with a 10 percent bleach solution or disinfectant wipe. Separate the clump into sections that have one or two leaf fans each and a healthy rhizome that is about as big around as your finger with white, healthy-looking roots. Toss out any rhizomes or roots that are soft, mushy, smelly, shriveled, or lightweight for their size, or any that don't have leaf fans. Inspect each rhizome completely for signs of damage from borers (the white larvae of the iris borer moth, which tunnel into the rhizomes) and throw out any damaged rhizomes.

Once you have all the rhizomes divided, cleaned, and inspected, you're ready to replant them. Clip off the leaf fans (the strappy leaves that sprout in a fan-like array from the rhizomes) to 4 to 6 inches in length. This helps the plant redirect its energy into growing more roots. Plant the rhizomes about 16 inches apart, with the roots fanned out and the top part of the rhizome just above the soil line. Water well right after planting.

SHRUBS

Cut back hydrangeas that have just finished blooming, but don't go too crazy with the pruners or you could be taking away some of next year's blooms. Leave at last three buds on each stem. If you want to encourage bigger blooms, cut a few stems all the way to the ground.

WATER

ALL

Even a slight slope in a lawn or flowerbed can lead to a lot of water runoff unless you take steps to prevent it. Not only does that waste water and money, but it also results in uneven watering that can lead to drought-stressed plants at the top of the slope and overwatered plants at the bottom.

■ *Mulching 3 to 4 inches and edging will slow the runoff of water on a hillside garden.*

HERE'S HOW

TO DIVIDE PERENNIALS

Most perennial plants will benefit from being divided every three or four years. Dividing prevents overcrowding and keeps the plants healthy, vigorous, and more prone to flower production. Some plants with deep taproots do not respond well to attempts to divide or replant them. Be sure to give careful thought to using these plants before planting, especially in a small garden.

The best time to divide most plants is spring so they have a full growing season to recover, but some plants are better divided in fall.

Water the soil around the plant a few hours before dividing. Prepare the new planting site before digging so you can plant the new divisions right away. Transplant on a cloudy or even rainy day.

1. *Cut back the foliage on an overgrown perennial by about half to reduce water loss in the transplanting process.*

2. *Use a sharp spade to cut around the plant and gently lift as much of the rootball out of the ground as possible.*

In a dry month like August, any watering you do must be more efficient than that. Follow these tips to water sloping grounds more effectively and evenly:

- For lawns on a slope, regularly aerating and dethatching will improve drainage and allow the water to percolate down through the turf and soil before it runs off.

- In flowerbeds, create one or more berms along the slope to reduce runoff by slowing the downward path of the water. Containers or large stones can also slow the water's run and perhaps hold some back.

- Reset the timer on your irrigation system to water in short bursts with off periods in between when the water can sink in.

- Apply a layer of mulch 3 to 4 inches thick over the area. A woody mulch will have the advantage of absorbing some of the water as it runs down, but even a gravel mulch would slow the course of the water, allowing more of it to seep down into the soil.

It may seem as if watering the landscape will help deter wildfires, but the fire season is so long that watering the landscape is not an effective deterrent. What's really important is to clear dry brush (see October).

FERTILIZE

ANNUALS, PERENNIALS, AND SHRUBS

Continue feeding all plants in flower or in bud. Feed azaleas, camellias, rhododendrons, hydrangeas, and other acid-loving plants with a fertilizer specially formulated for them.

EDIBLES

Add another sidedressing of compost to warm-season annuals, such as tomatoes, peppers, and eggplants.

If you planted peas in July and if your soil is sandy, you can apply a balanced fertilizer now (six

3 *Smaller rootballs can usually be cut into pieces using a sharp knife. Larger clumps can be sliced with a sharp spade or pried apart using two back-to-back garden forks.*

4 *Remove excess soil from the rootball so you can see what you are working with and remove any rotted or damaged roots.*

5 *Replant the new plants as soon as possible at the same depth the plant was growing at or slightly higher to allow for settling, and water the soil thoroughly. If you can't replant the same day, pot up the divisions and keep well watered until they are established.*

weeks following planting). If your soil isn't sandy, however, skip the feeding. Peas can generally create enough nitrogen on their own.

ROSES

Apply the monthly feeding for all roses. In cooler parts of the state (zones 7 and below), this will be the last feeding for the year so that roses can get ready to harden off for winter.

PROBLEM-SOLVE

HOUSEPLANTS

In the warmer weather you may find tiny black flying insects creating a nuisance in your home. If you trace them back to the soil in your houseplant containers, the problem is most likely fungus gnats (*Orfelia* and *Bradysia* species). Female fungus gnats like to lay their eggs in moist environments like potting soil. The adult fungus gnats aren't themselves a threat to plants, but the larvae that hatch from their eggs will feed on plant roots, and if the infestation is severe enough, they can do serious damage to a plant.

There are several ways to control fungus gnat infestations, depending on how severe the situation is. You can use yellow sticky traps to trap the adult flying gnats. Because the life cycle of the gnats runs about seventeen days, this kind of control will reduce or eliminate the population over two to three weeks. You can also remove the top ½ to 1 inch of topsoil in your houseplant containers, replace it with fresh sterile potting soil, and top it with a layer of a mulch-like gravel or decorative marbles that prevent the adult gnats from getting to the soil surface to lay eggs.

For more severe infestations there are three organic solutions. One is the application of *Bacillus thuringiensis* subspecies *israelensis* (Bti), also called Gnatrol. This is a naturally occurring bacterium that is toxic only to the fungus gnat larvae, not the adults or eggs, so it will need to be applied repeatedly for continued control. Other options are the release of *Hypoaspis* predatory mites or *Steinernema feltiae* nematodes, which must be purchased by mail order. Of these options, the nematodes are best for long-term control.

To make your houseplants less gnat-friendly, make sure the soil is well-draining and that you remove standing water from saucers as well as any decaying vegetation.

LAWNS

Most lawn diseases are usually preventable with regular lawn maintenance, but sometimes fungi, the most common cause of lawn diseases, get the upper hand. Often, dethatching and aeration are enough to keep diseases in check, but sometimes you'll need to apply a fungicide. Be aware, however, that fungicides will not only kill the fungus causing the disease but also the beneficial insects and other organisms that a healthy lawn depends on. For that reason, fungicides should be applied as a last resort and sparingly.

But before you can treat a diseased lawn, you must first identify the disease. Use the following information to help you pinpoint what's ailing your lawn and plan an appropriate course of action:

- **Brown patch:** The primary symptom is brown patches that grow up to 2 feet across, sometimes with the center of the patch recovering to create a ring effect. This disease is commonly found in areas with high humidity and on shaded lawns. Bermuda, Kentucky bluegrass, centipedegrass, bentgrass, St. Augustine, and ryegrasses are all susceptible. A regular practice of aeration and dethatching will usually disrupt the cycle, but you can all reseed with disease-resistant turfgrass varieties.

- **Fairy rings:** Appearing in lawns that are heavy with organic matter or wood debris, fairy rings show as circular patches of dark green grass surrounding lighter green grass. There may or may not be mushrooms present in the ring. The best treatment is aeration and dethatching, watering well, and maintaining a fertilizing schedule. There is no fungicidal treatment for fairy rings.

- **Rust:** If your lawn has an orange, rusty appearance, then it probably has rust. To tell for sure, take a white tissue and rub some

◼ *Fairy rings can be treated with aeration and dethatching to improve drainage.*

of the affected blades of grass. If it shows an orange dust on the tissue, then it is certainly rust. Follow the usual maintenance techniques of aeration and morning watering to control the problem in addition to more frequent mowing and removing the clippings. Fertilize but be careful not to overdo it.

• **Powdery mildew:** The same fungus that can affect your roses can also bedevil your lawn. Powdery mildew appears as though your lawn has been sprinkled with a light coating of flour. It is most common in lawns that are shaded, and Kentucky bluegrass is the most susceptible. While roses and other plants are usually not seriously harmed by powdery mildew, it can cause lawns to wither and

die where affected. Improving drainage and reducing the shade over the lawn can help, as can watering in the morning so there is time for the water to be absorbed during the day.

Sometimes, though, brown patches are due to pests rather than disease. White grubs are the larvae of beetles, usually 1 inch to 1½ inch long with six legs. The grubs attack the roots of grasses, leaving dead, brown patches that can be pulled up easily, and become most prevalent in late summer. After removing the dead patch, if you find more than one grub per square foot in the area, you will need to treat the lawn with parasitic nematodes. (See April for information on controlling pests using parasitic nematodes.)

August ◼ 161

September

It's time to get reacquainted with your shovel. If you think that spring was a flurry of planting and that your shovel and trowel had become permanent fixtures in your hands, you ain't seen nothing yet. Fall is the hands-down best time for planting most landscape plants. Perennials, shrubs, trees, vines, groundcovers, even lawns—all do best when planted in the fall. And in most parts of the state, edible gardening gets a second life as cool-season vegetables and season-extending cold frames and row covers continue the bounty through autumn and into winter.

I like to think of autumn gardening as a kind of do-over. It's a chance to take another run at correcting problems or improving disappointing views. By adding or subtracting plants, we can breathe fresh life into a garden scene that's become static or overwhelming. Dividing and transplanting perennials has the same effect as rearranging the furniture in your house—old things become new again and what might have seemed cluttered before now appears tidy. Planting trees or hedges can change the bones of a garden—like adding a new wall that redirects the flow of a room. And all those changes can take place with the aid of just one tool—your shovel.

As we enter the final months of the dry season, you may feel both a sense of urgency and a renewed energy regarding your garden plans. You may need to hire help to complete a big project or consult a professional to work out a design problem you haven't been able to solve on your own. But you might be surprised at the new solutions that suddenly appear so clearly in the autumn light when all seemed murky and confused in the spring.

This is a good time to revisit the garden plans you made back in January. What projects remain undone? What dreams are still yet to be achieved? And with your shovel in hand, what can you accomplish in these last few months of the year that will bring you closer to the garden of your dreams?

PLAN

ALL

As the days are beginning to get noticeably shorter this is a good time to evaluate the outdoor lighting, especially around walkways and entryways. Installing more lighting or adjusting the timer schedule can prevent a mishap or dangerous slip-and-fall. Consider installing energy-efficient LED lighting or solar lighting.

BULBS

This is one of those times that makes gardeners rub their hands together with glee. It's time to shop for spring-blooming bulbs, such as daffodils, tulips,

BAD BULB

GOOD BULB

■ *Select bulbs that are full and firm, and reject those that have cracks or soft spots.*

and hyacinths. If you order bulbs from a catalog, choose a reputable dealer and keep in mind that paying more for bigger bulbs will mean bigger and healthier blooms in the spring. If you shop from a local garden center, choose bulbs that are firm and heavy for their size. It's not necessary for them to have their onion skin-like covering (fancifully called a "tunic") intact, but avoid bulbs that looked scarred. They may have had wounds that allowed viruses or other pathogens to enter. Store your bulbs in a dry, well-ventilated area until you're ready to plant them.

EDIBLES

As you clear out the warm-season crops and prepare to plant cool-season crops, it's important to have a crop-rotation plan in place. To really achieve the main goal of crop rotation (that is, breaking the cycle of pests and diseases), you need to consider not just individual plants but plant *families*. By siting plants so that they don't grow in the same spot where another member of the same plant family grew the previous season (that is, alternating plant families), pests and diseases that attack a particular plant family are less likely to lurk in the soil from one season to the next. Refer to this list of plant families when mapping out your rotation plan:

- Amaranth family (*Amaranthaceae*): Beet, spinach, Swiss chard

- Onion family (*Amaryllidaceae*): Garlic, leek, onion, shallot

- Carrot family (*Apiaceae*): Carrot, celery, cilantro, dill, parsley, parsnip

- Cole family (*Brassicaceae*): Broccoli, cabbage, cauliflower, collard, kale, mustard, radish, turnip

- Sunflower family (*Compositae*): Artichoke, chickory, endive, lettuce

- Gourd family (*Cucurbitaceae*): Cucumber, melon, pumpkin, squash

- Legume family (*Leguminosae*): Bean, pea, soybean (edamame)

- Grass family (*Poaceae*): Corn, popcorn

- Nightshade family (*Solanaceae*): Eggplant, pepper, potato, tomatillo, tomato

LAWNS

Having survived another long, dry summer and the accompanying water bills, maybe you're ready now to consider reducing the size of your lawn or replacing it with a more drought-tolerant planting of succulents or Mediterranean plants. Check with your local water utility to see if you can qualify for a rebate or other assistance for replacing a water-thirsty lawn with more sustainable landscaping.

PERENNIALS, ROSES, AND SHRUBS

Identify the plants that will need to be transplanted this fall. You may choose to transplant a plant because it has outgrown its location, because the sun exposure has changed where it is, or because it's just not thriving in its current spot. I sometimes find that my transplant plans look like a long chain reaction where I want to move one plant to a spot that will be vacated by another plant, which will move to a spot to be vacated by a different plant, and so on. Writing out or drawing up how each stage of the move will happen helps to keep it all straight so that each plant lands exactly where you intended with the least overall disturbance.

PLANT

ALL

This month begins the best time of year for planting, particularly for permanent landscape plants. Anything planted in September, October, and November will get the benefit of the rainy season to follow to help establish a healthy root system before spring induces the plant to grow. Fall planting also allows you the financial benefit of buying smaller plants: A plant from a 1-gallon container planted in the fall will quickly catch up in size to a more expensive plant from a 5-gallon container. By midspring you would probably not even notice a difference in size, but the savings can be substantial.

HERE'S HOW

TO IDENTIFY INVASIVE PLANTS

In the flurry of fall planting, take the time to make sure that what you're planting is not considered invasive in your region. Nurseries are getting better at not stocking, or at least labeling, plants that are super-aggressive growers, but you should do your own research before planting.

The best resource is the California Invasive Plant Council (Cal-IPC). The council identifies plants that have proven to be problems in terms of displacing native plants and wildlife, consuming too much water, or enhancing flood or wildfire risk. Some of the most troublesome invasive plants in California include crimson fountaingrass (*Pennisetum setaceum*), Scotch broom (*Cystius scoparius*), fennel (*Foeniculum vulgare*), and English ivy (*Hedera helix*). Look to the Cal-IPC website (www.cal-ipc.org) to search the current inventory of invasive plants, find out what's invasive in your area, and identify noninvasive alternatives.

■ *Crimson fountaingrass,* Pennisetum setaceum, *may look nice, but it's highly invasive in California.*

ANNUALS

Plant seeds of cool-season annuals like calendula, Iceland poppies, and pansies. In mild-winter areas, sow seeds of sweet peas now. (In cold-winter regions, wait until February to April.) Establish a support structure (trellis or netting) before planting. Work compost into the soil, then plant seeds 1 inch deep and 2 to 3 inches apart. When seedlings are few inches tall, thin to 4 to 5 inches apart and mulch.

BULBS

You can start planting many spring-flowering bulbs now (see October for more information on planting bulbs), but it's most important to get the earlier flowering ones in the ground this month. This includes many of the South African plants that will bloom as early as January. Start planting babiana, chasmanthe, crocosmia, freesia, ixia, sparaxis, tritonia, and watsonia. For smaller bulbs like these, the general rule is to plant them a little more deeply than twice the height of the bulb.

EDIBLES

It's time to swap out those worn-out warm-season crops that have given their all for you and replace them with new cool-season plants. Fall is the time to grow vegetables that can't take the heat. Here are some of the best choices for an autumn vegetable garden:

- Arugula
- Beet
- Broccoli
- Broccoli rabe
- Cabbage
- Carrot
- Cauliflower
- Kale
- Leeks
- Lettuce
- Onion
- Radish
- Spinach
- Swiss chard
- Turnip

■ *For flowers as early as January, plant bulbs like this crocosmia now.*

■ *Root vegetables, such as carrots, parsnips, radishes, turnips, and beets, are easy to grow from seed, as long as you have relatively loose, crumbly soil. If there are a lot of rocks in your soil, pick them out before planting. If, when your soil is wet, a handful of it feels sticky like pottery clay, mix some sand and compost into the soil to loosen it up.*

■ *Check the soil pH before planting seeds. If it is lower than 6.0, sprinkle garden lime on the soil according to the package instructions and rake it in. Then, sow the seeds in garden rows according to package spacing instructions, and cover the seeds by sprinkling ¼ inch of seed-starting mix on top of them. Water the seeds daily until they sprout. Water two or three times a week after that.*

Whether you plant seeds or seedlings, the process of preparing the bed is essentially the same. As with your summer vegetable garden, find a planting area with as much sunlight as possible. When selecting a site for cool-season crops, however, keep in mind that areas previously shaded by deciduous trees and shrubs may get sufficient sunlight when those plants have shed their leaves. Those spots can be perfect for crops like Swiss chard, spinach, lettuce, and other greens that would bolt (send up a seed stalk) with too much heat.

It's usually not necessary to rototill a new bed. Just clear the area of weeds and other debris and make sure the soil is loose. If you'll be planting root crops, however, make sure the soil is loose to a depth of as much as 12 inches and free of rocks and other materials that could deform the roots. Add generous amounts of garden compost or composted chicken or cattle manure and work it lightly into the soil. Map out your plantings, leaving paths to access the entire bed if the area is large. Once the plants are in the ground, spread 3 to 4 inches of mulch around the plants to suppress weeds and cover the paths.

■ *Swiss chard is considered to be one of the healthiest vegetables you can grow.*

Plant Swiss chard now and you should be able to harvest leaves through the autumn and beyond. A relative of the beet, Swiss chard (*Beta vulgaris chicla*) is grown for its nutrient-rich leaves and stalks, which are loaded with Vitamins A, C, E, and K plus fiber, magnesium, manganese, and potassium. It's a great-looking plant besides, especially in its more colorful forms, and works well tucked in among ornamental plants.

Chard prefers cool, mild conditions and can tolerate light frosts. In colder areas, it can also be grown as a container plant or under floating row covers to sustain it through heavier frosts.

At this time of year, it's best to direct-seed Swiss chard outdoors in full sun. Work compost into the soil before planting, then sow seeds ½ inch deep and 2 inches apart in rows 10 inches apart. You can also broadcast seeds over a bed. Tamp soil down firmly over seeds to make sure they make good contact with the soil. Apply a fish emulsion solution and keep the bed evenly moist. Seeds

should germinate in five to seven days. When seedlings are 2 to 3 inches high, thin plants to 1 foot apart. Don't let the thinnings go to waste. You can use them as you would any baby greens.

Swiss chard is available in the classic white-stemmed varieties as well as shades of deep red, golden yellow, and vivid orange. If there is a difference in taste between the white and the colored stems, I have not been able to discern it. Aside from the color of the stem, and in some cases the darkness of the green leaves, the main difference is that the white-stemmed varieties often have wide stems. Favored white-stemmed varieties include 'Barese', 'Fordhook Giant', 'French Swiss', and 'Italian Silver Rib'. Colored-rib varieties include 'Bright Yellow', 'Golden Sunrise', 'Rhubarb', 'Ruby', 'Scarlet Charlotte', 'Pot of Gold', and the rainbow mixes 'Bright Lights', 'Rainbow', and 'Neon Glow'.

Autumn is a great time to plant lettuces. There are four main types of lettuces. Crisphead

TO PLANT COOL-SEASON TRANSPLANTS

Vegetable gardening doesn't end when summer fades and cool temperatures return. Fall and spring are second seasons for gardeners. Cool-weather vegetables grow fast, and most of them are easy to start from seed right in the garden. Here's how to get more out of your vegetable gardens by growing greens, broccoli, cabbage, and cover crops from seeds or from transplants.

1 Prepare the soil and set out the plants according to spacing instructions on the plant tag. Broccoli, cabbage, and kale plants need 12 to 18 inches of space between them. Lettuce only needs 8 inches of space between plants.

2 Spread mulch around the vegetable transplants. This will help keep water in the soil during those hot, Indian summer fall days. In cooler areas, the mulch acts to insulate the vegetables, helping them stay warmer longer into the fall. Straw is good for vegetable gardens because it is lightweight. Most garden centers and home-improvement stores sell bales of wheat straw. Just ask for it if you don't see it.

lettuces are tight, round heads like 'Great Lakes', 'Summertime', and 'Nevada'. Butterheads are looser heads like 'Bibb', 'Buttercrunch', 'Tom Thumb', and 'Mignonette'. Loose-leaf lettuces are very loose leaves in a rosette, such as 'Black-Seeded Simpson', 'Green Ice', 'Oak Leaf', 'Salad Bowl', 'Prizehead', and 'Ruby'. The last group is romaine, which grows in erect, cylindrical bunches and includes 'Medallion', 'Olga', and 'Parris Island' varieties. While all lettuces prefer cooler weather, loose-leaf and romaine varieties are more heat-tolerant than the others.

Plant in full sun or in partial shade in the hottest regions. The soil should be loose, well-drained, and amended with organic matter. Before planting, add compost or an all-purpose fertilizer and work it several inches into the soil. Broadcast the seed and barely cover it with a light sprinkling of soil. Tamp down to ensure seeds make contact with the soil and water until moist. Seeds germinate in five to fourteen days. Thin seedlings to 6 inches apart or more, depending on the variety.

Mesclun mixes are an assortment of young salad greens. Broadcast seed in blocks and do not thin since they will be harvested while still young. To prolong the harvest, repeat the sowings every two weeks throughout the cool spring and fall weather.

Keep the lettuce bed lightly but consistently moist. Feed with a light fish emulsion at the time of planting and again six weeks later. Lettuce beds can be very appealing to snails, slugs, and earwigs, which would just love to beat you to the harvest. Liberal sprinkling of diatomaceous earth can keep them in check.

One of the biggest challenges to growing lettuce can be dealing with sudden heat waves that can quickly cause the lettuce to bolt. There are a few varieties, however, that are more heat-tolerant than others, such as 'Deer Tongue' and 'Marvel of Four Seasons', both butterheads; 'Reine de Glace', a crisphead; and 'Slowbolt', a loose-leaf lettuce.

If you want to add a little more zing to your salads, consider adding some other gourmet greens. Arugula (*Eruca sativa*, also called "rocket") is a peppery green that you can grow and harvest much the same way you do mesclun. If you leave a plant or two to grow to maturity and go to seed, it will reseed, and you'll have a ready-made crop coming up the next growing season. A nutty-flavored alternative is mache (*Valerianella locusta*, also called "lamb's lettuce" or "corn salad"). This is another cool-weather crop that can be sown in midsummer in cold-winter regions or fall through winter in mild-winter regions. It's slower growing than lettuce, taking up to 90 days to mature, but it is more cold-hardy, resistant to mildew, and it will reseed.

In most parts of the state there is also time to get in another crop of potatoes. (See March for information on planting potatoes.)

PERENNIALS & SHRUBS

In fall you almost have carte blanche to plant perennials. Many of the perennials and shrubs that you'll see in the nurseries throughout the year when they're in bloom can be planted now for later bloom.

If you're looking for plants that can provide multiple seasons of color, try *Euphorbia polychroma*, which has springtime flowers and bracts that change from yellow-green to shades of red, purple, and orange in the fall. Or try a sedum like the popular 'Autumn Joy', which has a long bloom period (August to November) during which the blooms change from pink to copper.

This is also a good time to bring new textures and forms into the garden by planting ornamental grasses. There are a number of grasses that grow in feathery or strappy clumps that stand out strikingly among other landscape plants, but do some investigating before planting any kind of fountain grass (*Pennisetum setaceum*). Some varieties can be invasive in some regions. Mexican fountain grass in particular is lovely, especially when planted *en masse*. But those feathery fronds are loaded with seeds and you (and your neighbors) will soon have Mexican fountain grass growing out of every nook and cranny in your garden.

ROSES

In warmer parts of the state (zones 7 and above) you can plant container-grown roses. Do not

fertilize following planting to avoid encouraging a lot of tender new growth before the colder weather comes.

CARE

ALL

Begin the fall cleanup this month and clear away as much debris as possible early. Remove fading annual plants as well as fallen leaves, flowers, and fruit. In cooler regions, you may want to start cleaning and covering or storing outdoor furniture.

Do not do heavy pruning at this time. Pruning will stimulate new growth right at the time when many plants should be slowing down or going dormant.

BULBS

Potted amaryllis bulbs that you want to rebloom should begin their dormancy period now. Help

NEMATODES: FRIEND OR FOE?

Sometimes the reason that plants thrive or die has something to do with an agent you'll never actually be able to see, at least not with the naked eye. Lurking in your soil are microscopic worms, some of which are beneficial and some of which are parasitic. The beneficial nematodes are predators of other soil pests, like cutworms. Parasitic nematodes, such as root-knot nematodes, suck the sap from roots, inhibiting a plant's ability to take in nutrients, and can also spread viruses. If you have a serious problem with nematodes, you can steam or solarize the soil, but that will kill the beneficials as well as the parasites.

A better approach is to try to achieve a balance with nematodes. You do this by planting nematode- and disease-resistant plant varieties and by rotating crops annually. Adding organic matter or planting cover crops that fix nitrogen into the soil (such as fava beans, an edible cover crop) also helps to keep the parasitic nematode population in check and the soil healthy.

■ *Tomatoes that aren't fully ripe can be harvested by the branch and ripened indoors.*

them along by withholding water and moving them where rainfall won't hit them. Remove all foliage after it has died back.

EDIBLES

Tomatoes are reaching the end of their productive season. Keep one eye on the ripening fruits so you can pick them as soon as they're ready and one eye on the weather forecast. If the temperatures are starting to dip, you may want to clip off entire branches of still-green fruit and bring them indoors to finish ripening. The flavor will probably not be as good as those ripened on the bush in the sun, but they'll certainly taste better than a store-bought tomato. You can then discard the tomato plant.

LAWNS

If you have a Bermudagrass lawn and you didn't dethatch it in the spring, do it now. If the thatch is especially thick it may be necessary to dethatch twice a year.

PERENNIALS

Keep cutting back, dividing, and cleaning up perennials. Clivia, iris, daylily, and agapanthus are among the perennials that need dividing every three to four years. You'll know it's time to divide when they start producing fewer flowers and just appear much too crowded. Most perennials can be divided by simply digging up the clump with a garden fork and separating the clump into sections using your fingers, or a knife or shovel. Closely examine all sections before replanting and discard any parts that look mushy, shriveled, diseased, or damaged. The section at the center of the clump may be spent and, if so, can be discarded as well.

ROSES

Stop deadheading roses in cooler parts of the state (zones 6 and below). In warmer areas, you can continue deadheading to encourage repeat blooms for the rest of the month.

■ *Lift and divide bearded irises every few years, about six weeks after blooming.*

WATER

ALL

September is often the hottest month in California so special attention should be paid to watering throughout the garden. Continue to water in the early mornings. During a heat wave, be prepared to adjust the irrigation schedule or do some hand-watering to supplement the usual schedule. Container plants are particularly vulnerable to the heat and dry out quicker than plants in the ground. Water them more frequently and watch closely for signs of wilt.

New plantings should also be watered regularly and monitored closely for drought stress. Even native plants and other plants that are considered "drought tolerant" should be watered regularly for the first year in order to get well established.

EDIBLES

In cold-winter regions, stop watering grape vines at this time to help nudge the plants into dormancy before the really cold weather arrives.

You can be a little stingier with water for warm-season crops that are coming to the end of their life cycle. Tomatoes, peppers, eggplants, and other vegetables that have almost completed their harvests don't need a lot more water at this point, and you'll soon be removing the plants all together, so there's no point in wasting too much water on them.

LAWNS

Continue watering the lawn regularly, particularly if you will be fertilizing it this month. It's important that the lawn not be drought-stressed when the fertilizer is applied.

FERTILIZE

ALL

Newly planted annuals and perennials can be fertilized, but wait until they've been in the ground for at least two weeks and make sure they are well watered and showing no signs of transplant shock before feeding.

LAWNS

Fall fertilizing should accomplish two things: Greening up a lawn that's been stressed from summer heat, and getting the roots in the best shape to survive the winter and come back healthy in the spring. Something like a 20-8-8 fertilizer will take care of the first job, but a 13-25-12 formula will do the trick for the roots. You may not find fertilizers with these exact numbers, but that's fine. It's the proportions that matter most.

The best approach is to feed your lawn once in September with a high-nitrogen fertilizer and then again in November with the high-phosphorous formula. Follow the directions on the fertilizer package for how to apply it and how much to use. Never apply fertilizer to a dry lawn; always make sure it has been watered well in advance of feeding.

HERE'S HOW

TO CRACK THE N-P-K CODE

To determine what kind of fertilizer to use, you have to understand the meaning behind the N-P-K numbers you'll see on the fertilizer packages. N is for nitrogen, which promotes green growth; P is for phosphorous, which helps aids root development; and K is for potassium, which supports overall health and vigor. While the N-P-K numbers don't strictly translate to the exact elemental composition, they do represent the general make-up of the fertilizer. So a 20-0-0 fertilizer is heavy in nitrogen but without phosphorous or potassium. A 10-10-10 fertilizer would be considered a balanced fertilizer, with roughly equal proportions of each nutrient. (See April for more information on choosing and using fertilizers.)

1 Ready to Use

2 FERTIFEED

3 *All Purpose Plant Food*

4 12-4-8

FertiFeed Ready To Use All-Purpose Plant Food
Net Weight 4lb. 12oz. (2.15kg)

GUARANTEED ANALYSIS

5 Total Nitrogen (N)..12%
    12.0% Urea Nitrogen

6 Available Phosphate (P_2O_5)....................................4%

7 Soluable Potash (K2O)..8%

Manganese (Mn)...0.05%
    0.05% Chelated Manganese (Mn)

8 Zinc (Zn) 0.05%
    0.05% Chelated Zinc (Zn)

9 Inert Ingredients..76%

Information regarding the contents and levels of metals in this product is available on the Internet at http://www.regulatory-info-sc.com.

KEEP OUT OF REACH OF CHILDREN

1 **Type of fertilizer:** *"Ready to use" means that you can directly apply according to the instructions. Fertilizer marked as "concentrated" has to be mixed with water before spreading it on plants.*

2 **The fertilizer brand name:** *There are different brands of fertilizer, just as there are different brands of clothes.*

3 **Intended use:** *This tells you which plants the fertilizer is for. Use different fertilizers for grass, vegetables, and flowers.*

4 **Fertilizer analysis:** *Every fertilizer has three numbers on the bag, separated by dashes. This is called the analysis, or sometimes the N-P-K number. The first number is the percentage of nitrogen in the fertilizer, the second number is the percentage of phosphorous, and the third number is the percentage of potassium. This number is also a ratio. For example, a fertilizer with analysis 10-10-10 has a ratio of 1:1:1; in other words, the same percentage of available nitrogen, phosphorous, and potassium in the fertilizer. A 12-4-8 fertilizer has three parts nitrogen to one part phosphorous and two parts potassium.*

5 **Nitrogen content:** *This number indicates the percentage of nitrogen in the contents of the package. In this example, a 4-pound bag with 12 percent nitrogen has .48 pounds of nitrogen.*

6 **Phosphorous content:** *This shows the amount of phosphorous in the fertilizer.*

7 **Potassium content:** *This number shows the amount of potassium in the fertilizer. This fertilizer example has .32 pounds of potassium in a 4-pound bag. If you need to apply 2 pounds of potassium per 1,000 square feet, you would need 6.25 bags of this fertilizer.*

8 **Nutrients other than N-P-K:** *These are micronutrients, other nutrients that plants need in smaller amounts than nitrogen, phosphorous, and potassium.*

9 **Other ingredients:** *Other ingredients make the fertilizer easier to spread.*

One easy way to make sure that your lawn is getting a steady diet all year long is to use a mulching mower and leave the grass clippings on the lawn. They'll break down and slowly feed the grass, keeping it healthier and greener and reducing the need to add supplemental nutrients.

PERENNIALS

Give tropical plants their last feeding of the year this month. Next month they will need to slow down their growing so that they're not producing tender new foliage just as the cold weather and possibility of frosts descend. Do not use a timed-release fertilizer for this feeding; instead feed them with something fast-acting

and preferably higher in potassium and lower in nitrogen. The potassium will contribute to their overall vigor and health without encouraging green growth.

ROSES

In warmer parts of the state (zones 8 and above), apply the last feeding for the year to all roses. After this final feeding, the roses will need to begin hardening off for winter.

TREES

Citrus trees should get their last feeding of the year this month. It's best to use a fertilizer specially formulated for citrus, and if the tree is showing signs of chlorosis (yellowing between the leaf veins), a foliar feeding will get the nutrients into the plant more quickly.

PROBLEM-SOLVE

ALL

Sometimes the biggest pests are the tiniest. Spider mites are so small that they're nearly impossible to see with the naked eye. You can use a small magnifying glass to see the spider mites themselves, but you can easily recognize the sticky webs they spin around the leaves and stems of your plants with no help at all.

The webbing isn't really the problem, however. The damage comes from the holes the mites pierce into the undersides of leaves in order to suck out juices. These pests may be tiny and the holes they make may be tiny as well, but they reproduce rapidly, with females laying hundreds of eggs at a time. As their population explodes, you'll find that more of your plants suffer damage. In addition, spider mites can spread a number of diseases from plant to plant. They feed on a wide range of plants, both ornamental and edible, and evergreen and deciduous. They thrive more in warm, dry climates than cold, moist ones so California summers are perfect for spider mites to set up camp.

If you see tiny brown spots on the undersides of yellowing leaves, you can suspect spider mites as the culprits. The presence of their webbing

■ *Yellowing leaves is a sign of chlorosis.*

■ *Spider mites are tiny but can cause big damage to plants.*

on the plants will confirm it. If you find them on only one or two plants, you can wash them away with a blast of the hose, or a more careful washing of the leaves (on both sides) and stems with insecticidal soap. For more serious infestations, you can spray with Neem oil or (during the dormant season) horticultural oil or release some of the spider mite's natural predators, such as lacewings, lady beetles, and minute pirate bugs.

TREES

Citrus trees will always drop the occasional fruit, but if you find that the fruit drop on your tree is getting excessive, it's most likely due to over- or underwatering. In summer when weather turns hot, dry and windy, flowers and fruit may drop if the tree is drought-stressed. If fruit drops but also splits, that's more likely a sign of overwatering.

Leaf drop may also indicate a watering problem. Watering a drought-stressed tree too much all at once can cause leaves to turn yellow and drop within a few days of watering.

To correct the problem, follow these guidelines:

- For trees in the ground, water deeply once a week.

- For trees in containers outdoors, water thoroughly once or twice a week.

- For citrus grown indoors, provide ¼ to ½ gallon one or twice a week.

October

Gardens are made for sharing. We may appreciate them most often for the privacy and serenity they provide, but in the midst of the bounty that October brings, the blessings of a garden are really just too abundant to keep to ourselves. They must be shared.

You may share your garden first of all with your family, but not just as a place to relax, to play, or to party. Involve your children in maintaining the garden and it becomes a family affair. As more children are introduced to gardening through their school gardens, they will likely take more of an interest in their home garden and you can tend it together.

Perhaps you share your garden with your neighbors by creating a lovely, lively front yard for them to enjoy walking by, or by offering free divisions or cuttings or seeds from some of your favorite plants for them to include in their own gardens.

If you're happy to share your harvest, keep in mind that your local food bank would be happy to receive your excess fruits and vegetables. The nonprofit Ample Harvest (www.ampleharvest.org) makes it easy for you to connect with a food bank in your community and determine where and when they're open to receive your donations.

You could share your entire garden by opening it for a garden tour. This is the time of year when garden clubs, schools, and other organizations are planning next spring's garden tours. If you're really pleased with how your garden is shaping up or if you've successfully incorporated native plants and sustainable practices, let people take a look and learn from your experiences.

This month you'll be busy planting, cleaning, raking, and harvesting, but as you work, keep an eye open for what you can pass along to someone else. When you share from your garden, you experience it differently and appreciate all it offers even more. What you give away will make what you keep seem even more bountiful.

PLAN

ALL

Your soil has been working hard all spring and summer, and this is a good time to give it another checkup. If you ran a soil test earlier in the year and added amendments, retesting now will tell you how well those amendments are working. If you haven't tested it yet, do it now so you can make adjustments that will have time to take effect before spring. (See March for information on testing your soil's pH and nutrient levels.)

If you've been keeping a garden journal, this is a good time to make sure your notes are up to date. Note when different plants were installed and when they were fertilized or pruned. For your edible garden, note the varieties you planted and how successful they were. Did they yield as much as you expected? If not, do you know why? Was the quality what you hoped for or should you try another variety next year? Tracking successes, failures, and problems to watch will help you make better choices for your garden in the future.

PLANT

ANNUALS

Fall is the best time for sowing California poppy (*Eschscholtzia californica*) seeds in most parts of the state. (Cold-winter regions do best to wait until April.) If the traditional bright orange California poppy doesn't suit your color palette, there are many more options now from which to choose. Colors range from cream to rosy pink and copper to deep red. Broadcast the seeds over cleared, prepared soil, cover with a light layer (no more than ¼ inch) of soil, and press to make contact between the soil and seeds. Water well and keep the soil moist as the seedlings emerge. Seeds should germinate in seven to fourteen days. Keep watered until established; mature plants will be very drought tolerant but will be helped by occasional watering. If flowers the following spring and summer are left to set seed, the plants will self-sow seeds for another year's blooms.

■ *California poppies will reseed easily and return year after year.*

BULBS

I confess that for one reason or another I am *always* late getting my spring bulbs planted. More than once I have seen January roll around with my bulbs still sitting on the shelf, patiently waiting to get in the ground. I have found that they are remarkably forgiving of my tardiness, and they still reward me with remarkable blooms each year, but this is one of those "do as I say, not as I do" moments—this is the best time for planting spring bulbs, and you'll find (as I do when I finally get my act together) that it doesn't take very long. Unless, of course, you've shown absolutely no sales resistance and purchased hundreds of bulbs, in which case you should resign yourself to having some very dirty knees this month.

Bulbs need excellent drainage. If you have sandy soil, as I do, you're golden, but if you have heavy clay soil, be prepared to amend with organic matter (to a depth of at least 12 inches) to improve soil drainage, or plant your bulbs only in containers. Plant the bulbs at a depth that is two to three times the diameter of a bulb. In other words, a daffodil bulb that is 3 inches wide should be planted 6 to 9 inches deep. It's a good idea to plant them even a bit deeper in sandy soil. It's a good idea to mix a little granular fertilizer (not bone meal, which is no longer as nutrient-rich as it was in the past) into the soil at the bottom of the hole before placing the bulbs.

Aside from spring-blooming bulbs, there is a late summer, early autumn bloomer that can be planted now as well—the belladonna lily (*Amaryllis belladonna*). Also known provocatively as naked ladies, these South African bulbs send up a cluster of leaves in the winter that then die back completely in early summer. Then in late summer 2- to 3-foot tall bare stalks emerge with clusters of fragrant pink trumpet-shaped flowers.

Plant the bulbs now in full sun in well-draining soil about 1 foot apart with the tops of the bulbs at or slightly above the soil level. In cold-winter areas plant the bulbs slightly below soil level, preferably in a spot that is somewhat protected with a southern exposure. These bulbs will live a long time, don't require supplemental water except during periods of winter drought, and rarely need to be divided. You should get many years of blooms from one planting.

HERE'S HOW

TO PLANT LOTS OF BULBS FAST!

Here's my quick-and-dirty bulb-planting method: Dig a wide hole to the proper depth for the bulb you are planting. Mix the fertilizer into the soil, then take the bulbs in large handfuls and toss them in the air, allowing them to fall into the hole. Turn over any bulbs that land upside down or sideways (most spring bulbs should be planted pointed side up, flat side down), but leave them exactly where they fell. Cover with soil and you're done. In the spring you'll get natural-looking clusters of blooms rather than unnatural-looking rows of uniformly spaced flowers.

TO FORCE SPRING-BLOOMING BULBS

Forcing bulbs is a long-practiced way of thumbing our noses at winter by inducing a little spring to unfold right on our windowsills. It's an incredibly easy process, and it makes a wonderful holiday gift or just an effective talisman against the winter blues.

Most spring bulbs can be forced, but the ones most commonly used are hyacinths, tulips, narcissus, daffodils, grape hyacinths (muscari), and crocuses.

■ *There are special vases specifically for forcing hyacinth bulbs that allow you to see their roots.*

1. Plant the bulbs in shallow containers (usually a depth of 4 inches is sufficient) using a potting mix lightened with perlite or vermiculite (two parts potting mix to one part perlite/vermiculite) and water thoroughly. Some bulbs can be planted with no soil at all. Just fill a shallow container with clean pebbles and add water to the top of the pebbles and nestle the bulbs into the pebbles so that just the bottom of the bulb is touching the water. Similarly, forcing vases that hold a single bulb over the water are often used for hyacinths, allowing the roots to descend into the water while the bulb sits on top.

2. Most spring bulbs require a chilling period after planting; refer to the following table to determine how long to chill each flower type. Bulbs can be chilled in the refrigerator as long as they are protected from gases emitted by other produce that can affect the maturing process of the bulbs. Bulbs can also be chilled outdoors in a cold frame or other location where they will be protected from rain, snow, or wildlife.

Tulips	15–17 weeks chill
Crocus, daffodils, glory-of-the-snow, iris	15 weeks chill
Danford iris, *Iris danfordiae*	14–20 weeks chill
Grape hyacinths	14–15 weeks chill
Hyacinths	11–14 weeks chill
Paperwhite narcissus, *Iris reticulata*	No chilling required

3. After the chill period, move the pots indoors and begin watering regularly. Keep the pots in a cool area until the foliage begins to sprout, then move them to a warmer location with good light, like a sunny windowsill, and enjoy watching the blossoms open. To extend the bloom period, pot up bulbs every two weeks so that the flowering will be staggered over a longer time.

EDIBLES

Continue planting cool-season crops. In mild-winter regions, you can also plant strawberries. (See February for information on planting strawberries.) Artichokes can be planted as dormant roots. (See December for more information on growing artichokes.)

Alliums such as garlic and shallots can be planted now throughout the fall in mild-winter regions to harvest the following summer. (See November for information on planting leeks and onions.) In colder areas where there are hard frosts, plant one month before the ground freezes or in early spring for a fall harvest.

Garlic is divided into two categories: Hardneck and softneck. Hardneck is usually grown in cooler climates and includes 'Rocambole', 'Porcelain', and 'Purple Stripe'. Softneck garlic grows in warmer areas and includes 'Artichoke' (the kind most commonly sold in grocery stores), 'Silverskin', and 'Creole'. Each of those varieties has subvarieties as well. If you want to harvest the flower stalks called *scapes* as well as bulbs, you need to plant a hardneck 'Rocambole' type, such as 'Carpathian', 'German Red', and 'Spanish Roja'.

Garlic grows well throughout California. It appreciates full sun and requires well-draining soil rich in organic matter, but it's not particular about pH level. Garlic can be grown mixed into flower beds and containers. It appears to repel aphids and has natural antifungal and antibiotic properties that are said to make it a good companion plant for fruit trees, lettuces, cabbages, beets, tomatoes, and more. It appears to sometimes stunt the growth of beans and peas so should not be grown near those plants.

To plant garlic, break the bulbs into individual cloves and plant only the largest ones. Plant them with the pointed end facing up, 1 inch deep and 3 to 6 inches apart in rows 15 inches apart. The large fist-sized bulbs called giant or elephant garlic should be planted the same way, but spaced 8 to 12 inches apart. Water well and apply mulch to keep the moisture level even. You won't see it doing much until the spring when the green growth appears, but rest assured that the garlic is establishing a good root system through the fall and winter.

Plant shallots in much the same way as garlic, but with shallots good drainage is even more necessary. Unless your soil has excellent drainage, plant shallots and garlic in a raised bed.

In most of the state, this is the best time to plant blueberries. (Cold-winter regions should wait until early spring. Blueberries will grow in zones 3 to 10. Plant in full sun or partial shade in well-drained acidic soil (pH 4.5 to 5.5). If your soil is not that acidic, add peat. If the drainage isn't good, create a mound of soil to plant in or use a raised bed.

When planting blueberry shrubs, keep in mind that they have shallow roots. Dig a hole twice as wide but no deeper than the rootball. For bare-root blueberries, plant with the crown no more than ½ inch below the soil line. For better pollination and a higher yield, plant at least two varieties.

■ *Garlic can be planted in the fall for a summer harvest.*

Varieties that ripen at different times will give you a longer harvest. Plant taller varieties 6 feet apart; shorter types can be set 3 feet apart.

Northern highbush varieties are the type of blueberries you find in the grocery stores. Best suited for zones 4 to 7, they grow to about 6 feet high and produce a late-spring to late-summer harvest. Some popular varieties are 'Bluecrop', 'Earliblue', 'Elliott', 'Spartan', and 'Tophat' (a dwarf suitable for container-growing).

Southern highbush are good choices for zones 7 to 10. They are self-fertile but benefit from cross-pollination and produce a mid- to late-spring harvest. Try 'Jubilee', 'Misty', 'O'Neal', and 'Southmoon'.

Although not as flavorful as highbush types, rabbiteye blueberries are good for Central and Southern California and mild-winter regions (zones 7 to 9). They ripen from May to July. Recommended varieties include 'Bluebelle', 'Southland', and 'Tifblue'. They grow up to 10 feet high and should be planted 10 to 12 feet apart.

Hardy half-high varieties are hybrids of highbush and lowbush and are well-suited for zones 3 to 7. These include 'Chippewa', 'Polaris', 'St. Cloud', and 'Northcountry'. These shrubs are very compact (18 to 24 inches high) but can grow up to 4 feet wide.

In mild-winter areas artichokes can be planted as dormant roots now for a spring harvest. (Young plants can be planted in winter or early spring. See December for more information on growing artichokes.) Warmer parts of the state can also plant strawberries and bare-root brambleberries at this time. (See February for information on planting strawberries, and see April for information on brambleberries. Also see April for information on planting pomegranate trees.)

LAWNS

New lawns are best planted in fall when they are less likely to be drought-stressed. Cool-season grasses can be planted now from seed. Both warm- and cool-season grasses (or a mix of the two) can be laid as sod.

HERE'S HOW

TO PLANT A NEW LAWN FROM SEED

Sowing seed for a new lawn is best done on a dry, windless day. It's essential to properly prepare the ground before sowing the seed, so don't skip that important first step.

1. Remove all traces of previous lawn or other plantings, using a sod-cutter if necessary. Clear and level the ground using an iron rake.

2. Set the spreader rate on the seed-spreader to the appropriate setting for your seed. You will usually find instructions on the setting either on the seed package or the spreader itself.

3. Pour half the amount of seed for the total lawn area into the spreader.

4. Spread the first half of the seed walking back and forth over the length of the lawn area.

5. Spread the second half of the seed walking back and forth over the width of the area.

6. Follow up with an application of a complete granular starter fertilizer. Starter fertilizers are high in phosphorous, which aids germination.

7. To cover the seed, use a metal rake to lightly rake over the entire bed.

Alternatively, you can apply a thin layer (⅛ to ¼ inch) of a fine-grained organic mulch.

8. Fill a roller halfway with water and roll over the entire area to ensure contact between the seed and the soil.

9. Water the soil gently to a depth of 6 to 8 inches. Apply the water in three or four applications during the day to prevent it from pooling on the soil surface.

10. It's essential to keep the soil moist until the seeds germinate. If you see the color of the soil surface lighten noticeably, it's time to water.

11. Fence off the seeded area from dogs and foot traffic until the lawn is established.

12. As the grass grows in, lessen the frequency of watering, but continue to water deeply each time. If you see the grass turn from bright green to a duller shade, it needs water.

13. Mow the grass at a high setting when it reaches 3 to 4 inches in height.

14. Fertilize the lawn four to six weeks after the seed has germinated.

HERE'S HOW

TO PLANT A NEW LAWN BY LAYING SOD

The success of a new lawn depends heavily on the thoroughness of the preparation. Don't waste the expense and time spent installing new sod on ill-prepared ground. To do a good job, you'll probably need to rent a few heavy-duty pieces of equipment, such as a sod-cutter, a rototiller, and a water-filled roller. You may want to do all the prep on one day and then lay the sod the next day so that you can start each stage in the morning before it gets too hot and the sod dries out.

1. Begin by using the sod-cutter to remove all of the existing grass. Clear the area and level it with an iron rake.

2. Lay down 2 inches of compost over the entire area. If the soil is heavy clay, add 2 to 3 inches of sand to improve the drainage, then rototill the amendments into the soil.

3. Water the soil thoroughly. Allow the soil to dry to the point of being moist but not soggy before laying the sod.

4. Begin unrolling the sod, starting along a straight edge such as a sidewalk or driveway. If the planned lawn area has no straight edges, run a string tightly across the space and position the first piece of sod along the string.

5. Unroll and position each additional roll of sod to fill the space, staggering the ends as you would when laying bricks, and piecing the strips of sod together tightly. Use a sharp knife to cut the sod where necessary to fit or to make holes for sprinkler heads.

6. Fill in open seams or gaps with potting soil or sphagnum peat to keep the sod edges from drying out. You can water the first strips of sod you laid out before you've completed the entire lawn if needed to keep it moist.

7. Once the entire lawn is laid out and cut to fit, go over the entire lawn with the water roller (half-filled with water), rolling in a direction perpendicular to the strips of sod.

8. Finish by watering thoroughly to wet the soil 6 to 8 inches below the sod. Don't guess—use a probe to poke down into the soil to test the wetness to the proper depth.

9. Water well every morning for the first week.

10. Water every other morning for the second week.

11. Water twice a week for the third week.

12. After four weeks of growth, broadcast a fertilizer over the sod and water well.

PERENNIALS

This is a good time to start cuttings of the succulents that are winter-growers, such as senecios, aeoniums, and sempervivums. Cut back leggy plants, allow the cuttings to sit somewhere sheltered and dry for a week for the roots to callous over, then pot them up in a container with potting soil lightened with perlite or pumice stone. They will root in a matter of weeks, and the plants from which you took the cuttings will generate some new growth.

ROSES

In warmer parts of the state (zones 7 and above) you can plant container-grown roses. Do not fertilize after planting; you don't want to encourage a lot of tender new growth before the colder weather comes.

TREES

California is not known for having trees with fabulous fall color, but if color is what you're looking for in a tree, there are a few that stand out in providing that amazing blaze of scarlet, gold, and yellow. One is the Chinese pistache (*Pistacia chinensis*), a tree that in recent years has become a favorite of city planners throughout the West for its color as well as its adaptability and generally good behavior. In zones 6 to 9 it grows at a moderate rate to a height of 30 to 50 feet with a canopy spread of about the same dimensions. It likes full sun and good drainage, but it tolerates a variety of soil conditions. Bright green in spring and summer, the leaves take on the full range of autumn colors. In alternate years, female trees also produce red berries that ripen to a dark blue; if you don't want to deal with sweeping up berries, look for a male tree.

Next up is the ginkgo (*Ginkgo biloba*). Native to China, ginkgos have become much loved on the West Coast with their delicate, fan-shaped leaves that go from bright green in summer to a brilliant gold in autumn. Growing in zones 5 to 9, they will grow up to 50 feet high in full or partial shade. The most popular variety is 'Autumn Gold,' but if you want a smaller tree, look for 'Jade Butterfly' or 'Chi-Chi', both of which grow to about 10 feet. Female ginkgos set fruit in the fall that is notoriously smelly, so much

so that it's likely that you'll only find male trees in the nurseries (it's worth asking when you buy to make sure).

Another popular choice for fall color is the Japanese maple (*Acer palmatum*, *Acer japonicum*, and *Acer shirasawanum*). There are so many varieties of Japanese maple available you're sure to find one that will suit your size and foliage preferences. As small as low shrubs (or even bonsai-sized!) or as tall as 30 feet or higher, Japanese maples typically are understory plants, meaning they want partial shade and moist conditions and will tolerate most soil conditions except heavy clay. Foliage can range from large-lobed leaves to lacy, even spidery, leaves that turn to dazzling shades of yellow, orange, red or burgundy in the fall. Japanese maples can be a bit of an investment both in cash and commitment. They require careful pruning and can be vulnerable to certain diseases, but most gardeners consider them worth the cost and the effort.

When planting container-grown trees, dig a hole the same depth as the rootball but at least twice as wide. (For Japanese maples, which are very shallow-rooted trees, it's good to dig the hole three or four times as wide as the rootball, then add half the loose dirt back to the hole before placing the rootball in it). It's generally not necessary to amend the soil when planting and often doesn't help anyway. What is necessary is to water newly planted trees frequently and consistently for the first year. Mulching also helps to get them established by keeping moisture and soil temperatures more even.

CARE

ALL

Fire safety is always an issue in California and never more so than in October, often the driest month of the year. In the rural parts of the state, wildfire awareness tends to be a fact of life, but the massive Oakland Hills Fire of October 1991 was a lesson to all of us that landscaping for fire safety is necessary even in urban areas.

Fire-safe landscaping requires the removal of excess "fuel," that is, grasses, brush, dense shrubs,

■ *Fire-safe landscaping can help prevent the spread of wildfires, particularly in times of drought.*

woodpiles, or any flammable debris around your property. California state law requires that you keep a 100-foot "defensible space" around your house that not only will minimize fire risk but will also create a safer space for firefighters to defend your home in case fire does break out. They break it down into a 30-foot zone around your home called the "Lean, Clean and Green Zone," and a 70-foot zone around that called the "Reduced Fuel Zone."

In the "Lean, Clean and Green Zone" clear out stacks of firewood, compost piles, building materials, woodpiles, stacks of paper, or collections of other flammable items. It is essential in this zone that you eliminate any fire ladders, which are dense plantings increasing in height as they go toward your house. Landscapes should have lower plants near the house with shrubs and trees getting taller farther away from the house.

In the "Reduced Fuel Zone" cut down high grass, prune low-hanging limbs of trees and thin out dense shrubbery.

Here are some additional tips to create a more fire-safe landscape:

- Prune tree branches to keep them at least 10 feet away from the chimney.

- Clear roofs and gutters of piles of needles and leaves.

- Remove vines from exterior walls of the house.

- Take care when using power tools to remove dry brush. Have a water source at hand in case a spark ignites a fire.

- If cost is an issue regarding removing trees and brush that are a fire hazard, check with local agencies. Public funds may be available to homeowners and neighborhoods to help pay for removal.

In addition to clearing for fire safety, continue the fall cleanup that began last month by removing

HERE'S HOW

TO CLEAR BRUSH

1. Begin by using a tree pruner to cut woody brush that has a diameter of less than 1½ inch. Cut the brush and small trees as close to the ground as possible, dragging brush out of the way and into a pile as you clear.

2. Next, clear out larger plants—brush and trees with a diameter of about 1½ to 3½ inches. Use a bow saw or chainsaw to cut through the growth, and place the debris in a pile. Trees larger than 4 inches in diameter should be left to grow or removed under the supervision of a professional.

3. Use a heavy-duty string trimmer or a swing-blade-style weed cutter to cut tangled shoots, weeds, and any remaining underbrush from the area.

4. Clear the cut debris and dispose of it immediately. Curbside pickup of yard waste usually requires that sticks or branches be tied into bundles no more than 3 feet long. If you plan to install a hardscape surface, make sure the brush does not grow back by using a nonselective herbicide to kill off remaining shoots or laying landscape fabric.

spent annuals, raking up fallen leaves, and clearing fallen fruit or fruit mummies that are decaying on the tree. Lay down new mulch or refresh the mulch layer that's already there.

BULBS

Divide clumps of gladioli or belladonna lilies that have grown too dense. Use a garden fork to dig up the bulbs without piercing or slicing through them. Toss bulbs that show signs of damage or disease and replant the clean, healthy bulbs.

If you have potted amaryllis that you forced last year, you can now move them (still in their pots) to an area out of direct sunlight that is protected from freezing temperatures. Allow the bulbs to rest there for six to eight weeks.

EDIBLES

Keep the edible garden mulched and weeded so that late-season crops can still get sufficient water and light.

Chard is usually ready to begin harvesting about fifty days after planting. You can either cut the entire plant to the ground, or harvest only the outer leaves, leaving the inner leaves to grow. New leaves will grow in at the center and the plant will keep producing until the winter. In my Bay Area garden where the winters are mild, chard has continued to grow for well over a year.

Depending on the variety, lettuces can be ready to harvest in thirty-five to sixty-five days from sowing. Harvest head lettuces as soon as the heads reach a good size. If you leave them in the ground much beyond that point they will quickly bolt and become bitter. Loose-leaf and romaine lettuces can be harvested by clipping the outer leaves as needed so that new leaves can grow in the center, or by taking the entire bunch at once.

"Cut-and-come-again" lettuces are generally loose-leaf lettuces that are intended to be harvested well before maturity. When the leaves are a few inches high, cut across the leaves about ½ inch above the crowns of the plants. After harvesting apply a light fish emulsion solution to encourage re-growth.

Bananas will be ripening now (approximately seventy to one-hundred days after bloom). When the fruit at the top of the cluster starts to turn yellow, cut and remove the whole cluster to let them ripen inside at room temperature. If left on the tree, the fruit will split open and rot.

Each stalk will only bear fruit once. After the stalk blooms, let replacement stalks grow and then remove the stalk that has fruited after harvest. Wear old clothes when harvesting because sap from the bananas will permanently stain fabric.

In addition to using the edible flowers and fruit, you can also use the banana leaves to wrap fish and other food for grilling. The leaves perfume the food when heated, lending a tropical "luau" touch.

HOUSEPLANTS

If you have successfully kept a poinsettia alive from the previous winter, congratulations! Starting on October 1 and for the following 10 weeks, you must cover or move the poinsettia to keep it in complete darkness for twelve hours each night in order to stimulate blooming before Christmas.

PERENNIALS

Continue to divide perennials as needed when they become too dense. Daylilies can be dug up and divided. Before replanting, trim the leaves back to 4 inches in length. Trim the leaves of daylilies that don't yet need dividing in the same way.

ROSES

Stop deadheading roses in all parts of the state.

VINES & GROUNDCOVERS

Groundcovers that have become too dense can be thinned at this time. For trailing or rambling groundcovers, use pruners to thin out crowded areas. Clumping groundcovers that spread out, such as gazanias, need to be dug up and split into smaller sections and replanted.

WATER

ALL

If September is generally the hottest month in California, October is often a close runner-up.

Continue to watch for signs of wilt throughout the garden, particularly in the first half of the month. Adjust the schedule for your irrigation system as needed, or use hand-watering to supplement the regular schedule.

Continue to carefully watch and water new plantings, even of plants that are supposed to be drought tolerant.

EDIBLES

Back off watering warm-season crops that are nearing the end of their life cycle, but make sure recently planted cool-season crops, particularly greens and lettuces, are watered consistently.

HOUSEPLANTS

Water poinsettias that you are trying to rebloom every couple of weeks until mid-December.

TREES

Newly planted trees should be watered regularly and deeply enough that the water permeates to the depth of the entire rootball.

FERTILIZE

ALL

Fertilizers can be expensive, so the more compost you can produce yourself, the more money you'll save and the more sustainable your garden will be. In addition to maintaining an ongoing compost pile (see July), you can harvest the waste produced by worms (called *castings*) to feed your plants through vermicomposting. Just maintaining one bin of red worms can reduce your kitchen waste and supply you with healthy compost, loaded with nutrients, as well as a nutritious "worm tea" for occasional foliar feeding. You can start a worm bin anytime of the year, but it can be especially convenient to have it near or even in the house during the cool, wet months to come to save all those trips to the big compost bin outdoors with your kitchen scraps.

EDIBLES

Be sure to feed lettuces, chard, or any greens planted last month with a half-strength fish emulsion six weeks after planting.

TO START AND MAINTAIN A WORM BIN

Worms play a big part in the health of your garden's soil, and you can harness the benefits of their hard work by vermicomposting. If that term sounds intimidating, relax. It really just boils down to keeping worms in a bin, feeding them your scraps, and then making use of the nutrient-rich liquid and solid waste that results. Follow these steps to set up and maintain a vermicomposting worm bin:

1. Choose a bin to house the worms. You can purchase a commercially made worm bin that will be well-suited to worm-living, or you can adapt a lidded plastic box on your own. The bin should be 8 to 12 inches deep and have about a dozen or more ½-inch air holes. The size of the bin should be based on the size of your household and the amount of food scraps you generate. Two people typically produce enough scraps (about ½ pound) each day to feed 1 pound of worms, which need about 4 square feet of space, so a 2 × 2-foot bin would be just right. For every additional two people, add another pound of worms and another 4 square feet, either as a bigger bin or additional separate bins.

2. Once you have the right bin, look for the right place to set it up. Worms need ambient temperatures from 55 to 80 degrees Fahrenheit, so it's best not to put the bin

in full sun or near anything that may throw off too much heat. A spot that is sheltered and shady will work best. You should also consider convenience when choosing the location. You want to make it easy to feed your worms every day or every other day, so you may choose to keep your worm bin in the house (under the kitchen sink, in the laundry, or mud-room) or on the back porch or close to the back door. If, after you've established your worm bin, you find that the location isn't working well, you can move it, but take care. A full worm bin can be quite heavy.

3. With the bin in place, you're ready to make a bed for the worms. The simplest and most accessible bedding material is shredded newspaper, but you can also use shredded cardboard, coconut coir, or peat. Mix in a couple of cups of garden soil or some compost to add some healthy micro-organisms to the decomposition work.

4. Wet the bedding material with dechlorinated water. (To dechlorinate common tap water, pour a pitcher or bucket of water and just let it sit for a day or two to let the chlorine dissipate.) The bedding material should be completely moist but not sopping. If you squeeze a handful of it and only get a couple of drops of water, that's just right.

5. You're ready to add the worms. You should use red worms for composting, not earthworms. Red worms (typically *Eisenia fetida* or *Lumbricus rubellus*) tend to dwell in shallow soil, but earthworms like to dig much deeper. You can order red worms by the pound through mail-order sources or sometimes find them at your local nursery. Scatter the worms over the top of the moist bedding material, then give them a day or two to settle in before feeding them.

To feed your worms, collect food scraps from your kitchen including the following:

- Fruits and vegetables
- Cereals and grains
- Used teabags, coffee grounds, and coffee filters
- Egg shells
- Food-soiled paper towels, cardboard, and paper containers (as long as they are not chemically treated and are torn into small pieces)

Avoid adding the following items:

- Meat
- Dairy products
- Citrus fruits or hard rinds such as melon
- Bread, pasta, or processed grain products
- Fats and oils

You can add limited amounts of green waste from the garden, as long as it's chemical-free, broken into small pieces, and added in very small amounts. Adding a substantial amount of lawn clippings or plant debris can lead to the temperature in the worm bin growing too high as it decomposes. Food waste, on the other hand, tends to break down faster through the work of bacteria first and then the worms finish the job.

Whenever you add food scraps to the bin, cover it with more bedding material and wet it sufficiently to get it back to the original state of moistness. Don't add more food until what you've already given them is mostly gone. As the population of your worm bin grows, the food will disappear more quickly and you'll need to feed them more often.

(continued)

Sometimes something goes awry in the worm bin and you'll notice a problem. Here are a few tips for troubleshooting worm bin situations:

- **The worms disappear.** I've had this happen. Usually, it's because the bin got too wet, or because something was added that was too acidic or contained chemicals. If only some of the worms have fled, adjust the moisture by mixing in more dry newspaper or remove the uneaten food that may have bothered them. If all the worms have disappeared, remove all the contents of the bin and start over with fresh bedding material and new worms.

- **The worm bin is attracting insects.** Whether or not this is really a problem depends on the type of insect. Insects you may not want hanging around can still be helpful in the composting process, but clouds of fruit flies or trails of ants in and around your bin can easily be taken care of. Ants will not go into a bin that is properly moistened so if they're in your bin, it's a sign that it's too dry. Fruit flies will only lay eggs on the surface of decaying food, so if you see significant numbers of fruit flies it's an indication that you are leaving the food scraps exposed instead of covering them with more bedding material. Most of the other insects that you may find in your bin are harmless and may actually help with the decomposition process, but if they're appearing in large numbers it may indicate that something in the food scraps is too acidic or otherwise unsuitable.

- **The worm bin is starting to smell.** This is caused by food that is rotting before the worms can eat it. You may have added too much food at one time for the size of your worm population, or the ratio of carbon to nitrogen may be off. Adding brown material such as dead leaves, chemical-free sawdust, or shredded newspaper will usually fix this problem.

- **You need to leave your worm bin untended while you're on vacation.** This isn't a problem. The worms can take care of themselves for a week or two, probably even up to a month. It's a good idea, however, to add more bedding material to the bin before you leave and make sure that it is sufficiently moistened.

After a few months, your worms should have created a substantial amount of compost, and there may be little bedding or food left. It's then time to harvest the compost using one of the following methods:

- Dump the entire contents of the bin onto a large sheet of plastic and start building numerous little piles. Rather than be exposed to the light, the worms will burrow to the bottom of the piles. You can scrape off the top of the piles to use as compost and return the bottom of the piles back to the worm bin with fresh bedding.

- Set a medium-fine screen over a large tub or box and move the bin contents onto the screen a shovelful at a time. The screen will catch undecomposed bedding and food scraps as well as the worms, which you can set aside to be returned to the worm bin with fresh bedding. What will fall through the screen is the fresh compost.

- Stop adding food scraps to the bin for a couple of weeks. Then push the contents of the bin to one half of the bin, and fill the other half with fresh bedding and food scraps. Add food scraps only to the new bedding. After a couple of weeks the worms should have all shifted over to the new bedding where the food is. You can then scoop out the finished compost on the other side.

Finished vermicompost can be used like other compost—as a side- or topdressing on plants or mixed into potting soil for containers. It's loaded with nutrients your plants will love and microorganisms that will keep your soil healthy.

HOUSEPLANTS

Feed poinsettia plants that you're trying to rebloom with a liquid fertilizer every couple weeks until mid-December.

PROBLEM-SOLVE

ALL

If you have heavy clay soil in your garden, you may have experienced the pain of trying to dig when it has turned rock hard in the dry summer heat. It was long considered that the best approach to improving clay soil was to add gypsum, which has long been used in agricultural settings. In the home garden, however, this isn't necessary and isn't particularly suitable. A better approach to improving the structure and lessening the compaction of clay soil is just to add organic matter, such as compost. Add the compost now and the fall and winter rains to come will help work it into the soil. It is not an overnight fix, but with continued applications of organic matter, you can help clay soil become more workable when dry with improved drainage when wet.

BULBS

If your spring bulbs put on a less-than-stellar show this year, test the pH level of your soil. Most bulbs prefer a slightly acidic pH level between 5.5 and 6.5; more alkaline soil may inhibit blooming. There are a number of amendments you can use to acidify your soil before planting more bulbs, such as sulfur, aluminum sulfate or iron sulfate, but the easiest to add is sphagnum peat. Whatever amendment you use, work it into the soil to a depth of 12 to 18 inches where the roots will be.

HERE'S HOW

TO DETERMINE YOUR SOIL TEXTURE

Soils come partly from the earth's mineral crust and partly from the remains of living things. The mineral (inorganic) part is rock that has been worn down to particles. Clay (left photo) is simply stone that has worn down to microscopically small particles. Clay soils are dense and slow draining. Clay soils compact easily when wet. Compacted clay soils resist root penetration and do not support grass well. Most clay soils form a tight wad that does not easily crumble when squeezed in your hand.

The inorganic part of loam soils (center photo) is a mixture of clay, silt, and sand particles. Loam is the best soil for lawns because it doesn't compact like clay or dry out like sand. A handful of moist loam will form a ball when squeezed, but the ball will crumble as you handle it.

Sand soils (right photo) are gritty and resist forming a cohesive ball. Sand soil resists compaction better than clay and loam but dries out quickly unless generously amended with organic matter. Heavy clay and dry sand soils are best improved with the addition of compost or other organic matter.

November

Let us now give thanks. As the days shorten and the year's end hovers just out of view, it is worth taking some time to acknowledge and feel gratitude for all that our gardens have given us and continue to give us even as autumn strips them bare and winter breathes down our necks.

What does the garden give? Beauty, of course. And wonder. Food, perhaps; maybe a lot of food. A place to relax or meditate. A chance to exercise and breathe fresh air deep into our lungs. A playground for our children. A spot to entertain our friends. An opportunity to marvel at the intricacies of nature as life and death are played out every day in a million ways both great and small in our tiny patches of earth.

As we complete and check off the tasks we do each month, it's easy to allow a garden to become little more than another to-do list, a record of our efforts rather than a reward in itself. We brave cold and wet to plant bulbs that won't show themselves for months, or rake piles of leaves on the weekend only to have the next week's winds scatter a new layer over the lawn. Chores need repeating and the payoff is often long-term. Gardening is a lesson in patience, learned again and again.

But when we bring gratitude into the garden, the lesson becomes easier. The rake is no longer a tool of labor, but a way of uncovering beauty and order beneath chaos and detritus. The bulbs we bury in chilled, damp soil with fingers numb with cold are as much an investment in the future as money saved for a rainy day, a reminder that winter will come and it will go, as it has always done, as it always will do. And the flowers those bulbs will push out in the spring are not the reward for our efforts; it's the certainty that those flowers will indeed arrive that we carry with us into and beyond the hard heart of winter. That is the reward.

And for that we should be truly grateful.

PLAN

ALL

Are your house and garden ready for the holidays? If you decorate for Christmas or other holidays, it's best to make sure your landscape is clean and trimmed so that lights and other decorations can go on with a minimum of fuss. Pay particular attention to the front walkway, porch, and entrance. If anything is broken, fix it now. If any landscape plants need to be transplanted or pruned, get it out of the way this month so that next month you'll have a clean canvas ready for you to make your holiday magic.

Sometimes a gift from the garden is the most welcomed gift. If there are plants in your garden that you'd like to share with friends, take cuttings to root or divide them and pot them up. Label them as completely as possible, including planting and growing information. Doing this now will give the plant time to get established in the new container and get over any transplant shock before you give it away as a holiday gift.

Next year's seed catalogs are now available for your viewing pleasure. Visit websites of seed companies to get your name on their mailing list for a printed catalog or simply review their offerings online. You'll find introductions of new plants each year as well as the most popular varieties from recent years. It's best to place your orders as early as possible. Some popular choices will inevitably sell out. You can depend on the nurseries to hold off on shipping your order until the appropriate planting time for your area.

PLANT

ANNUALS

Continue to sow wildflower seeds and plant cool-season annuals. Iceland poppies are a vibrant addition at this time of year, usually appearing in shades of yellow or orange. In general, poppies are temperamental about being transplanted, so it's best to get them in the ground as early in their life cycle as possible. You'll most often see them in 4-inch pots in the nurseries, but if you can find them in six-packs, grab them. The younger they

■ *Amaryllis like to fit snugly in a pot.*

are, the better they will handle the transplant. Give them well-draining soil and consistent moisture to get settled in. They appreciate regular feeding and the more you deadhead, the longer they will stay in bloom.

BULBS

Keep planting spring-blooming bulbs. (See October for guidance on planting bulbs quickly and easily.) To make an even more stunning show, layer different types of bulbs in a bed or a container. Start with the bigger bulbs (daffodils or tulips) at the bottom layer, add some soil, and then add another layer of a smaller bulb, such as anemones, crocus, or muscari. You can build up three or four layers of bulbs and then cover with soil. In the spring, the bulbs may bloom one layer at a time or the layers may overlap, but either way you will have a colorful show that can extend all the way through the season.

Potted amaryllis bulbs in full bloom are one of the loveliest sights of winter, so if you hope to see some of those gorgeous blossoms in your home or have some ready to give as gifts, it's time to get them planted.

Amaryllis bulbs like to feel cozy in their containers so choose pots that will leave no more than an inch of space surrounding the bulb. Use a good-quality potting mix and lighten it with one part perlite to two parts potting mix. Plant the bulb, leaving the top third above the soil line, then water it well, and place it in a cool indoor location. Keep the bulb watered throughout the growing period, but don't overwater so that it is sitting in soggy soil.

It's best not to rush the forcing process, so don't move the container until leaf shoots or a flower stalk begins to show. When that happens, move it to a warm and bright location indoors. Keep turning the container so that the flower stalk grows straight. Apply a water-soluble fertilizer every two to three weeks through the bloom period. Flowers should open seven to ten weeks after planting. For continuous blooms over a longer period, plant multiple containers every two weeks.

EDIBLES

Continue planting cool-season crops for continuous harvesting. In Southern California, you can plant rhubarb now. (See April for information on growing rhubarb.) In mild-winter areas, you can also plant strawberries now. (See February for planting information.)

If you think your soil may be a little tired after a productive growing season, plant a cover crop that will keep down weeds and feed the soil through the winter so that it's in better shape for planting in the spring. There are several good options for cover crops: Vetch, rye, buckwheat, and clover, but one cover crop that does double duty is fava beans. Double duty means it not only feeds the soil but

■ *Fava beans can be planted for the winter as a cover crop.*

you as well since both the beans and the greens are edible. And fava beans, like all legumes, have nitrogen-fixing nodules on their roots that actually release nitrogen into the soil.

Plant cover crops at least four weeks before killing frosts are expected so they have time to get established. For grassy crops like rye and clover, rake over the soil, broadcast the seed over it, and then rake it in lightly. When using fava beans as a cover crop, plant the seeds 1 to 2 inches deep, and space them so that you'll have one plant per square foot. Water well after planting and water regularly until the rainy season takes over.

Continue planting alliums such as garlic, shallots (see September), leeks, and onions. In cold-winter regions, you can direct-sow leek seeds in fall for harvest the next year or set out transplants in early spring for harvest in the fall. In milder regions, you can set out transplants. In cool-summer areas, plant in full sun. In hotter areas, you can plant in partial shade. Leeks need very rich soil, so amend heavily with compost before planting. Sow seeds ½ inch deep and 1 inch apart. Seeds germinate in fourteen to twenty-one days. When setting out seedlings, space them 2 to 4 inches apart in a furrow 5 inches deep. As the plants grow, mound up soil around the leeks to blanch the stems and keep the flavor mild. Keep mounding the soil to the point just below the leaf joints. Keep evenly watered.

Recommended leek varieties include 'Dawn Giant' (maturing in 98 days), 'Blue Solaise' (100 to 120 days), 'Titan' (110 days), 'Broad London' (130 days), 'Hannibal Organic' (75 days), 'King Richard' (75 days), 'Megaton' (90 days), 'Lexton' (110 days), 'Tadorna' (100 days), 'Bandit' (120 days), 'Pandora' (90 days), and 'Lancelot' (95 days).

Onions are categorized by the amount of hours of daylight they require in order to form a bulb. Long-day varieties require fourteen to sixteen hours of daylight and really are not suited for California growing, except to harvest as scallions. Intermediate-day varieties need twelve to fourteen hours and grow well in Central California. Short-day onions, which are usually sweeter than long-day types, require only ten to twelve hours of sunlight; they are suitable for

■ *Onion sets are more reliable than seeds for beginning gardeners.*

Southern California gardens. Recommended short-day varieties include 'Bermuda', 'California Red', 'Granex', 'Grano', 'Super Sweet', and 'Cipollini'. Intermediate-day varieties include 'Autumn Spice', 'Red Torpedo', and 'Ringmaker'. Bunching onions (also called scallions) never form an actual bulb. They can grow anywhere.

Onions can be grown from seed, sets (small bulbs), or transplants. Growing from seed gives you a much larger crop for less money, and you'll have a greater choice of varieties. Gardeners who are new to edible growing may have greater success with sets and transplants. (More often than not, sets are available only in long-day varieties, but these can be grown in California to the green onion—or scallion—stage and harvested that way.)

Sow onion seeds from fall to early winter in mild-winter regions. Sets and transplants can be planted into early spring. Gardeners in cold-winter areas should wait until late winter to start seeds indoors or early spring to plant sets and transplants.

Plant onions in full sun (at least six hours a day) in loose, well-drained soil that is high in organic matter. Sow seeds ¼ inch deep in rows 15 to 18 inches apart. When seedlings are a few inches tall, thin to 4 to 5 inches apart. Sets and transplants should be planted 4 to 5 inches apart, or closer if you want to harvest some early as green onions. Bury sets just below the soil surface so that the

point of the bulb is visible. Water well. Seeds will mature in 110 to 125 days, transplants in 70 to 90 days, and sets in 50 to 60 days.

PERENNIALS

Cyclamens are a dependable brightener for the late fall and winter landscape. In containers or in the ground, they add bold splashes of color in shades of red, pink, lavender, and fuchsia but also make a dramatic display in winter white. Plant cyclamens in a spot where they'll get morning shade or sun only in the morning or late afternoon. Plant them with the crown slightly above the soil level in well-draining soil. Although they like moist conditions, too much water can cause the tubers to rot and water splash on the blossoms can cause spotting on the petals. Cyclamen are hardy to zone 5; in colder areas they can be grown as houseplants.

Another striking winter bloomer to add to the garden now is hellebore, also known as the Lenten rose. With leathery leaves and clusters of long-lasting flowers in shades of white, green, pink, apricot, purple, or even "black" (really a very dark purple), hellebores will bloom steadily from midwinter to early spring. Earlier hybrids had downward-facing blooms, but newer varieties have more outward-facing flowers, which I think make them much more appealing. Hellebores are also reported to be generally ignored by deer and rabbits. Depending on the cultivar, they can be hardy to zone 4 and tolerate full sun to partial shade.

SHRUBS AND TREES

Your winter landscape will be much brighter if you plant some beautiful holiday greens now. Not only will you have vibrant evergreens to perk up the drab winter months, but you'll be able to use cuttings to decorate inside as well. If you're looking for the best evergreens for that holiday look, consider these choices:

- **Holly (*Ilex opaca*):** The spiny leaves and red berries of this holiday classic make it a standout outdoors and indoors. The foliage comes in a range of dark to lighter greens as well as variegated leaves. Hollies are dioecious, meaning that plants are either male or female, and are hardy in zones 5 to 9. If you want a holly with berries, you need to plant a female

■ *Most holly berries are red, but this is* Ilex opaca *'Canary', which has yellow berries.*

plant with a male plant nearby. Plant in full sun to light shade in well-draining, slightly acidic soil.

- **Dwarf Alberta spruce (*Picea glauca*):** These compact, cone-shaped trees, also called dwarf white spruce, will eventually grow to 10–12 feet, but it will take about twenty-five years to achieve that full height. Hardy in zones 2 through 8, dwarf Alberta spruce prefers full sun but can tolerate some shade, and it does well as a container plant.

- **Boxwood (*Buxus*):** As a formal hedge or shaped shrub, boxwood is a great addition to the landscape, but it also is a great source of cuttings for holiday arrangements. Boxwoods will grow in full sun but do best in partial shade and are hardy in zones 5 through 8. Plant in well-draining, slightly acidic soil, and mulch well.

- **Dwarf fir (*Abies*):** With needles ranging from dark green to frosty blue, dwarf firs keep a compact, pyramidal shape and can grow in the ground or in containers. Firs are slow-growing, but some can grow quite tall so make sure you're buying a cultivar appropriate for your space. They prefer full sun but can tolerate light shade and require well-draining,

■ *Dwarf Alberta spruce are slow-growing evergreens with a compact shape.*

slightly acidic soil. There are many varieties of fir to choose from, including balsam firs (zones 3 to 6), Fraser firs (zones 4 to 7), and Korean firs (zones 5 to 8).

- **Dwarf Pine (*Pinus*):** Pines also come in shades of green and blue as well as shapes ranging from prostrate to conical. Pine is one of the scents most associated with the holidays, and pine cuttings make great additions to floral arrangements. Mugo pines are compact, mounded shrubs, hardy in zones 3 to 7. Plant in full sun in well-drained, slightly acidic soil.

Keep in mind that "dwarf" is a relative term, so be sure that the tree you select will still be appropriately sized for your garden when it reaches maturity.

VINES & GROUNDCOVERS

If you have a slope in your garden and are concerned about soil erosion, planting a groundcover along the slope is your best chance of stabilizing the ground. Groundcover plants are sufficient to stabilize mild slopes (up to a 33 percent grade). For steeper slopes, you need to employ other measures to prevent erosion. Given California's dry summers, groundcovers planted on slopes without irrigation don't have much of a chance of getting established unless they're planted in the fall. You may need to provide supplemental water until the rainy season begins, but at that point their roots should have begun to settle in.

For large planting areas, a combination of plants with shallow and deeper root systems will provide the best coverage and stabilization. Succulents like *Delosperma cooperi* (iceplant) and *Sedum rubrotinctum* (pork and beans) are quick to establish and fill in and can provide a wave of color. Other options include creeping rosemary, woolly thyme, osteospermum, and ivory star jasmine.

■ *Sedum can be used as a groundcover to prevent soil erosion.*

TO PLANT A GROUNDCOVER ON A SLOPE

Before planting on sloping ground, make sure the area is completely clear of weeds so the new plants won't be competing for water. If the slope has little soil or if the soil is sandy, work in some compost first so water won't run off before it can get to the roots. Stagger the rows of plants, making an individual terrace with a low spot behind each plant to catch water. Provide water until the rainy season starts and the plants are beginning to fill out.

■ *Delosperma cooperi as a groundcover in bloom*

CARE

ALL

For much of California, frosts are most likely to start occurring in November. Be prepared to protect your most tender and vulnerable plants. That means not only having protective materials at the ready but also knowing in advance which plants are most in need of protection.

The first step should be to water the entire garden well, especially container plants. Plants that are adequately hydrated will be better able to withstand the frost. Water at the soil level; don't spray the foliage because any water left on the leaves will freeze and burn the plant.

Next, relocate container plants that are small enough to move. Sheltering them in a garage, shed, or even under the eaves of the house can be the easiest and safest course of action. For plants that can't be moved, you'll have to shield or wrap them using one of the following methods:

- **"Frost blankets" or Reemay cloth:** These spun-polyester fabrics can be draped directly over plants or "floated" over PVC hoops or stakes to provide insulation against frost. Reemay cloth, also sold as "floating row covers," are sold in different weights; be sure you have a heavy enough fabric weight for cold weather rather than the lighter-weight summer fabrics.

- **Antitranspirant sprays:** These sprays, sold under several brand names, can be sprayed on tender plants before a frost to coat it with a thin polymer film that minimizes the moisture loss plants experience during a frost. The sprays will last up to three months but will not protect any new foliage that emerges after spraying.

- **Improvised protection:** Container-grown trees or other smaller plants can be covered with sheets or lightweight blankets, but any foliage coming in direct contact with the fabric may still sustain some frost damage. Large tomato cages can be placed over smaller plants and filled with dried leaves or straw for insulation. You can even use strings of Christmas lights to protect small trees and shrubs. Wrap the strings of tiny lights around the trunk and branches, don't just drape them over the canopy. The lights generate just enough heat to make the difference on nights of light frost.

You can never protect your entire garden, of course, so which plants should you target for attention? The following list should help you set your priorities:

- Any nonherbaceous perennial, shrub, or tree that has been planted in the past six months

- Any tropical plants such as bougainvillea, palms, and most orchids

■ *A cold frame is a great way to protect plants from frost or cold damage.*

- Citrus and avocado trees

- Most succulents

- Container plants, which can be susceptible to root freezing as well

Traditionally, gardeners have been advised to wrap the trunks of thick-barked trees, like citrus and avocado, with paper to protect them from frost, but I'm not going to advise that. Tree-wrapping is one of those things that people remember to do but often forget to undo, and leaving layers of cold, wet paper tightly wrapped around a tree trunk for an extended period of time is a good way to hold excess moisture against the bark, causing the tree to rot. The paper can also provide a layer of protection for pests. Assuming your tree is hardy in your zone, the trunk will probably survive a night or two of frost well enough. If the tree is small, it's better to cover the entire tree with a frost blanket or use an antitranspirant spray on it. If the tree is large, odds are it's survived frosts in the past and will do so again. If you do decide to wrap the trunk, remove the wrapping as soon as the immediate threat of frost has passed.

If some plants appear to sustain some frost damage, don't prune away the affected branches or dig up the plant right away. It's amazing how resilient some plants can be, and you may find that they have sufficiently recovered by the spring so that they can be tidied up a bit and be ready for another year.

BULBS

One of the happier days in my gardening life was when I found that with my climate (the mild-weathered Bay Area) and my soil (sandy, sandy, sandy), I didn't have to worry about digging up summer-blooming bulbs like dahlias, cannas, tuberous begonias, or gladioli. In gardens like mine, where there is no danger of killing frosts or freezes and where the fast-draining soil will ensure that the bulbs won't rot, it's perfectly fine to leave summer-blooming bulbs right where they are. It's a good idea to mark their place so that you don't disturb them when you're planting or digging around them. With dahlias, you can cut the plants right down to the ground and cover them with an overturned terracotta saucer so that water can't run into the hollow stems and rot the bulbs.

In areas that do have harsher winters with killing frosts, digging up the bulbs and storing them safely for the winter is the only way to ensure their survival. Refer to Here's How to Store Summer-Blooming Bulbs for more information.

For potted amaryllis that you forced last year and want to rebloom, you can now move them to a cool location and begin watering them again. Follow the instructions in the Plant section for this month to coax out that next stunning blossom.

EDIBLES

Prune blackberry and raspberry canes after their last harvests. For summer-bearing plants, prune canes that bore fruit all the way to the ground. For everbearing plants, prune off the tops of canes that bore fruit after the fall harvest. Those canes will produce lateral branches that will bear the spring crop. After the spring harvest, those canes should be pruned to the ground. In areas with harsh winters, mulch the canes with a 12-inch layer of straw.

In some areas by the coast, artichokes should have finished a second harvest by now. When leaves get yellow, cut stalks almost to the ground. In cold-winter areas, cut the tops to 1 foot high, tie the leaves down over the root crowns, and pile on the mulch for protection.

Make sure you harvest any frost-tender edibles before your first frost date, but some vegetables can be left in the ground into winter. Some edibles such as kale will improve in flavor with frosty weather, and in mild-winter areas, you can leave carrots in the ground and dig them up as needed, even after the green tops die off.

HOUSEPLANTS

Move houseplants that have been near north- or east-facing windows through the summer and fall to a south- or west-facing window, where they can get the most light.

If you are overwintering any outdoor plants indoors, give them a close inspection and wipe-down before bringing them in the house. Make sure no insects or other garden creatures are hitching a ride under the leaves or in the soil and that the containers are clean. Trim off any damaged or diseased foliage. In fact, if there is any suspicion of disease on a plant, it's best to quarantine it. Most plants moved in from the garden want bright, indirect light. If you don't have enough sunny windowsills to go around, you may need to hook up a grow light. Some plants will inevitably get leggy when moved indoors. In those cases, it's best to pinch them back and perhaps try to root some of the cuttings. That way, if the parent plant doesn't make it through the winter, you'll have some new plants to keep growing.

If you're trying to rebloom a poinsettia, cover or move it to keep it in complete darkness for 12 hours each night in order to stimulate blooming before Christmas. Continue watering and fertilizing every couple of weeks until mid-December.

■ *Move houseplants to south- or west-facing windows to get the most light through the winter.*

HERE'S HOW

TO STORE SUMMER-BLOOMING BULBS

For dahlias, cannas, tuberous begonias, gladioli, or other summer-blooming bulbs and tubers, follow these steps:

1. Allow the foliage to die back completely, then carefully dig up the bulbs. If the bulbs have multiplied, you can divide them now or wait until spring.

2. Before storing the bulbs, allow them to "cure" first. Brush away dirt and remove any foliage left, then spread them out somewhere dry and well-ventilated for a few days. (Some bulbs, such as gladioli and ismenes, prefer a curing period as long as three weeks.)

3. Once cured, most bulbs can be placed in a paper or plastic bag with holes cut into it, a potato sack, or a plastic mesh bag like the ones that produce is sometimes packaged in at the grocery store. Be sure to label them.

4. Store the bulbs somewhere dry where the temperature will not go below freezing. Some really tender bulbs, like dahlias, will dry up, however, in dry storage. Store these bulbs in containers of dry peat moss, vermiculite, or a similar material that will allow air circulation while still allowing the bulb to retain its natural moisture.

LAWNS

With the hot, dry season behind us, reset your lawn mower for a shorter cut. Some types of grasses should be trimmed shorter than others; check this table for the ideal cool-season setting for your type of lawn:

2 inches	Bahiagrass Fescue Blue grama Buffalograss
1¾ inches	Kentucky bluegrass
1½ inches	St. Augustinegrass Ryegrass
1 inch	Centipedegrass Zoysiagrass
¾ inches	Bermudagrass
¼ inch	Bentgrass

PERENNIALS

Continue dividing and transplanting perennials as needed. Most perennials need to be divided only every three to four years. A good way to remember when to do it is to do all your plant divisions during the election years. (It also makes for a pleasant escape from all the political ads on TV.)

SHRUBS, VINES, & GROUNDCOVERS

For spring-blooming woody plants like lilac or wisteria that have been experiencing disappointing bloom periods, there is a little trick called root-pruning that may help "shock" the plant into heavier flowering next year. For a shrub, take a spade and insert it about 18 inches deep into the soil at the drip line all the way around the trunk. For well-established vines, do the same thing about 4 feet out from the trunk all the way around. Severing the ends of the roots in this way stresses the plant and it responds by being more productive—in other words, flowering more abundantly.

TREES

Don't wait to clean up storm damage caused by falling branches; be proactive and prune now to prevent that damage from occurring. Remove any dead wood or diseased limbs. Thin out branches that are rubbing against other branches or ones that are poorly attached. Look for *included bark*, a term for a bulging ring of bark surrounding the area where a branch is attached to the tree trunk. The thin branches extending from an area of included bark are generally weakly attached and more likely to break off in a storm.

Now through February is a good time to do structural pruning on Japanese maples. Some varieties may "bleed" when pruned at this time; if that occurs, you may want to stop and wait until February to continue. (The "bleeding" doesn't harm the tree, but it can appear unsightly.) There is a bit of an art to pruning Japanese maples and it can be intimidating to the novice pruner. Keep in mind that these are trees that are meant to be pruned repeatedly, removing a small amount each time. Japanese maples should always be pruned to have an open, airy form that allows you to see light through the branches and appreciate the lacy foliage. Many a valuable Japanese maple has been ruined by a gardener shearing the tree into a full, round lollipop shape. Remember to prune "coarse to fine," meaning you remove bigger, coarser branches first, then move on to trimming thinner, shorter branches. If you don't want to handle pruning your Japanese maple yourself or want to learn from a pro how it's done, look for an arborist or garden coach who is experienced at aesthetic pruning.

WATER GARDENS

In mild climates, cold-weather care of a water garden generally amounts to keeping a watchful eye and doing the routine maintenance that is done the rest of the year. In areas where ponds are likely to either partially or completely freeze, you basically have two choices: drain the pond or water feature and store the fish and plants until the spring, or take steps to keep the ice in check throughout the winter.

If you opt to drain the pond, remove the fish, snails, and other aquatic animals and move them to an indoor aquarium or give them away and buy new ones in the spring. Lift the water plants and cut their stems back to within a couple of inches of the soil line. Wrap them in wet newspapers and store them in plastic trash bags someplace cool

TO CREATE A DRAINAGE SWALE

Swales work much like rain gardens: Both are designed to direct water run-off to an area of capture so water can slowly drain back into the soil or be redirected to an appropriate outlet, such as a storm water sewer. The difference is, a swale is basically a shallow, vegetated collection trench and a rain garden requires establishing an entire drainage environment. Depending on the run-off severity, a simple swale might be all you'll need to keep your lawn from turning into swampland.

2   *Remove soil from the marked zone using a shovel. If you must remove grass before digging, consider cutting grass pieces carefully and setting them aside so you can use the turf as sod squares to finish the trench. You can rent or buy a sod cutter to improve your chances of getting reusable cuttings. Otherwise, pile dirt on one side of the trench for a berm.*

3   *Shape the trench so it slopes gradually downward toward the outlet, and smooth the sides.*

4   *Level the trench by laying a 2 × 4 board with a carpenter's level on the foundation. Distribute soil so the base is level, moving the board to different areas of the trench to check for levelness. Crack the bottom of the swale with a spading fork to aid in percolation (optional).*

1   *Use stakes to mark a swale route that directs water away from the problem area toward a run-off zone. Place stakes slightly uphill from the drainage area.*

5   *Lay sod in the trench to complete the swale. Compress the sod and water the area thoroughly to check drainage.*

but not freezing. Then drain the water, making sure the water does not empty onto other plants in your garden.

If you don't want to drain your pond, you can install a deicer to maintain an open hole in the ice, but they can be costly to run. If the ice is not likely to be too thick on the surface, and if it only ices over periodically, you can set a pot of boiling water on top of the ice to melt a hole in it. Floating a piece of wood or a rubber ball on the water is another way to keep the surface from freezing completely and preventing excessive pressure from the ice from damaging the pond liner.

WATER

ALL

As much as October can be incredibly dry, November can quickly turn on the waterworks. Depending on how soon the rainy season kicks in, you'll need to be on water watch to make sure plants are getting sufficient hydration (but not too much). This becomes even more crucial when frost threatens. Water plants well when frost is predicted, preferably early in the day and without getting water on the foliage.

Adjust your irrigation system as the rains kick in and as some plants begin to go dormant. You may want to investigate adding a smart controller to your existing irrigation system, which will use weather data from satellites to adjust the irrigation schedule as needed. The controllers can be purchased for a couple of hundred dollars but could save you at least that much over the course of a year if you have a large garden and high water-usage costs.

You should also check the downspouts on your house to make sure they won't be emptying into beds that can't handle excessive water. You can add extensions to the downspouts to carry the water to a different area where it won't overwhelm any plants.

HOUSEPLANTS

Water poinsettia plants that you're trying to rebloom every couple of weeks until mid-December.

PERENNIALS

Summer-growing succulents such as agave, echeveria, euphorbia, ficus, lithops, and tillandsia will start entering dormancy this month through February and will require less water than usual. If grown in containers or any situation with limited drainage, try to control their water by relocating them to an area where they'll get limited or no rainfall.

FERTILIZE

ANNUALS

Feed fall- and winter-blooming annuals like pansies and calendulas once a month with a complete fertilizer to keep the bloom period going strong. For flowering kale and cabbage, a liquid fertilizer like fish emulsion or sea kelp is sufficient.

BULBS

Spring-blooming bulbs have just begun sending out new roots and will need feeding. Use a complete fertilizer that is high in phosphorus (such as one marked 10-10-10) to help the flower inside finish its development. As an alternative, you can apply half the fertilizer now and the other half in the spring when the buds begin to emerge, but I consider that too much work. Spring brings enough chores to get on with so I suggest giving the full feeding now.

HOUSEPLANTS

Most indoor plants will enter a cycle of little or no growth for the next few months, so stop fertilizing them until the spring. Continue feeding any blooming plants until they complete their bloom period.

Feed poinsettia plants that you're trying to rebloom with a liquid fertilizer every couple of weeks until mid-December.

LAWNS

If you fed your lawn in September with a high-nitrogen fertilizer, then you should do a follow-up feeding now with a high-phosphorous formula. Follow the directions on the fertilizer package for how to apply it and how much to use. Never apply fertilizer to a dry lawn; always make sure it has been watered well in advance of feeding.

■ *Spray trees for peach leaf curl once they are completely dormant.*

If you planted a new lawn from seed or laid sod in September, fertilize it four to six weeks later.

PROBLEM-SOLVE

EDIBLES

If your peach or nectarine trees showed signs of peach leaf curl the prior spring, take action now.

Peach leaf curl is a common fungal disease affecting both peach and nectarine trees. The fungus, called *Taphina deformans*, lives through the winter on the bark of the trees, but you won't notice its effects until spring. The symptoms appear about two weeks after leaves begin to emerge as red spots on the leaves, which become thick and puckered. Whitish spores appear on the leaves, which then turn yellow and fall off. New, healthy leaves will generally follow, but the cycle tends to take a toll on the overall health and vigor of the tree. You will probably find that some years there will be little or no problem with peach leaf curl, while other years it can be quite severe. That's because the prime environment for the fungus is when there is a period of cool, wet weather just when the leaves begin to emerge. The rain splashes the fungal spores around, spreading the disease. But whether the tree is lightly affected or more severely affected, repeated cases of peach leaf curl will reduce fruit production and eventually cause the tree to decline.

The only treatment for peach leaf curl is the application of a copper-based fungicide when the tree is dormant. Use a fungicide that contains at least 50 percent copper and spray the tree completely in late November and a second time in early February. (See February for information on spraying trees.)

Some varieties have been developed that have some resistance to peach leaf curl. 'Autumn Rose', 'Frost',

'Indian Free', 'Muir', 'Nanaimo', and 'Oregon Curl Free' are all resistant yellow peaches. 'Q-1-8' is a resistant white peach. 'Kreibich' is the only nectarine shown to have resistance to peach leaf curl. Many gardeners report, however, that even the resistant varieties benefit from spraying.

LAWNS

Even if you keep your lawn watered, mowed, and fertilized, ugly, stubborn weeds can spoil the look.

First, identify what type of weeds you have. One type is broadleaf weeds, including plants such as buttercup, chickweed, clovers, dandelions, English lawn daisies, pearlwort, plantain, speedwell (creeping Veronica), and yarrow. The second category is annual weeds, which include henbit, lamb's quarter, mallow, pigweed, and prostrate knotweed. Last, there are weedy grasses, which include annual bluegrass, crabgrass, pasture grasses, bentgrasses, Bermudagrass, quackgrass, and velvetgrass. For help identifying the weeds you have, search the Internet for "weeds" and look through photos until you find the type you have.

The simplest way to rid your lawn of weeds is to handpick them. It's important that you remove the entire plant, including the complete root. Leaving behind part of a dandelion's taproot or a rooting node of a buttercup or speedwell stem will make it possible for the plant to grow back. Using a hand

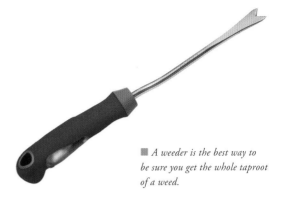

■ *A weeder is the best way to be sure you get the whole taproot of a weed.*

tool called a weeder makes it easier to pull out the complete weed.

For more pervasive weeds, consider how they reproduce in order to determine how best to control them. Weeds can be annual, biennial, or perennial. Annuals and biennials reproduce by setting seed. Most perennials also set seed but once mature they can additionally spread by stolons, rhizomes, bulbs, or tubers, making them even more pernicious. To halt the reproduction of weed seeds, apply a pre-emergent herbicide, which will prevent the seeds from germinating. To get rid of the weeds themselves, including their root systems, you need a post-emergent herbicide, which kills a weed by interfering with its metabolism.

Once you determine a strategy for controlling the weeds, you're ready to choose your weapon and attack. Because weeds can be an ongoing problem for lawns, it's best to try natural remedies first and save the chemical controls for only the most serious and tenacious weed problems. Corn-gluten meal is an effective pre-emergent herbicide. Sprays containing vinegar can be effective as post-emergent herbicides. Whether you use natural or chemical herbicides, *read the directions completely* before applying and follow all instructions regarding application as well as protecting yourself and the surrounding environment.

With the proper approach you can keep weeds from spreading throughout your lawn and stealing water and nutrients from the grass. But keep in mind that your goal should be to control weeds to keep them from becoming an unsightly problem for your lawn—not to eradicate them completely.

■ *Be sure to remove the entire taproot of a dandelion or else it will keep growing back.*

December

Close the year but not the garden. The advice you will most often hear at this time of year is about how to close the garden, implying that it's out of business or at least on hiatus. It's important, of course, to ready a garden for winter, cleaning and clearing out the dead or faded plants, covering furniture, and turning off irrigation systems as the rains take over the job of watering.

But in much of California, winter never gets harsh enough to really shut down a garden. Instead the garden downshifts into neutral in December, like an engine that never turns off but idles quietly through the short days and long nights. Manzanitas and other natives burst into bloom, evergreens maintain their composure, and succulents soldier on, all cheered on by cool-season annuals in hot shades. Even in areas blanketed by snow, while the outdoor garden rests, the indoor garden moves to the fore as bulbs are forced into bloom and tender plants take up their winter residence indoors.

Gardens are not meant to be merely blue-sky endeavors. Enjoying the garden year-round should be our goal. To do that, we have to keep the gate open and the path clear so that the garden can beckon us in at every moment. Even on days that are too cold to linger outside, the garden can comfort and delight us from a window, reminding us that even on the shortest of days the rewards of a garden stretch out long before us.

So tear the last page off the calendar and make your final entries in your garden journal. Remember the sweetest-smelling blossoms, the most successful harvests, the most eye-catching plants. Note the new bed you planted that now flourishes below your window and the bare-root tree you planted last winter, now taller than you and bare of leaves once again. Take a picture to mark your progress. Then close the book on the year and take up your daydreams for next year's garden. But leave the garden open, always waiting for your footstep and the next plunge of your fingers into the soil.

PLAN

ALL

As you clean and organize tools and gardening accessories this month, make a list of items that you need or that need to be replaced or repaired. You may find holiday sales on some of the items, or maybe you can add them to your Christmas wish list.

EDIBLES

If you hope to increase the productivity of your edible garden next year, check out some high-density planting plans for fruit trees. High-density planting offers several ways to plant and prune fruit trees to produce bigger and longer harvests by including cross-pollinators and varieties that bear at earlier and later times. The most common methods are planting two, three, or four trees in one hole; espaliering trees against a wall or fence; and planting multiple trees in a hedgerow. For diagrams of example high-density plantings, check out the California Rare Fruit Growers' (CRFG) website at www.crfg.org/tidbits/byo-examples.html.

■ *An espaliered tree can be grown against a wall (above) or as a standalone (below).*

Another technique for multiplying your harvest is to graft cuttings from compatible cross-pollinating varieties onto one tree. Some nurseries offer pre-grafted multiple-variety trees (apple trees are the most common trees sold this way), but you can also do the grafting yourself. Every winter (usually in January) the California Rare Fruit Growers local chapters hold a Scion Exchange where you can find cuttings from a wide range of fruit trees, as well as information and demonstrations on how to graft. Contact CRFG (www.crfg.org) for information.

ROSES

Start shopping early for bare-root roses to get the best selection. New introductions, particularly award-winning varieties such as the All-America Rose Selections, can sell out quickly in bare-root form and will cost more when purchased already potted.

TREES

Shop catalogs and online nurseries for bare-root fruit trees for the best selection. Pay close attention to the potential size of the variety you buy. While you can keep a standard tree pruned to 6 feet high, it's much easier to keep a dwarf cultivar within those limits. For small-space gardens, look for trees grafted with multiple varieties (sometimes called "fruit salad trees"), columnar-form trees (also called "fastigiate"), or trees that are already trained into an espalier form.

PLANT

ALL

There's still time to do plenty of planting in December but only if the soil is dry. Planting in soggy soil is a good way to get plants off to an unhealthy start, drowning tender roots before they've had a chance to settle in. Want to know how to tell if the soil is dry enough to work? Stick a shovel in to a depth of about 6 inches and pull it back out. If clumps of soil are still sticking to the shovel, the ground is too wet for planting.

ANNUALS

Quick and colorful containers or beds can still be planted with cool-season annuals like pansies, primroses, and calendulas.

■ *Soil that is too wet (which will stick together) will compact when you work it, destroying its structure. Wait until it's dry.*

BULBS

This is the final month for planting spring-flowering bulbs. The rule of thumb is that you should have them in the ground by Christmas, although I confess that I planted daffodils as late as early January during one particularly hectic fall and winter. Be sure to add either compost or a slow-release fertilizer to the hole when planting the bulbs.

EDIBLES

For coastal gardens, particularly in the Central Coast region, artichokes are a great addition to the edible and ornamental garden. Although sometimes grown as annuals, artichokes (*Cynara scolymus*) are herbaceous perennials, meaning that the plants die back to the ground in the winter, but regrow from the living root crowns the following spring. With silvery green foliage and edible flower buds that open to lavender thistles if left unharvested, they make beautiful accent plants that grow 3 to 5 feet tall.

Artichokes can be grown in zones 8 to 9 and are happiest in climates with cool, moist summers. They require full sun, but like afternoon shade in the hottest areas.

Plant container-grown artichokes in winter or early spring. (Dormant roots can be planted earlier, in the fall.) Space them 4 feet apart in mild climates or 2 feet apart in colder regions and plant with the shoots just above the soil level. Water well and mulch heavily; artichokes are thirsty plants.

Artichoke plants are generally productive for about five years and then must be replaced. 'Green Globe' is the favorite California artichoke, but 'Imperial Star' is also popular. 'Violetto' is an attractive purple variety that's smaller and turns green when cooked.

Kiwis are not only one of the most delicious fuzzy fruits you'll find, they're also a popular addition to edible gardens. Depending on the variety, kiwi vines can grow well even in some of the coldest parts of the state, and late fall or winter (just before or during their dormant period) is the best time to plant.

If you're going to grow kiwis, plant more than one. Most kiwis need a male plant nearby to pollinate the female (fruit-bearing) vines. One male can pollinate up to eight females. There are some self-fruitful varieties, but even with those you'll get a greater yield from each vine if you plant more than one. In addition to cross-pollination needs, pay attention to the required chill hours when choosing a variety. They can vary widely in how much cold they need to set fruit.

The type seen in supermarkets is fuzzy kiwi, but there are also hardy and arctic beauty kiwi, which are hardier, sweeter, and require no peeling. Fuzzy kiwi varieties (hardy in zones 7 to 9) include 'Elmwood' (needs 'Matua' to cross-pollinate), 'Hayward' (800 chill hours, needs a male), 'Tomuri Male' (low chill, cross-pollinate to 'Vincent'), 'Vincent' (100 chill hours, cross-pollinates with 'Tomuri Male'), 'Saanichton' (needs 'Matua' to cross-pollinate), and 'Matua' (cross-pollinates to 'Elmwood', 'Hayward', and 'Saanichton'). Recommended hardy varieties (hardy to zone 4)

include 'Ananasnaja', 'Dumbarton Oaks', 'Issai' (self-fruitful), 'Ken's Red', and 'Meyer's Cordifolia'. 'Male' will pollinate any female hardy kiwi. For arctic beauty kiwis (hardy to zone 3), try 'Frost', 'September Sun', and 'Male Kolomikta', which pollinates all female arctic beauty vines.

When planting, select a site with full sun (kiwis can tolerate partial shade but much prefer full sun). In hot-summer areas, they require afternoon shade. Kiwis need slightly acidic soil (pH 5.0–6.5) with excellent drainage.

Kiwi vines require a sturdy support structure, such as a pergola, fence, or trellis at least 6 feet high. Have the structure in place first, then plant the vine in a hole twice as wide but no deeper than the rootball. Water well and mulch. Refer to information on training kiwi vines for optimum fruiting later in this chapter.

It's not uncommon for Californians to harbor secret fantasies of owning their own vineyards. But even if you can't have a vineyard, you can successfully grow a grape vine or two (or more). In the milder parts of the state, this is the time to start planting bare-root vines. Cold-winter regions should hold off until three weeks before their last expected frost date. (Container-grown vines can sometimes be found in nurseries and can be planted throughout the year.)

■ *Kiwi vines need a sturdy support structure to keep them upright.*

Grapes can be grown in zones 4 to 10 but do especially well in hot-summer climates. If you live in an area that doesn't have particularly hot summers, try planting the vines against a south-facing wall or fence. Plant in full sun in deep, well-drained soil. Rich soil will make all the difference in the quality of the fruit.

Before planting bare-root vines, trim the roots back to just 6 inches. Plant the vines up to the soil line on the vine, spreading out the roots in all directions. Space the vines 8 to 10 feet apart. If planting near a support structure such as a pergola, fence, or arbor, leave 1½ feet between the structure and the vine and set the vine at a 45-degree angle, leaning toward the support structure. Once planted, cut back the top growth to leave just two or three buds.

There are four main types of grapes: American, European, muscadine, and hybrids. Except for muscadines, most grapes are self-fruitful. Check before buying to see if the variety needs a cross-pollinizer. Recommended American varieties include 'America', 'Champanel', 'Concord', 'Price', and 'Swenson Red'. For European grapes, try 'Black Monukka', 'Delight', 'Flame', and 'Olivette Blanche'. 'Cowart', 'Regale', and 'Sterling' are some good muscadine varieties. Recommended hybrids include 'Baco Noir', 'Foch Grape', and 'Missouri Riesling'.

Grapes can be targeted by grape leafhoppers, grape mealybugs, grape berry moths, and Japanese beetles, as well as birds and deer, but diseases such as anthracnose, black rot, and mildew are an even bigger worry. Pierce's disease, which is spread by the sharpshooter insect and can cause vines to wilt and die, has become a serious problem in California. Buying disease-resistant vines is your best bet, and American, muscadine, and hybrid grapes are the most disease resistant.

HOUSEPLANTS

Pot up an indoor herb garden that will add flavor, fragrance, and variety to your meals at the same time it brightens and scents your home through the winter. See Here's How to Grow an Indoor Herb Garden.

PERENNIALS AND SHRUBS

Winter is a good time to plant California native perennials and shrubs, particularly in the interior regions of the state. As long as temperatures stay above 15 degrees Fahrenheit long enough for plants to harden off, they should do well and winter rains will help them get established. In times of winter drought, however, newly planted natives still need watering every week deeply enough that the water penetrates to the entire depth of the rootball.

ROSES

In warmer parts of the state (zones 8 and above) plant container-grown roses and bare-root roses as soon as they're available. Do not fertilize following planting to avoid encouraging a lot of tender new growth that might be vulnerable to frosts.

TREES

Nut trees are a terrific addition to the garden, both as an edible and as a focal point. They require a fair amount of space as they usually require a second tree for cross-pollination, and even the dwarf varieties are not all that small. But if you have the space, consider adding one of these beauties to your landscape.

Almonds (*Prunus dulcis*) are so well-suited to growing in California that 80 percent of the world's almond supply comes from our state. Almonds are hardy to 10 degrees Fahrenheit, but require 250 to 500 chill hours and do best in zones 5 to 9. They require full sun and well-drained soil, but dwarf trees can be planted in large containers.

Plant in a hole twice as wide but no deeper than the rootball. Make sure that soil does not cover the graft union. Take care that roots do not dry out before planting and water well once planted. Once it's in the ground, prune off the top third of the tree; this will encourage better root formation and a healthier tree structure.

Most standard trees require a second tree of a compatible variety for cross-pollination. If space is tight, you can plant two varieties of standard trees in the same hole (18 to 24 inches apart) or plant a dwarf variety nearby as the cross-pollinizer.

HERE'S HOW

TO GROW AN INDOOR HERB GARDEN

1. Begin with healthy seedlings that are full and bushy; leggy seedlings are already showing the effects of insufficient light. Good choices for indoor growing include basil, bay, chervil, chives, lemon balm, mint, oregano, parsley, rosemary, sage, tarragon, and thyme. Plant the seedlings in clean containers with a drainage hole using a sterile potting mix. Using dirty pots or regular garden soil is an invitation for disease and pests to decimate your fresh herbs.

2. Place the potted herbs where they will get six hours of sunlight each day. A south-facing window usually provides the best light. If you don't have a spot with enough natural light, you can substitute with two 40-watt cool white fluorescent bulbs. Place the plants 6 to 12 inches from the lights for 14 to 16 hours a day.

3. Keep herbs at approximately 65 to 70 degrees Fahrenheit during the day and 55 to 60 degrees at night. Herbs will not survive indoors at temperatures below 50 degrees.

4. Water regularly. Don't let the soil become soggy or completely dry out. Dry indoor air can take a toll on herbs; try sitting the pots on a tray of pebbles with water to keep enough moisture in the air. Good air circulation also helps to keep them from getting stressed.

5. Feed your herbs every couple of weeks with a low-dose, water-soluble fertilizer. Don't go overboard, as too much fertilizer can affect the flavor and fragrance of the herbs.

6. If you should find any pests making a home in your herb garden, spray the plants with a weak dishwashing liquid solution (1 to 2 tablespoons dish soap in 1 gallon of water). Make sure you wash any leaves you harvest before cooking and eating.

Almonds bloom in early spring. Frosts occurring during or soon after bloom time can reduce the yield, so if your area is prone to early spring frosts, choose a later-blooming variety, such as 'Butte', 'Mission', or 'Titan'. Recommended dwarf varieties include 'Garden Prince' and 'All-in-One' (semi-dwarf). For standard trees, consider the following varieties: 'Butte' (pollinate with 'All-in-One', 'Nonpareil', or 'Mission'); 'Mission' (pollinate with 'Nonpareil' or 'Hall's Hardy'); 'Ne Plus Ultra' or 'Nonpareil' (pollinate each other); or 'Titan' (pollinate with 'Hall's Hardy', or any peach (a close relative to the almond) blooming at the same time. A mature standard tree yields 20 to 25 pounds of nuts per year.

Pound for pound, planting a pecan tree (*Carya illinoensis*) might be one of the most cost-efficient things you could do in your garden. Growing up to 100 feet tall, these large, stately trees are not only beautiful in the landscape, but they produce prodigious amounts of expensive nuts that are high in protein, omega-6 fatty acids, and antioxidants.

Pecans do best in the inland areas where summers are long and hot, but they can be grown anywhere in zones 5 to 9. Plant in full sun in well-drained soil; they can't tolerate salt in the soil. Pecans have very deep roots ,so they should be planted only where the root systems will be able to grow to a depth of 6 to 10 feet. Plant the trees at least 40 feet apart and 20 feet away from other structures (foundations, sidewalks, driveways, or power lines).

Pecan trees have a long taproot and must be handled carefully when planting. Make sure the hole is as deep as the rootball and twice as wide and that the graft union is above the soil level. Fill in the soil around the rootball, making sure the tree is straight, and water well.

Pecans are divided into Type 1 and Type 2 varieties. Generally, you need one tree of each type for cross-pollination. Type 1 varieties that do well in California include 'Cheyenne' and 'Pawnee'. Recommended Type 2 varieties include 'Western-Schley', 'Burkett', 'Mohawk', 'Wichita', 'Shoshani', and 'Kanza'. Pecan trees do not produce nuts for the first five to seven years and they produce a light or no crop in alternate years. A ten-year-old tree produces about 10 pounds of nuts, but a fully mature tree can yield a substantial harvest—up to 100 pounds.

CARE

ALL

Mulch is a good addition to the garden any time of year, but in the colder months it has a special purpose: It protects plants from extreme temperature fluctuations and helps them to stay dormant. Sudden drops in temperature can cause shallow-rooted plants and newly planted specimens that have not yet developed sturdy root systems to be heaved out of the ground and exposed to the cold. A layer of mulch helps maintain an even soil temperature to avoid that heaving. This even soil temperature also helps keep the plant from breaking dormancy too early when freezing temperatures or frost could kill tender leaf buds.

Timing is important when it comes to mulching for the winter. Wait until plants are fully dormant and nighttime temperatures are consistently below freezing. If you spread mulch before that, you can create an environment that is conducive to breeding pests and diseases.

A healthy mulch is a 2- to 4-inch layer of organic material, such as pine needles, dead leaves, straw, or small wood chips. Spread the material evenly, making sure not to pile the mulch up around tree trunks, which can cause them to rot. (See June for information on choosing the best mulch material.)

Some plants, such as strawberries, should be completely covered in cold-winter regions in order to protect the tender crowns. In these cases, cover the plants with a 4-inch layer of a lightweight mulch that won't mat together, such as straw or pine needles. For taller plants that need such protection, you can create a wire cage around the plant and fill it with leaves or straw.

◼ *In winter mulch protects plants from extreme temperature fluctuations.*

HERE'S HOW

TO ADD WOOD MULCH TO LANDSCAPE BEDS

1   *Before adding any mulch, spread a pre-emergent herbicide. There are organic and conventional choices for pre-emergents, which work by preventing weed seeds from sprouting. You'll save yourself a lot of time and backaches if you use a pre-emergent. (If you have an area where you like to let plants go to seed, and you leave the seeds to resprout, don't use pre-emergent.)*

2   *Next, add the mulch by creating little piles around your landscape beds. You can buy mulch two ways: in bags or in bulk. Most home-improvement stores sell bagged mulch, and they'll probably have several brands of the same type of mulch. Some home improvement stores and garden centers sell bulk mulch. To buy bulk mulch, you usually need a truck so you can bring home a big load. If you're buying more than 3 cubic yards of mulch, you will want to consider delivery. A pitchfork and wheelbarrow are handy for moving bulk mulch.*

3   *Use a hard rake or a four-tine claw to rake the mulch around the bed. Start raking from either the back or one side of the bed so you can leave "fluffy" mulch behind you. You will want to put mulch across the entire bed, at least 3 inches deep.*

4   *After spreading the mulch in the landscape bed, pull it slightly away from plant stems and leaves. Mulch is usually warm and moist—the perfect environment for bacteria and fungi to live and thrive. These microorganisms can rot your plant stems, so leave a little breathing room between the mulch and plants.*

EDIBLES

Prune kiwi vines during winter while they are still dormant. In the first year train one strong shoot up the support structure and tie it in place. Prune out all the other shoots coming from the crown. When the shoot grows to the top of the structure, pinch the tip to encourage lateral growth and tie it in place. Train two lateral branches, and take off any other lateral branches coming off the main stem.

In the second year train two shoots at the top of the main stem horizontally and tie in place. In the second winter, trim each one back to twelve to eighteen buds. The next year, clean up the vine, removing water sprouts and dead or weak wood, but be sure not to remove the fruiting spurs on the lateral branches. In later years, thin the fruiting lateral branches to 6 inches apart and cut the remaining laterals to 18 inches.

Cut asparagus stems down to the ground and clear away the debris to prevent asparagus beetles from overwintering. In areas with snowfall, you can leave the stems up until spring to catch some of the snow and keep it off of the plant crowns.

Make a final pass through your edible garden to clean up fallen fruit and clear out debris. This sanitation practice will go a long way to preventing problems in next year's garden.

HOUSEPLANTS

To maintain a potted poinsettia (*Euphorbia pulcherrima*), place it near a sunny south- or west-facing window. Keep it at 65 to 70 degrees Fahrenheit during the daytime and about 5 degrees cooler at night. Blasts of cold or hot air can cause the leaves to drop. Do not let the soil dry out completely, but do not let the plant sit in a saucer of standing water. Following these procedures should maintain the blossoms and healthy foliage through the holiday season and somewhat beyond.

Poinsettias are fussy plants when it comes to getting them to reflower the following year. For best results, continue watering until April 1, then begin to withhold water, allowing the plant to dry out gradually. Once it's dry, store it in a cool, well-ventilated area (but not below 60 degrees Fahrenheit).

In June begin hardening the plant off by moving it outdoors to a shady location. Keep watering and fertilizing. In early July pinch back each stem, then pinch it back again in late August, leaving three or four leaves on each stem. After the second pinch, return the plant to the same light and temperature conditions it had previously indoors. Keep watering and fertilizing.

Starting on October 1 and for the following ten weeks, the poinsettia must be kept in complete darkness for twelve hours each night in order to stimulate blooming. Continue fertilizing until mid-December.

For all that, there's a good chance your poinsettia will not reflower successfully. Like I said, they're fussy, but give it your best shot.

Many other flowering houseplants are given at this time of year. If you find yourself with containers of cyclamen, azaleas, or other flowering container plants that you want to maintain indoors for a while, find a spot for them with bright indirect light with temperatures that stay above 60 degrees Fahrenheit. Avoid keeping them near heater vents or doorways with cold-air drafts.

To maintain holiday greenery such as evergreen wreaths and garlands indoors, choose one of the longer-lasting evergreens—pine, cedar, and the longest-lasting, fir. It helps to soak greenery for a few hours before hanging it, but you can also spritz it with water every few days to keep it fresh or spray it with an antitranspirant to help it retain its natural moisture. (It's best to spray it before bringing it in the house.) Keep greenery away from heater vents, fireplaces, and bright windows. If you'll be decorating it with lights, use LED lights, as they stay cooler and are more energy-efficient. Be aware that berries on holiday greenery such as holly and mistletoe can be poisonous and should be kept away from children and pets.

LAWNS

In the parts of the state where there's enough snow on the ground to cover the lawn during winter or if you have a cool-season grass that dies back in the winter, you should clean and store your lawn mower for the winter. Even in areas where lawn

HERE'S HOW

TO SPREAD PINE STRAW MULCH

1 *Buy the mulch. Pine straw is sold in bales, just like hay. Bales can be prickly, and spiders and other insects like to hang out in pine straw, so use gloves when handling the bales. Look for bales that don't appear to have a lot of other material in them—cones, twigs, or pieces of ferns. Pine straw is raked and baled from yards and commercial forests, and sometimes it comes with hitchhiking plants or weeds. Nutsedge is one type of weed that tends to come along, so if you can, put down a pre-emergent herbicide before using pine straw. If you need to control nutsedge that is already sprouting, Image® is the best chemical product to use. It is virtually the only thing that will kill nutsedge.*

2 *To add the pine straw to the landscape, simply snip the twine holding a bale together, and the bale will break apart into clumps called "flakes." Sprinkle the flakes around the landscape bed or trees, being careful to keep*

the straw near the ground. If you fling pine straw around above your waist, you'll end up with needles hanging all over your shrubs, and that's annoying to clean up.

3 *The newly spread straw will be fluffy, and it will most likely escape the landscape beds. To tidy up the beds, you'll want to rake and tuck the straw to keep it in place. Using a hard rake, pull the straw into the edge of the landscape bed. Step on the straw on top of the rake, and then, leaving your foot where it is, pull the rake out. This bunches up the straw at the edge of the bed.*

4 *To tuck the straw, after raking, plunge a sharpened spade or shovel into the ground about 1 inch inside the landscape bed. This will trap the edge of the straw in the soil and keep it from blowing out of the bed. You can use a chopping motion to do this.*

■ *You can keep holiday greens fresher by spritzing them with water every few days*

mowing is necessary year-round, this is a good time to give your lawn mower a once-over to ensure it's in good shape for the coming year.

PERENNIALS

Some succulents need extra protection not just from freezes but also from heavy rains, particularly in zones 8 and below. Move container plants where they have some shelter under the eaves of the house or under taller trees and shrubs. Since many succulents go dormant during winter, keep them fairly dry during this time (and withhold fertilizer).

This is a good time to lightly prune hellebores so they will be clean and in prime shape when their flowers start to open. Hellebores can be prone to a fungal leaf spot disease that causes unattractive brown lesions on the leaves. It's not likely to be severe enough to damage the plant, but it's more of a cosmetic problem, so just trim the affected

leaves and clean up any fallen plant debris to avoid spreading the fungal spores. Aphids can also be a problem on hellebores but can be removed with a blast of the hose or just wiping them off the plant with a damp paper towel. Avoid overfertilizing hellebores, which can cause a flush of tender growth that attracts aphids.

SHRUBS & TREES

People sometimes think that evergreens are maintenance-free plants, but while they often require less care than other plants, they still need some extra help to get through the winter without damage from the elements.

Late autumn or early winter is the time to make sure that your evergreens have enough water to get them through cold months, particularly if you live in a dry winter climate. Water the plants deeply and apply a 3-inch layer of mulch to keep the moisture in the ground and accessible to the roots.

HERE'S HOW

TO CLEAN AND STORE A LAWN MOWER FOR THE WINTER

1. It's not good for the engine to sit with a partially filled gas tank, which can cause moisture that leads to rust. Begin by adding a fuel stabilizer and running the motor for a few minutes to distribute it throughout the carburetor and the rest of the system. Turn the engine off and let it cool. You can then either fill the tank completely or empty it. To empty it, siphon out as much of the gas as you can into a clean can. Restart the engine and let it run until it stops. Repeat until it won't start again. Whether you keep the gas in the engine or store it separately in a can, the stabilizer should keep the gas fresh for up to six months.

2. Change the oil and oil filter. Refer to the manual for your mower for instructions on doing oil changes.

3. Disconnect the negative battery cable and remove the battery from the battery terminal. Clean the terminal with a terminal cleaning fluid. Store the battery in a cool, dry location away from any flammable liquids or any appliance with a pilot light.

4. Detach the mower blade and sharpen it.

5. Wipe off all lawn clippings, dirt, and debris from the top and undercarriage of the mower, using a wire brush or putty knife to remove more stubborn build-up.

6. Reattach the blade.

7. Replace the air filter and make sure the cooling vents are clear of dirt and debris.

8. Replace the spark plug with a fresh one.

■ *Check the air filter.*

■ *Check the oil.*

One of the biggest winter threats to evergreens isn't so much the cold, but the drying effects of wind. Newly planted evergreens are particularly susceptible to this kind of damage. The best way to protect a tender evergreen from wind damage is to build a windbreak around it. Drive four strong stakes or poles into the ground around the plant, then wrap chicken wire around it and fasten it closed. Wrap the wire cage in burlap and fasten the burlap securely to the chicken wire. If this kind of windbreak seems like more protection than you need or too unsightly, you can try spraying the plant with an antidesiccant to minimize the drying effects of the wind. Antidesiccants should

Change the oil.

Clean out the bag and undercarriage.

9. Store the mower and any cans of gas or oil in a cool, dry location away from any water heater, furnace, or other appliance with a pilot light.

With your mower cleaned and safely stored, it will be ready to be put into action again in the spring.

be applied before temperatures regularly reach freezing levels.

After wind damage, the next biggest threat that winter presents is the weight of snow or ice breaking branches. To protect smaller evergreens like junipers and cedars, pull the branches up

against the trunk and working from the bottom up, wrap the tree with twine, the same way commercial growers wrap up Christmas trees for transport. With the branches cinched in tight, the snow or ice won't have horizontal branches to pile up on.

Another option is to use commercial tree wraps, which are basically burlap netting that you wrap around a plant and tie into place. Make sure you buy the tree wraps intended for winter use, not the cardboard or paper ones that are used to prevent sunburn. It's important that the wrap be applied loosely enough to allow some air circulation through the branches and that it be removed as soon as the threat of snow or ice damage has passed.

To shield plants from frost damage, see November for suggestions on protective coverings.

Keep fallen camellia blossoms raked up from beneath the plant, particularly during periods of rainfall. Leaving them in place encourages the fungal spores that cause petal blight to settle into the soil, causing future blossoms to appear with ugly brown lesions. Applying a 3- to 4-inch layer of mulch beneath the plant also helps to keep the spores from surviving and breaks the disease cycle.

Tree wraps can help protect trees from snow, ice, and freezing.

You can begin winter pruning of deciduous trees and shrubs as soon as they appear to enter dormancy. (See January for information on winter pruning.)

WATER

ALL

Make sure plants are watered well whenever there's a frost warning. Sufficient hydration can make all the difference in surviving a frost or freeze.

You may be able to adjust your irrigation schedule again or, if there is sufficient rainfall, turn your irrigation system off completely. If you live in an area that has hard freezes, winterize your irrigation system by draining the pipes manually or automatically, depending on the system, or blowing out the pipes to remove any water remaining in the system, which could freeze and break the pipes. If you have never winterized your system before, it's best to consult an irrigation professional to make sure your particular system is managed correctly.

If you have enough storage space, you may want to consider setting up rain barrels to harvest the rainfall. If you collect rain that runs off your roof, be sure to use that water only for ornamental plants. The water may have collected toxins as it ran off the roof that would make it unusable for watering edible plants. Rain harvesting makes more sense in places where rains are intermittent throughout the year, so rain barrels are constantly filling up and being used for watering. Here where we have wet winters and dry summers, the barrels fill up fast and empty fast and then may remain empty for months. But if you have the space and the barrels, it's a shame to let that rainfall go to waste.

HOUSEPLANTS

Many houseplants are not growing much at this time of year and therefore need less water. Home heaters, however, can dry out plants faster than usual, so you have to take care to get houseplants the right amount of water without overdoing it. The best way is to give it the finger test: Stick your finger into the soil to the depth of the full rootball. If the soil is dry all the way down, it's time to water.

Water poinsettia plants that you're trying to rebloom every couple of weeks until mid-December.

FERTILIZE

ALL

Although native California plants generally don't require additional fertilization, especially when planted in heavy clay soil, winter-blooming natives growing in sandy soil can benefit from a light feeding now. Apply a sidedressing of compost or, if using a commercial fertilizer, choose one with a low-nitrogen formula and apply half the recommended amount.

ANNUALS

Apply a balanced fertilizer to cool-season annuals early in the month to encourage blooming before Christmas. Annuals not in bloom by that time will have a harder time flowering in the later winter. Use a liquid fertilizer for faster action.

BULBS

Begin fertilizing spring-flowering bulbs as soon as the leaves begin to appear, but avoid a high-nitrogen fertilizer, which will only stimulate green growth rather than flowering and can lead to bulb rot.

HOUSEPLANTS

Feed poinsettia plants that you're trying to rebloom with a liquid fertilizer every couple of weeks until the middle of the month.

PROBLEM-SOLVE

ALL

If you have roses, shrubs, or small trees that appear to be wasting away and you dig them up to find that they have almost no roots left, you may have a gopher problem. Gophers are furry rodents, 5 to 14 inches long, that dig tunnels and feed off of the roots of many kinds of plants. In addition, they'll venture short distances out of their burrows to feed on vegetation nearby and

■ *Pocket gopher in its burrow.*

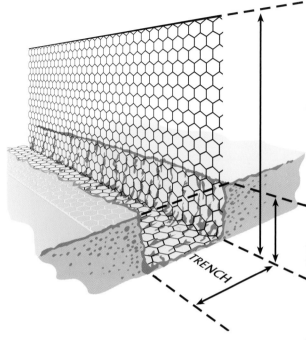

■ *To protect beds from gophers (and rabbits) bury wire mesh fencing under the bed and up the sides (about 6 inches).*

even pull entire plants back into their tunnels to eat. In addition to the damage that the gophers do, they attract larger predators like moles, which will do even more damage digging to reach the gophers. If you have a gopher problem, you're not likely to ever actually see a gopher since they spend most of their time below ground. What you will see, in addition to the plant damage, are fan-shaped mounds of freshly turned dirt with a plugged hole on one side of the mound. (If you find unplugged holes with no mounds of dirt, the problem is more likely to be ground squirrels, not gophers.)

In California, gophers are classified as nongame animals, which means you can control them on your property by any legal means, including trapping, baiting, fumigation, or repellents. Each of these methods has its problems, however. Commercial fumigants can be dropped into the tunnels, but gophers are sometimes able to seal off their tunnels quickly enough to evade the gas. Toxic baits can be dropped into the burrows, but you may not feel comfortable leaving feed laced with strychnine or other lethal poisons

around your garden. Commercially sold traps are effective, but you need to be fairly diligent about setting multiple traps to really reduce the gopher population. Some people have installed owl boxes to attract the gophers' natural predators to the area, but owls have such large hunting territories that it's unlikely that they'll have much effect in controlling the gophers in your garden.

Repellents have limited success but may be the best method to start with. The most effective repellent seems to be granular castor oil. Broadcast the granules at a rate of 1 pound per 1,000 square feet and water them in. The granules will dissolve into the soil and the scent of the castor oil should send the gophers scurrying out of your garden.

You can take the extra step of protecting some of your more precious plants in wire baskets in the ground. Bulbs, roses, bamboo, and fig tree roots are reportedly some of their favorites, but gophers are herbivores and will eat whatever plant material is available. Keeping your garden free of weeds will also help to discourage gophers from turning your garden into their smorgasbord.

Glossary

Acidic soil: Soil with a pH level lower than 5.5. Most flowering and fruiting plants prefer a soil a bit on the acidic side.

Afternoon sun: Full sun from 1 to 5 p.m. daily, with more shade during the morning hours.

Alkaline soil: Soil with a pH level higher than 7.0. Many desert plants thrive in slightly alkaline soils.

Annual: A plant that germinates (sprouts), flowers, and dies within one year or season (spring, summer, winter, or fall).

Bacillus thuringiensis (B.t.): An organic pest control based on naturally occurring soil bacteria, often used to control harmful caterpillars such as cutworms, leaf rollers, and webworms.

Bare-root plants: Plants that are shipped dormant, without being planted in soil or having soil around their roots. Roses are often shipped bare root.

Beneficial insects: Insects that perform valuable services such as pollination and pest control. Ladybugs, soldier beetles, and some bees are examples.

Biennial: A plant that blooms during its second year and then dies.

Bolting: The process when a plant switches from leaf growth to producing flowers and seeds. Bolting often occurs quite suddenly and is usually undesirable, because the plant usually dies shortly after bolting.

Brown materials: High-carbon materials such as brown leaves and grass, woody plant stems, dryer lint, and sawdust used in composting.

Bud: An undeveloped shoot nestled between the leaf and the stem that will eventually produce a flower or plant branch.

Bulb: A plant with a large, rounded underground storage organ formed by the plant stem and leaves. Examples are tulips, daffodils, and hyacinths. Bulbs that flower in spring are typically planted in fall.

Bush: *See* shrub.

Cane: A stem on a fruit shrub; usually blackberry or raspberry stems are called canes, but blueberry stems can also be referred to as canes.

Central leader: The term for the center trunk of a fruit tree.

Chill hours: Hours when the air temperature is below 45°F; chilling hours are related to fruit production.

Container: Any pot or vessel that is used for planting; containers can be ceramic, clay, steel, or plastic—or a teacup, bucket, or barrel.

Container garden: A garden that is created primarily by growing plants in containers instead of in the ground.

Container-grown: A plant that is grown, sold, and shipped while in a pot.

Cool-season annual: A flowering plant, such as snapdragon or pansy, that thrives during cooler months.

Cool-season vegetable: A vegetable, such as spinach, broccoli, and peas, that thrives during cooler months.

Cover crop: Plants grown specifically to enrich the soil, prevent erosion, suppress weeds, and control pests and diseases.

Cross-pollinate: The transfer of pollen from one plant to another plant.

Cut-and-come-again crop: Plants such as lettuces and other greens that can be grown from seed and harvested with scissors when only a few inches high and still tender, leaving the roots intact to keep sending up new leaves for future harvests.

Dappled shade: Bright shade created by high tree branches or tree foliage, where patches of sunlight and shade intermingle.

Day-neutral plant: A plant that flowers when it reaches a certain size, regardless of the day length.

Deadhead: Removing dead flowers to encourage further bloom and prevent the plant from going to seed.

Deciduous plant: A plant that loses its leaves seasonally, typically in fall or early winter.

Diatomaceous earth: A natural control for snails, slugs, flea beetles, and other garden pests, consisting of ground-up fossilized remains of sea creatures.

Dibber: A tool consisting of a pointed wooden stick with a handle. Used for poking holes in the ground so seedlings, seeds, and small bulbs can be planted.

Dividing: A technique consisting of digging up clumping perennials, separating the roots, and replanting. Dividing plants encourages vigorous growth and is typically performed in the spring or fall.

Dormancy: The period when plants stop growing in order to conserve energy; this happens naturally and seasonally, usually in winter.

Drip line: The ground area under the outer circumference of tree branches. This is where most of the tree's roots that absorb water and nutrients are found.

Dwarf: A tree that grows no taller than 10 feet tall and is usually a dwarf as a result of the rootstock of the tree.

Evergreen: A plant that keeps its leaves year-round, instead of dropping them seasonally.

Floating row covers: Lightweight fabric that can be used to protect plants from pests. Usually white in color.

Flower stalk: The stem that supports the flower and elevates it so that insects can reach the flower and pollinate it.

Four-inch pot: The 4-inch-by-4-inch pots that many annuals and small perennials are sold in. Four-inch pots can also be sold in flats of 18 or 20.

Frost: Ice crystals that form when the temperature falls below freezing (32°F).

Full sun: Areas of the garden that receive direct sunlight for six to eight hours a day or more, with no shade.

Fungicide: A chemical compound used to control fungal diseases.

Gallon container: A standard nursery-sized container for plants, roughly equivalent to a gallon container of milk.

Garden fork: A garden implement with a long handle and short tines, used for loosening and turning soil.

Garden lime: A soil amendment that lowers soil acidity and raises the pH.

Garden soil: The existing soil in a garden bed; it is generally evaluated by its nutrient content and texture. Garden soil is also sold as a bagged item at garden centers and home improvement stores.

Germination: The process by which a plant emerges from a seed or a spore.

Grafted tree: A tree composed of two parts: the top, or scion, which bears fruit, and the bottom, or rootstock.

Graft union: The place on a fruit tree trunk where the rootstock and the scion have been joined.

Granular fertilizer: A type of fertilizer that comes in a dry, pellet-like form rather than a liquid or powder.

Grass clippings: The parts of grass that are removed when mowing. Grass clippings are a valuable source of nitrogen for the lawn or the compost pile.

Green materials: An essential element in composting that includes grass clippings, kitchen scraps, and manure and provides valuable nitrogen in the pile.

Hand pruners: An important hand tool that consists of two sharp blades that perform a scissoring motion, used for light pruning, clipping, and cutting.

Hardening off: The process of slowly acclimating seedlings and young plants grown in an indoor environment to the outdoors.

Hardiness Zone Map: A map listing average annual minimum temperature ranges of a particular area. This information is helpful in determining appropriate plants for the garden.

Hard rake: A tool with a long handle and rigid tines at the bottom, used for moving a variety of garden debris, such as soil, mulch, leaves, and pebbles.

Hedging: The practice of trimming a line of plants to create a solid mass for privacy or garden definition.

Heirloom: A plant that was more commonly grown pre-World War II.

Hoe: A long-handled garden tool with a short, narrow, flat steel blade, used for breaking up hard soil and removing weeds.

Hose breaker: A device that screws onto the end of a garden hose to disperse the flow of water from the hose.

Host plant: A plant grown to feed caterpillars that will eventually morph into butterflies.

Hybrid: Plants produced by crossing two genetically different plants, often bred to have desirable characteristics such as disease resistance.

Insecticide: A substance used for destroying or controlling insects that are harmful to plants. Insecticides are available in organic and synthetic forms.

Irrigation: A system of watering the landscape. Irrigation can be an in-ground automatic system, soaker or drip hoses, or hand-held hoses with nozzles.

Jute twine: A natural-fiber twine, jute is used for gently staking plants or tying them to plant supports.

Landscape fabric: A synthetic material that is laid on the soil surface to control weeds and prevent erosion.

Larva: The immature stage of an insect that goes through complete metamorphosis; caterpillars are butterfly or moth larvae.

Leaf rake: A long-handled rake with flexible tines on the head, used for easily and efficiently raking leaves into piles.

Liquid fertilizer: Plant fertilizer in a liquid form. Some types need to be mixed with water, and some types are ready to use from the bottle.

Long-day plant: Plants that flower when the days are longer than their critical photoperiod. Long-day plants typically flower in early summer, when the days are still getting longer.

Loppers: One of the largest manual gardening tools, used for pruning branches of 1 to 3 inches in diameter with a scissoring motion.

Morning sun: Direct sunlight during morning hours that hits garden areas that have an eastern exposure.

Mulch: Any type of material that is spread over the soil surface around the base of plants to suppress weeds and retain soil moisture.

Nematode: Microscopic, wormlike organisms that live in the soil; some nematodes are beneficial, while others are harmful.

Naturalized: Plants that are introduced into an area, as opposed to being native to it.

Nectar plant: Plants that have flowers that produce nectar that attracts and feeds butterflies, encouraging a succession of blooms throughout the season.

New wood (new growth): The new growth on plants characterized by a greener, more tender form than older, woodier growth.

Nozzle: A device that attaches to the end of a hose and disperses water through a number of small holes; the resulting spray covers a wider area.

Offset: A small plant that is produced naturally and asexually on the parent plant and is genetically identical to the parent. It can be removed from the parent plant and rooted to grow as a separate adult plant.

Old wood: Growth that is more than one year old. Some plants flower and fruit on old wood. If you prune these plants in spring before they flower, you will cut off the wood that will produce fruit.

Organic: Derived from naturally occurring materials instead of materials synthesized in a lab.

Part shade: Areas of the garden that receive three to six hours of sun a day. Plants requiring part shade will often require protection from the more intense afternoon sun, either from tree leaves or from a building.

Part sun: Areas of the garden that receive three to six hours of sun a day. Although the term is often used interchangeably with "part shade," a "part sun" designation places greater emphasis on the minimal sun requirements.

Perennial: A plant that lives for more than two years. Examples include trees, shrubs, and some flowering plants.

Pesticide: A substance used for destroying or controlling insects that are harmful to plants. Pesticides are available in organic and synthetic forms.

pH: A figure designating the acidity or the alkalinity of garden soil, measured on a scale of 1 to 14, with 7.0 being neutral.

Pinch: A method to remove unwanted plant growth with your fingers, promoting bushier growth and increased blooming.

Pitchfork: A hand tool with a long handle and sharp metal prongs, typically used for moving loose material such as mulch or hay.

Plant label: A label or sticker on a plant container that provides a description of the plant and information on its care and growth habits.

Pollination: The transfer of pollen for fertilization from the male pollen-bearing structure (stamen) to the female structure (pistil), usually by wind, bees, butterflies, moths, or hummingbirds; this process is required for fruit production.

Potting soil: A mixture used to grow flowers, herbs, and vegetables in containers. Potting soil provides proper drainage and extra nutrients for healthy growth.

Powdery mildew: A fungal disease characterized by white powdery spots on plant leaves and stems. This disease is worse during times of drought or when plants have poor air circulation.

Pre-emergent herbicide: A weedkiller that works by preventing weed seeds from sprouting.

Pruning: A garden task in which a variety of hand tools are used to remove dead or overgrown branches to increase plant fullness and health.

Pruning saw: A hand tool for pruning smaller branches and limbs that features a long, serrated blade with an elongated handle.

Push mower: A lawn mower that is propelled by the user rather than a motor, typically having between five to eight steel blades that turn and cut as the mower is pushed.

Reel mower: A mower in which the blades spin vertically with a scissoring motion to cut grass blades.

Rhizome: An underground horizontal stem that grows side shoots, a rhizome is similar to a bulb.

Rootball: The network of roots and soil clinging to a plant when it is lifted out of the ground.

Rootstock: The bottom part of a grafted fruit tree, rootstocks are often used to create dwarf fruit trees, impart pest or disease resistance, or make a plant more cold hardy.

Rotary spreader: A garden tool that distributes seed and herbicides in a pattern wider than the base of the spreader.

Runner: A stem sprouting from the center of a strawberry plant; a runner produces fruit in its second year.

Scaffold branch: A horizontal branch that emerges almost perpendicular to the trunk.

Scion: The top, fruit-bearing part of a grafted fruit tree.

Seed packet: The package in which vegetable and flower seeds are sold; it typically includes growing instructions, a planting chart, and harvesting information.

Seed-starting mix: Typically a soilless blend of perlite, vermiculite, peat moss, and other ingredients, specifically formulated for growing plants from seed.

Self-fertile: A plant that does not require cross-pollination from another plant in order to produce fruit.

Semidwarf: A fruit tree grafted onto a rootstock that restricts growth of the tree to one-half to two-thirds of its natural size.

Shade: The absence of any direct sunlight in a given area, usually due to tree foliage or building shadows.

Short-day plant: Flowering when the length of day is shorter than its critical photoperiod, short-day plants typically bloom during fall, winter, or early spring.

Shovel: A handled tool with a broad, flat blade and slightly upturned sides, used for moving soil and other garden materials.

Shredded hardwood mulch: A mulch consisting of shredded wood that interlocks, resisting washout and suppressing weeds, hardwood mulch can change soil pH.

Shrub: A woody plant that is distinguished from a tree by its multiple trunks and branches and its shorter height of less than 15 feet tall.

Shrub rake: A long-handled rake with a narrow head that fits easily into tight spaces between plants.

Sidedress: To sprinkle compost or slow-release fertilizer along the side of a plant row or plant stem.

Slow-release fertilizer: A form of fertilizer that releases nutrients at a slower rate throughout the season, requiring less-frequent applications.

Snips: A hand tool used for snipping small plants and flowers as well as harvesting fruits, vegetables, and flowers.

Soaker hose: An efficient watering system in which a porous hose, usually made from recycled rubber, allows water to seep out around plant roots.

Soil knife: A garden knife with a sharp, serrated edge, used for cutting twine, plant roots, turf, and other garden materials.

Soil test: An analysis of a soil sample that determines the level of nutrients (to identify deficiencies) and detects pH.

Spade: A short-handled tool with a sharp, rectangular metal blade that is used for cutting and digging soil or turf.

Spur: A small, compressed, fruit-bearing branch on a fruit tree.

Standard: Describing a fruit tree grown on its own seedling rootstock or a nondwarfing rootstock, this is the largest of the three sizes of fruit trees.

String trimmer: A hand-held tool that uses monofilament line instead of a blade to trim grass.

Succulent: A type of plant that stores water in its leaves, stems, and roots and is acclimated for arid climates and soil conditions.

Sucker: The odd growth from the base of a tree or a woody plant, often caused by stress, this also refers to sprouts from below the graft of a rose or fruit tree. Suckers divert energy away from the desirable tree growth and should be removed.

Summer annual: Annuals that thrive during the warmer months of the growing season.

Systemic herbicide: A type of weedkiller that is absorbed by the plant's roots and destroys all parts of the plant.

Taproot: An enlarged, tapered plant root that grows vertically downward.

Thinning: The practice of removing excess seedlings to leave more room for the remaining plants to grow; also refers to the practice of removing fruits when still small from fruit trees so that the remaining fruits can grow larger.

Topdress: To spread fertilizer on top of the soil (usually around fruit trees or vegetables).

Transplants: Plants that are grown in one location and then moved to and replanted in another; seeds started indoors and nursery plants are two examples.

Tree: A woody perennial plant typically consisting of a single trunk with multiple lateral branches.

Tree canopy: The upper layer of growth, consisting of the tree's branches and leaves.

Tropical plant: A plant that is native to a tropical region of the world and thus acclimated to a warm, humid climate and not hardy to frost.

Trowel: A shovel-like hand tool used for digging or moving small amounts of soil.

Turf: Grass and the surface layer of soil that is held together by its roots.

Variegated: The appearance of differently colored areas on plant leaves, usually white, yellow, or a brighter green.

Warm-season vegetable: A vegetable that thrives during the warmer months. Examples are tomatoes, okra, and peppers. These vegetables do not tolerate frost.

Watering wand: A hose attachment featuring a longer handle for watering plants beyond reach.

Water sprout: A vertical shoot that emerges from a scaffold branch. It is usually nonfruiting and undesirable.

Weed and feed: A product containing both an herbicide for weed control and a fertilizer for grass growth.

Weeping: A growth habit in plants that features drooping or downward-curving branches.

Wheat straw: Dry stalks of wheat that are used for mulch, retain soil moisture, and suppress weeds.

Wood chips: Small pieces of wood made by cutting or chipping, wood chips are used as mulch in the garden.

Resources

SEEDS

Baker Creek Petaluma Seed Bank
www.rareseeds.com
199 Petaluma Blvd. North
Petaluma, CA 94952
Phone: 707-509-5171

Kitazawa Seed Co.
www.kitazawaseed.com
PO Box 13220
Oakland, CA 94661-3220
Phone: 510-595-1188
Fax: 510-595-1860

Peaceful Valley Farm & Garden Supply
www.groworganic.com
P.O. Box 2209
Grass Valley, CA 95945
Phone: 888-784-1722

Renee's Garden Seeds
www.reeneesgarden.com
6060A Graham Hill Rd.
Felton, CA 95018
Phone: 888-880-7228

Sustainable Seed Co.
www.sustainableseedco.com
P.O. Box 38
Covelo, CA 95428
Phone: 877-620-SEED

Territorial Seed Company
www.territorialseed.com
P.O. Box 158
Cottage Grove, OR 97424
Phone: 800-626-0866

ONLINE NURSERIES

Annie's Annuals
www.anniesannuals.com
801 Chesley Ave.
Richmond, CA 94801
Phone: 888-266-4370
Ornamentals and edibles

Digging Dog Nursery
www.diggingdog.com
31101 Middle Ridge Rd.
Albion, CA 95410
Phone: 707-937-1130
Ornamentals and edibles

Four Winds Growers
www.fourwindsgrowers.com
Phone: 877-449-4637, ext. 1.
Citrus and fruit trees and more

Heavenly Greens
www.heavenlygreens.com
370 Umbarger Rd.
San Jose, CA 95111
Phone: 888-254-5503
Artificial turf

Regan Nursery
www.regannursery.com
4268 Decoto Road
Fremont, CA 94555-3204
Phone: 510-797-3222
Roses

One Green World
www.onegreenworld.com
28696 S. Cramer Rd.
Molalla, Oregon 97038-8576
Phone: 877-353-4028
Fruit and nut trees and more

NETWORKS & INFORMATION

Ample Harvest
www.ampleharvest.org
This is a national organization that works to connect home gardeners with local food pantries that can use their surplus crops. Just plug in your zip code and it gives you contact information for participating food banks near you.

California Rare Fruit Growers
www.crfg.org
This organization's website is a treasure trove of information on growing fruit in California. Check out the local chapter events in your area and meet the CRFG members—they're some of the most knowledgeable gardeners you'll ever meet.

Plant Maps
http://www.plantmaps.com/index.php
Plug in your zip code in this site and it will show you not only your USDA hardiness zone, but also first and last average frost dates, minimum and maximum monthly temperatures, and average monthly precipitation.

Bibliography

American Horticultural Society. *Roses*. New York: DK Publishing, Inc., 1999.

Baldwin, Debra Lee. *Succulents Simplified*. Portland, OR: Timber Press, 2013.

Bale, Sharon. "Spring, Summer & Fall Bulbs." Cooperative Extension Service, University of Kentucky, College of Agriculture.

Brenzel, Kathleen Norris, ed. *The New Sunset Western Garden Book*. New York: Time Home Entertainment Inc., 2012.

"Care and Maintenance of Bulb Flowers." University of Idaho Extension. 2013.

Endicott, Katherine Grace. *Northern California Gardening: A Month-by-Month Guide*. San Francisco: Chronicle Books, 1996.

Garden Trends Research Report, October 2013 Survey. Conducted for the Garden Writers Association Foundation.

Meyer, Mary H. "Storing Tender Bulbs and Bulblike Structures." University of Minnesota Extension, Department of Horticultural Science. Reviewed 2009, copyright 2013.

Pleasant, Barbara. *The Complete Houseplant Survival Manual*. North Adams, MA: Storey Publishing, 2005.

Rosenthal, Ed. *Protect Your Garden*. Oakland, CA: Quick American Publishing, 2013.

Schmidt, Genevieve. "Stop! Don't Prune that Grass." *Fine Gardening*, October 2013. No. 153.

Smaus, Robert. *52 Weeks in the California Garden*. Los Angeles: Los Angeles Times, 1996.

Speichert, Greg, and Sue Speichert. *Ortho's All About Water Gardening*. Des Moines, IA: Meredith Books, 2001.

Splan, Claire. *California Fruit and Vegetable Gardening*. Minneapolis, MN: Cool Springs Press, 2012.

Stapleton, J. J., C. A. Wilen, and R. H. Molinar. "Pest Notes: Soil Solarization for Gardens and Landscapes." UC ANR Publication 74145. 10/08. UC Statewide IPM Program, University of California, Davis.

Swindells, Philip. *The Master Book of the Water Garden*. London: Salamander Books, Ltd., 2000.

Welsh, Pat. *Southern California Gardening: A Month-by-Month Guide*. San Francisco: Chronicle Books, 2000.

Wilde, Barbara. *Growing Roses Organically*. Erasmus, PA: Rodale, 2002.

Index